W9-AWG-020

PRAISE FOR *THE BIG STRETCH*

"If readers take in at least half of what Teneshia shares in *The Big Stretch: 90 Days to Expand Your Dreams, Crush Your Goals, and Create Your Own Success*, they should do very well!"

LUVVIE AJAYI, speaker, host of the *Rants and Randomness* podcast, and *New York Times* bestselling author of *I'm Judging You*

"Teneshia has created a powerful blueprint for not only imagining the impossible, but activating powerful values and virtues to personalize the success of our dreams. Every reader will walk away triggered into action by the truth that the reality of our dreams is only one blueprint away."

SYBIL CLARK-AMUTI, creator and host of *The Great Girlfriends Show* podcast

"*The Big Stretch* is a must-read for anyone who has ever had a dream they've wanted to fulfill but didn't know how. Begin your journey to make your dream a reality with Coach T. Get ready to be stretched by someone who's been there and done it!"

LORI GEORGE BILLINGSLEY, Global Chief Diversity and Inclusion Officer of The Coca-Cola Company

"I loved this book. It is truly, truly incredibly engaging, inspiring, and practical at the same time. I tried THE STRETCH on for me and garnered so many insights. It came right on time for me!"

ESI EGGLESTON BRACEY, EVP and COO of North America Beauty and Personal Care of Unilever

"*The Big Stretch* digs deep and pushes the reader to think, to dream, and to stretch! If you are stuck and wondering what's next for you, *The Big Stretch* allows you to determine your Dreamer profile with tools to help you bring the dream into a vision and ultimately a reality!"

DR. KARMETRIA BURTON, General Manager of Strategic Programs of Delta Air Lines

"I wish I had *The Big Stretch* earlier in my career because it would have made my climb up the corporate ladder and the building of my nonprofit so much easier. This book provides clarity and the understanding of how to see your dreams through to the finish line."

VALEISHA BUTTERFIELD JONES, Fortune 100 Executive and cofounder and CEO of the Women in Entertainment Empowerment Network

"*The Big Stretch* is truly uplifting, inspirational and a kick start we all need no matter where we are on our journey of greatness. This is not just any business book, it is a playbook to empower us to go big or go home."

SARAH CARBERRY, Head of US Multicultural Strategy & Sales of Google

"The principles in *The Big Stretch* are key to success in any industry. I filmed several Dream Project conferences over the years and witnessed, firsthand, Teneshia's vision transform thousands of attendees. On a personal level, I applied what I learned to my own journey and am proud to say that my stretch from running a production company to directing episodic television was powered by the tools that Teneshia shares."

PETE CHAPMAN, director of *Insecure*, *Grey's Anatomy*, *Black-ish*, *Silicon Valley*, *The Last O.G.*, *It's Always Sunny in Philadelphia*, *Greenleaf*, and more

"A deeply insightful, yet practical, piece of work on how to realize dreams and create a business with soul and purpose. A must in today's global economy. Now you really can live your dreams. Teneshia shows you how."

JUSTIN THOMAS-COPELAND, CEO of RAPP New York and Global Executive Board Member

"Wow, this is what I wish I had when I started my business. So often, we're given a fairytale or nightmare as to what it means to go after your dreams, but Teneshia really addresses every emotion and fear that people go through as they consider going after the dream!"

BRANDICE DANIEL, CEO and founder of Harlem Fashion Row

"Over the years I've attended several events celebrating Teneshia and EGAMI Group's accomplishments, and now with *The Big Stretch* I have the secret sauce that made all those achievements possible. Read this book if you want to experience the phenomenal success that all dreamers wish for."

KYLE DONOVAN, inventor, entrepreneur, CEO of iFork (as seen on *Shark Tank*), and publisher of *NV Magazine*

"*The Big Stretch* has principles that are core for any entrepreneur and business owner, especially in the entertainment industry. *The Big Stretch* is a must-read for all people looking to create extraordinary results in their professional and creative endeavors."

ESTELLE, Grammy Award–winning singer

"Teneshia Warner has put together one of the best books I've read on achieving your dreams in record time. *The Big Stretch* is a great year-round read, but start now—there is no time to waste before your dreams turn to nightmares. Thank you, Teneshia, for this labor of love and masterwork."

DR. GEORGE C. FRASER, bestselling author of *Success Runs In Our Race* and *Click* and Chairman and CEO of Frasernet

"As I was reading, I could hear Teneshia's voice gently saying each word. It was as if she were speaking specifically to me, and I felt like she was truly committed to my realizing 'My Dream.' The tone of the book is authentic, and the purposeful approach makes it even more impactful."

CONSTANCE CANNON FRAZIER, Chief Operating Officer of American Advertising Federation

"I found *The Big Stretch* BEYOND MOTIVATING!! It made me think double-time about my purpose and my dreams. It is extremely insightful, though provoking, motivating, and inspirational—and it gave me hope that I can do anything!!!"

SANDRA KRUT, Portfolio Director of Italian Estates, Castello Banfi

"Teneshia Jackson Warner (aka Coach T) strikes again! If you're ready for 90 days of inspiration, self-reflection, behavior modification, purpose-driven action, and execution of your wildest dreams, then this book is for YOU! The practical tools and assessments are invaluable and have helped me, a 14-year business owner, reenergize and refocus the path for my next Big Stretch!"

MICHELLE D. HARE, Multicultural Business Development of State Farm

"This hands-on practical guide delivers nuggets of wisdom that hold true for everyone from the business neophyte to the seasoned entrepreneurial pro. I've spent 10 years innovating and growing my venture, and Teneshia's lessons inspired me to dust off my playbook and start to dream even bigger. Thank you!"

SHEILA MARMON, founder and CEO of Mirror Digital

"*The Big Stretch* fills a BIG need for anyone looking to figure out what their dreams are and need a north star to get there. The exercises in the book give you the structure and the space to figure out what type of dreamer you are, the type of risk you can take, and then how to start making it happen today. This is a must-read for anyone looking to getting out of the 'I wish I could, but I don't have the time' rut and help you turn your 'shoulds' into 'musts' so that you can define and accomplish your dreams."

LAURA MIGNOTT, CEO of DFlash and host of the *Reset* podcast

"I wish I had *The Big Stretch* 20 years ago when I started my journey. Every single entrepreneur needs to read this book. But bigger than that, every dreamer, every child of a dreamer, every spouse of a dreamer needs this book. This book gives you permission to dream big, play big, and stretch in big ways."

LISA NICHOLS, founder and CEO of Motivating the Masses and *New York Times* bestselling author of *No Matter What*

"As a small business owner, I welcome a book that serves as a boot camp for business. There is always a long distance between our dreams and their realization. This useful bridge will help people like me get to where we need to be in business and in life."

SOLEDAD O'BRIEN, award-winning broadcast journalist and Executive Producer and CEO of Starfish Media Group

"I'm thrilled that Teneshia is now sharing the business insights and wisdom from that conference in the form of *The Big Stretch*. This book gives you the play-by-play to convert ideas into business successes. What a valuable tool for go-getters with big dreams."

DR. RANDAL PINKETT, winner of the show *The Apprentice* and Chairman and CEO of BCT Partners

"*The Big Stretch* is the opposite of the kind of one-size-fits-all, reductive, hustle-porn advice that neglects to appreciate that each reader's life, obligations, strengths, and most importantly dreams, are different . . . and instead celebrates that! If you're ready to put your dream into action, I can't think of a better companion than Teneshia Warner and her Big STRETCH 90-day program."

ELISA CAMAHORT PAGE, cofounder of BlogHer and founder and CEO Cygnus

"As a female entrepreneur, oftentimes I am "the only one" in certain rooms. With a book like *The Big Stretch* and authors like Teneshia, there can be more of us. Like the saying goes—'If you see it, you can be it.'"

LISA PRICE, founder of Carol's Daughter, a multimillion-dollar beauty business acquired by L'Oreal USA

"*The Big Stretch*, is an inspiring and motivating road map for dreaming big and jumpstarting the journey to achieve success with meaning. This book is a must-read for all of those who want to stretch themselves toward possibilities never imagined—and make their dreams come true."

MARC PRITCHARD, Chief Brand Officer of Procter & Gamble

"Why don't we teach these lessons in high school? That was my first thought when I read Teneshia Warner's terrific new book. If you want to test your big idea—and your personal commitment to winning—Teneshia's practical and spiritual coaching is for you. Stop dreaming and start doing."

LISA STONE, cofounder of BlogHer, serial entrepreneur, and advisor to start-ups

"Teneshia is a thoughtful leader who has crafted a blueprint for those daring enough to pursue their dreams. Full of strategic cumulative exercises and punctuated with encouragement and anecdotal stories, *The Big Stretch* is a book that helps cultivate true soul-centered business leadership."

LATHAM THOMAS, bestselling author of *Own Your Glow* and founder of Mama Glow

"From the entrepreneur with an idea on a napkin to the seasoned business owner, this book is a great blueprint for anyone wanting to turn their dreams into reality! Teneshia's ability to break down the steps to make it happen, backed up with real-life examples, is practical and easy for all!"

LILI GIL VALLETTA, CEO and cofounder of CulturIntel and Cien+

"The STRETCH is literally the blueprint for how to turn your dream into reality! The career profiles and exercises enable people from any industry to relate, innovate, plan, and take action! This book inspired me to begin a new stretch in pursuit of my dreams!"

DORINDA WALKER, founder and CEO of Cultural Solutions Group

"This book is fascinating and so informative. Teneshia had me rethinking my dream. The exercises are making it real, no dream deferred, and *The Big Stretch* is a quick study course on taking it to the end."

SANDRA SIMS-WILLIAMS, Chief Diversity Officer of Publicis Worldwide

THE BIG STRETCH

THE BIG STRETCH

90 DAYS TO EXPAND YOUR DREAMS, CRUSH YOUR GOALS, AND CREATE YOUR OWN SUCCESS

TENESHIA JACKSON WARNER

McGraw Hill

New York Chicago San Francisco Athens London
Madrid Mexico City Milan New Delhi
Singapore Sydney Toronto

Copyright © 2020 by Teneshia Jackson Warner. All rights reserved. Printed in the United States of America. Except as permitted under the United States Copyright Act of 1976, no part of this publication may be reproduced or distributed in any form or by any means, or stored in a database or retrieval system, without the prior written permission of the publisher.

1 2 3 4 5 6 7 8 9 LCR 24 23 22 21 20 19

ISBN 978-1-260-45680-6
MHID 1-260-45680-3

e-ISBN 978-1-260-45681-3
e-MHID 1-260-45681-1

Library of Congress Cataloging-in-Publication Data

Names: Warner, Teneshia Jackson, author.
Title: The big stretch : 90 days to expand your dreams, crush your goals, and create your own success / Teneshia Jackson Warner.
Description: New York : McGraw-Hill Education, [2020] | Includes bibliographical references and index.
Identifiers: LCCN 2019030692 (print) | LCCN 2019030693 (ebook)| ISBN 9781260456806 (hardcover) | ISBN 9781260456813 (ebook)
Subjects: LCSH: Success. | Goal (Psychology) | Success in business. | Self-actualization (Psychology)
Classification: LCC BF637.S8 W327 2020 (ebook) | LCC BF637.S8 (print) | DDC 650.1—dc23
LC record available at https://lccn.loc.gov/2019030692
LC ebook record available at https://lccn.loc.gov/2019030693

McGraw-Hill Education books are available at special quantity discounts to use as premiums and sales promotions or for use in corporate training programs. To contact a representative, please visit the Contact Us pages at www.mhprofessional.com.

To the Dreamer You're Becoming

This book is dedicated to the Dreamer
inside you who is more courageous,
more determined, more resourceful,
and more capable than you know.
May *The Big Stretch* guide you
to know this Dreamer intimately
and lead you to the future of your Dreams.

CONTENTS

ACKNOWLEDGMENTS

First and always, I must thank God, the ultimate giver of Dreams. Thank you for entrusting me with the idea for *The Big Stretch*.

My second acknowledgment is to *My Dream Team*, a dynamic group of people whom I believe were divinely united to deliver to the world a purposeful work:

- MY HUSBAND: **Michael Warner**. Thank you for being my Dream partner in business and in life. Thank you for once again helping to turn an idea into a Dream come true. I love you!
- MY LITERARY AGENT: Thank you to **Regina Brooks** and the **Serendipity Literary Agency Team** for helping develop the concept of *The Big Stretch* and then building a Dream team that included editors, collaborators, a publicist, and more. Thank you for securing a book deal with a world-class publisher, McGraw-Hill, and for being tireless strategists and skilled counselors.
- MY PUBLISHER: **McGraw-Hill**. To my Senior Editor **Cheryl Segura**—thank you so much not only for believing in this project but for having the exceptional editing skills to sharpen the manuscript while guiding me through the very complex publishing process. I'd also like to thank Donya Dickerson, Nora Hennick, Amanda Muller, Patricia Wallenburg, and the team at Matchbook Creative, Inc., for being valuable and resourceful members of my McGraw-Hill team.
- MY DEVELOPMENTAL EDITOR: **Jodi Fodor**. There are *no* words to thank you enough for your partnership. Your commitment to excellence, your work ethic, and your creative talents Stretched this

project into greatness. You've been a lifesaver, and now you have a writing partner for life.

- MY BUSINESS EDITOR: **Debbie Englander**. You ensured that this book's business content was original and relevant. And I thank you for scouring the Dream Project content to extract the most valuable excerpts for our readers.
- EDITOR: **Leah Lakins**. Thank you for your creative and editorial contribution to this project.
- MY RIGHT HAND: **Cybele Babayants**. Thank you for your signature excellence as you made sure we met every deadline and hit every mark. I can't imagine trying to go through such a process without your help.
- TO ALL THE DREAM ALL-STARS: Thank you for sharing your time and stories with the Dream Project Community. Because of your generosity, this book is filled with invaluable insight and wisdom.
- INSIGHTS/RESEARCH TEAM: **Renita Bryant** at Sight Set and **Brooke Gibbs** at Artyfact. Thank you for your strategic counsel on several of the book's exercises.
- TEAM EGAMI GROUP: Thank you for keeping the firm running in excellence during my time away to write. Special thanks to my invaluable executive leadership team of **Michael Warner**, **Cammillia Campbell**, **Liv Lewis**, and **Cheryl Overton**.
- EGAMI GROUP'S BUSINESS ADVISORS: Many thanks to **Dan Coleman** (EOS Implementor & Leadership Coach), **Mark Hodges** (Acresis), **Rick Gould**, and **Barry Collodi** who have supported our vision to scale the business. Much of the wisdom we've learned from working with you has been included in this book.
- MY FAMILY: Thank you for being my number one Dream team, always! Mom (Carolyn Hearns), Dad (Robert Jackson), Grandma Sweeny, Grandaddy, Coley, Chelle, Celeste, Chester, and many more. Also, *much* love to Bria, Aiden, and my entire Warner family.
- MY BFF AND SISTER GIRLS: Chelonnda Seryoer, Angianein Wallace, and the One Arm Up Crew: remember, girlfriends who Dream together reach the stars together.

- TO MY BLUE RIDGE FAMILY: Special thanks to Suzianne, Blake, Taber Pass, and Jerry for making me feel at home for months as I worked on the book in Blue Ridge.
- SPECIAL SHOUT OUT TO ESI: It was you who challenged me to take on the Stretch to run the New York City Marathon, a journey that symbolizes that I will always run toward my Dreams.

There are many people I haven't listed here but whose presence in my life makes me feel blessed every day. You know who you are, and I deeply appreciate you and your support.

INTRODUCTION

All Dreamers Stretch

WAITING AT THE STARTING LINE

The number 69645 will always have special meaning to me. This number was proof of my willingness to run, literally, toward a Dream. On a cold, crisp fall morning in Queens, I wore **69645** across my chest as I stood at the starting line of the New York City Marathon.

On that morning, I joined thousands of people from around the world—runners representing all races, ages, and nations. I felt an electrified connection to each person at that starting line. Inspiring rock music thundered from speakers everywhere. Some people warmed up by running in place, others held contorted yoga poses, while others lay on cement or grass, stealing final moments of rest. I also saw runners taking inventory of their energy bars, water, and Gatorade and checking for fully charged cell phones. We all busied ourselves with similar rituals and incidentals, but what really united us was our shared commitment. I felt connected to every single person at that starting line. Every one of us had made the commitment to Dream.

We said yes to the tiring and sometimes even grueling workouts. We said yes to the sacrifices of sleep, socializing, and the comfort of staying curled up on a big, comfy couch. We said yes to the determination necessary to reach the finish line. We were all united by willpower, strength, and discipline. We were willing to lean into the scary moments along the journey and keep going. And when the starting gun fired, we felt what it means to take the first step toward a Dream.

I'd been on a starting line just like this one 15 years earlier. One hot summer day in the parking lot of IBM Global Services in Minneapolis, I sat in my car ready to drive off the lot for the last time. My car was packed with my belongings and greeting cards from my colleagues wishing me the best. As I slid the key in the car's ignition and drove away from a "good, good job," as my Grandmama had called it, I knew that I was venturing into the unknown.

Was I nervous? Very.

Did I second-guess my decision to leave a relatively secure job in favor of an uncharted future? Yes. But I felt more excited than I'd ever felt about anything. I was feeling what it meant to start a journey based on passion and purpose. My career path would never again be traditional, and I didn't try to calm my fear by psyching myself into believing that nothing but victories and easy decisions lay ahead. No, as I drove away, I knew that I was leaving comfort and guarantees in the rearview mirror and that there was nothing to do but keep moving. As I turned from the parking lot onto the street, I felt I'd fired my own starting gun and entered a race. And I'm delighted to say that in the running of that race I discovered I can keep pace with some of the best in the world.

If you're reading this book, you're probably at the starting line of your own unique Dream. Maybe it's an idea that keeps you up at night. Maybe it fills your thoughts while you sit in traffic or stand in checkout lines. Maybe you find that you can't stop telling people about it. Or maybe you're haunted by questions relative to your ideas. Are you unsure exactly what to dream about, yet you feel that something is missing from your life? In all of these cases, something is telling you that you want more.

HOW THE STRETCH CAME TO BE

After being on my own Dream journey for several years, I wanted to create a formal means to help others reach for their Dreams. So I created The Dream Project, a conference that gives Dreamers the tools and insights to grow their ideas into real-life successful businesses. Since its inception, The Dream Project has inspired more than 100,000 entrepreneurs, creatives, and career Dreamers and has featured nearly 200 business moguls, influencers, and celebrity speakers. Just a few of the guest Dreamers who have joined us to share stories from their own goals, failures, and successes are NBA legend and entrepreneur Earvin "Magic" Johnson, Rent the Runway founder Jennifer Fleiss, *Shark Tank*'s Daymond John, BlogHer cofounder Elisa Camahort Page, CURLBOX founder and CEO **Myleik Teele**, digital strategist **Luvvie Ajayi**, *Apprentice* winner Randal Pinkett, Radio/TV One founder Cathy Hughes, and more.

Through The Dream Project, I've watched thousands of professionals manifest their Dreams, and I knew that I wanted to provide even more Dreamers with a road map for success. I call that road map The Stretch.

The Stretch is a soul-searching, life-transforming, 12-week boot camp created from principles and lessons at the heart of The Dream Project. The Stretch will show you how to get from where you are to where you dream to be—in business and in other aspects of your life.

Whether you want to start a small business, develop an innovative app, or build a nonprofit organization, this is your invitation to join me at the starting line and begin The Stretch to realize your Dream. From this point forward, consider me Coach T, your personal Dream coach who will support you all the way. But before you craft a new vision board, turn in your resignation, or rearrange your business plan, let me tell you a little more about what it means to say *yes!* to The Stretch.

The Stretch will help you:

- Begin a journey to reveal the greatness of your potential.
- Learn to extend beyond your comfort zone and reach for your goals.
- Be willing to think of, speak of, and execute ideas that others may find uncomfortable or risky.
- Develop the staying power to keep going despite doubt, disappointment, and boredom.
- Position your biggest Dreams for explosive growth.
- Make the necessary changes to become the best version of yourself.

IT'S ABOUT PLANNING AND PERSISTENCE

When I set out to run the New York City Marathon, I didn't plan to just step up to the starting line on the day of the race. The commitment required me to begin the journey six months earlier and embark upon a rigorous plan that included doing interval training, modifying my diet, creating dedicated time in my schedule, and putting my miles in whether I was home, on vacation, or across the world on a business trip. As we get ready to go on *this* journey, you'll also have to focus and commit to consistent, disciplined action. The Stretch will provide the motivation and the exercises to get you to the finish line.

When you step into this new Dream, focus on precisely why you're committing to this journey. Taking on a goal without a clear purpose will be a waste of your God-given energy. My purpose for running the New York City Marathon was to have my run serve as a reminder that I would always run toward my goals and inspire other people to do the same. Focusing on your *why* will inspire you to honor your commitment to Dream every day. The Stretch is designed to help you identify your *why* and step into your purpose.

As you tap into your *why*, you'll discover that you have a unique idea that can be realized only by you. You were put on earth, right here and right now, to deliver your service, your product, your message, and your gift as only you can do it. You must be willing to discover what motivates you to action, what stops you from moving to the next level, how tolerant you are when it comes to taking on new risks, and whom to invite along on the journey to support and inspire your visions to come to life. If you begin Stretching into a new goal while maintaining a full-time job, your steps will be different from the steps required of someone who has the flexibility to dedicate most of her time and resources to being an entrepreneur. This book will guide you through either scenario.

Stretching into your biggest goals also requires that you welcome a strong team to support you in your journey. Behind every marathon runner is a team of supporters that might include family, friends, colleagues, personal trainers, running groups, and sponsors. My support team included my husband, Mike; my friend, Esi; and lots of my relatives. Without their support and guidance, I wouldn't have made it past that first mile, let alone the other 25.2 miles. The Stretch will help you identify your team of supporters.

Your Dream journey will become more fulfilling when you invite your biggest supporters and champions along. Receiving supportive calls, texts, and hugs will be the balm that your mind and body need to keep you going when you hit roadblocks. Knowing that you can lean on a trusted mentor, friend, or spouse for support will give you the boost to keep going for another day. The Stretch will show you how to keep these trusted supporters engaged as you work to achieve your goals.

Now that I've learned how to lean on my support team, I've been able to Stretch toward my Dream for more than 15 years. But if you would have told me 15 years ago that my Stretch into building an award-winning integrated marketing firm would have included losing friendships, firing staff, and fighting it out for fair contracts, I might have stayed at my "good, good job" at IBM. But because I committed to The Stretch, I had to trust the entire process.

You can't say yes to The Stretch and then drop out of your training the first time you get turned down for a business loan. You can't abandon your idea just because your friend can't see your vision. You can't downsize your goal because it doesn't quite work in the community where you want to make a difference. **Big Dreams require unreasonable, radical action to catapult you from where you are to where you want to be.**

The Stretch demands that you hold onto this roller coaster called your Dream through every dip, curve, and twist along the path. But when you trust this process, you'll step into a more purposeful, meaningful, and intentional life that will be more satisfying and remarkable than what you can see now. You will be joining an elite group of courageous, imaginative, and world-shaping innovators and creators we call Dreamers. And as wide-ranging as our ideas are, all Dreamers are connected by one important event: we all said yes to The Stretch.

ALL DREAMERS SAY YES TO THE STRETCH

After speaking with some of my favorite Dream All-Stars at The Dream Project (you'll meet them later in the book!), I learned that **The Stretch** . . .

- Propelled Earvin "Magic" Johnson from one of the country's leading athletes into one of its most successful businesspeople
- Helped Christine Caine, whose birth certificate read "unwanted," to become an international speaker, author, and activist leading The A21 Campaign, one of the world's largest anti–human trafficking organizations
- Moved DeVon Franklin from successful movie executive to leading Hollywood producer and author
- Elevated Jennifer Fleiss from a business school student to a business force worthy of being named one of *Forbes* magazine's Most Powerful Women Entrepreneurs
- Advanced Luvvie Ajayi from passionate blogger with a knack for words to *New York Times* bestselling author
- Catapulted Yvonne Orji from struggling actress with a Dream to breakout star of the popular HBO series *Insecure*

I hope you're as excited as I am to meet the new you on the other side of this journey. But before we get too far down the road, I want to let you know that even if you think you're getting a late start, the train has *not* left without you. In today's fast-moving world of social media, it's easy to believe that your accomplishments don't measure up to those of your high school friend who became a CEO before age 30 or your fraternity brother who owns several successful franchises. **Your journey is yours alone, and if now is when you're starting, now is when you're supposed to be starting.**

I KNOW THE STRETCH FOR MYSELF

While I've interviewed hundreds of Dreamers and read countless inspiring biographies from incredible Dreamers, I also know this Stretch journey firsthand. As I mentioned earlier, my journey has required me to transform into bigger versions of myself over and over again, and the process is now part of my everyday lifestyle. **The Stretch has done much for me and my life including** . . .

- Made me admit that I was miserable at my first corporate job at IBM Global Services
- Gave me the courage to turn in my resignation to my "good, good job" without having another job lined up
- Pushed me to write and practice my one-minute pitch before I had any idea to whom I was going to pitch it
- Increased my faith in my vision that I would meet someone who would change the trajectory of my career
- Emboldened me to pitch my talent and my services for no fee (in exchange for an opportunity to learn) to an entertainment-business mogul after bumping into him at a trade show event
- Fueled me with the courage to offer the services of my company, EGAMI, even before my incorporation papers were signed
- Inspired me to grow EGAMI from a concept into a multimillion-dollar firm servicing Fortune 100 and 500 companies
- Compelled me to write the first-ever multicultural marketing book focused on purpose-driven marketing
- Landed me an opportunity to partner with Procter & Gamble to create a campaign called "The Talk" that raised awareness and fought against racial bias in African American communities, which led to EGAMI earning its first Emmy award and becoming the first African American, woman-led firm to win the Cannes Grand Prix award
- Motivated me to develop The Dream Project, which has empowered and inspired thousands of Dreamers across the nation
- Inspired me to create a portable 90-day boot camp to help Dreamers around the world expand their Dreams—and you are holding that very program in your hands right now

THE 90-DAY STRETCH-TO-ACTIVATE-YOUR-DREAMS-NOW PROGRAM

Now that you know what it means to say yes to The Stretch, what will this journey look like for you? This 90-day program is designed to provide you with a solid, soulful, practical, and rigorous plan to expand your biggest Dreams in just 12 weeks. This program will not be like a New Year's resolution that begins strong on January first and fades out by Valentine's Day. **Each week will take you through a guided set of life and business exercises that will keep you motivated, track your progress, help you navigate potential challenges, and ultimately direct you toward your goals.**

Each chapter will include lessons in which I share real-life experiences from my own Stretch journey and Stretch Exercises where you can begin visioning, planning, and working toward *your* Dream. How you access and execute these exercises is up to you, but I recommend one of these two options:

1. You can work through the exercises here in the book and/or in your Dream Notebook. When your Dream Notebook is required, you will see this icon:

2. You can download the entire exercise workbook or exercises individually at www.TheBigStretchBook.com. When an exercise is available for download, you will see this icon:

Throughout the chapters you'll also have access to bonus material featuring our Dream All-Stars who have Stretched to realize their Dreams.

DREAM, Weeks 1–3

In the first phase of The Stretch, you'll learn about the kind of Dreamer you are, how to develop your idea in vibrant detail, and how to detox poor habits to ensure your Dream's success.

STRETCH EXERCISES

WEEK 1	WEEK 2	WEEK 3
1. The Dreamer's Profile Assessment 2. Dreamer's Risk Tolerance Assessment 3. Discovering Your Dreamer's Ancestry	1. Dreaming Your Dream Environment 2. Dreaming in Childlike Wonder 3. Your One-Year Dream Projection 4. Create Your 90-Day Stretch Plan 5. Declare Your Dream	1. Identifying Dream Bullies 2. Time Audit

DESIGN, Weeks 4–6

After you've defined your Dream, The Stretch will introduce you to design exercises that will help you discover your purpose, define the opportunities for your Dream, and create your Dream blueprint.

STRETCH EXERCISES

WEEK 4	WEEK 5	WEEK 6
1. 10 Questions for Discovering Your Purpose from the Inside Out 2. Writing Your Personal Purpose Statement 3. 10 Questions to Discover Your Dream's Purpose 4. Developing Your Dream's Mission Statement	1. Becoming the Answer for Your Dream Irritant 2. Building Your Dream Audience 3. Finding Your Dream's Unique Position 4. Know Your Competition	1. High-Touch Dreaming: The Art of Networking 2. Finding Your Mentors 3. Six Degrees Toward Your Dream 4. Creating a Dream Culture 5. Building a Dream Team

DARE, Weeks 7–9

After you develop a solid foundation for your goal, you're ready to be daring. During this third phase of The Stretch, you'll learn how to be unconventional and bold in the interest of your Dream.

STRETCH EXERCISES

WEEK 7	WEEK 8	WEEK 9
1. 100 Nos and Counting 2. The Big Ask 3. Making Your Dream Pitch Perfect 4. The Uncomfortable Challenge	1. The Dream Extreme Challenge 2. First, Break All the Rules 3. Finding the Gap 4. Learning from Failure	1. Checkup and Refresh 2. Leveling Up into the Future 3. Taking Your Dream to the Next Level

DO, Weeks 10–12

Finally, after you complete this fourth phase of The Stretch, you'll have the tools you need to develop successful and profitable Dreams, find the value in imperfect Dreams, and leave room for your Dreams to grow beyond your wildest imagination.

STRETCH EXERCISES

WEEK 10	WEEK 11	WEEK 12
1. Discovering Your Financial DNA 2. Building a Strong Budget for Your Dream 3. Creating Cash Flow That Works for Your Dream	1. The Surrender Jar 2. Dream Warriors Expect the Best and Prepare for the Worst 3. Life Balance Tracker	1. Keeping Your Dream in Flight 2. Your Mega Dream Wild Card

The Stretch is a 12-week program that includes real-life stories, exercises, and training with All-Stars. To get the most from this program, I strongly advise that you follow the program weekly and resist the temptation to skip parts or jump ahead. Each component is important and is included for a reason. The *stories* are included so that you'll glean insight from real-life examples, the *exercises* show you how to apply important business concepts to your personal Stretch journey, and the Dream All-Star *training* that you can dive into at www.TheBigStretchBook.com lets you learn from others who have made it big. So take your time, take it all in, and enjoy.

THE STRETCH AGREEMENT

One last thing before we begin. I want you to make a commitment to yourself to take on The Stretch. The Stretch Agreement below will be your personal contract to commit to this journey. After you sign this agreement, take a picture of it, and keep a screenshot on your phone or make a copy and hang it prominently in your home or office.

I (*Your Name Here*), henceforth known throughout this process as "The Dreamer," will commit to the following terms of the Stretch Agreement:

1. The Dreamer will become aware of his or her Dream and pursue it.
2. The Dreamer is willing to Stretch and commit to the journey between his or her comfort zone and Dream.
3. The Dreamer will move forward in The Stretch in the face of fear.
4. The Dreamer will endure seasons of difficulty during The Stretch.
5. The Dreamer will be willing to fight the obstacles that confront the Dream.
6. Under no conditions will The Dreamer quit the journey of The Stretch in pursuit of the Dream.

DREAMER: ______________________________

DATE: ______________________________

I'm very excited to provide The Stretch as an intensive, life-changing, soul-stretching program that will transform your life, starting today. If you're ready to unleash your biggest, boldest, and brightest Dreams, join me at the starting line in Chapter One as you discover how all Dreams begin with a Stretch.

PART I

DREAM

Dreaming the Possible Dream

A Dreamer is an idealist, someone who believes in what hasn't yet been tried, invented, discovered, or explained. Every human being born with an imagination is a Dreamer, and one of our greatest gifts as Dreamers is our ability to see what doesn't yet exist and bring that forward to reality.

Take a moment to observe the things around you. Perhaps you're reading this book on a Kindle or an iPad. Maybe you're reading in a recliner in your home, maybe on an airplane. Perhaps you're stopping every few moments to check messages on your smartphone. All these inventions began in the minds of visionary Dreamers. Dreamers like SpaceX and Tesla's Elon Musk, Spanx's Sara Blakely, and *Hamilton*'s Lin Manuel Miranda. The Dreamers who created today's most popular wonders are the same as you and me. They're people with powerful imaginations and a powerful ability to bring forth what they imagine.

Dreams are inspiring. They can offer greater possibilities for you, your family, and your community. The idea you have yet to develop could be the answer to a problem someone else is facing right now.

HELLO! YOUR DREAM IS CALLING YOU NOW

What Dream is calling you? Don't overthink it. Don't worry about how to get from point A to point B. Simply bring your idea forward in your thoughts in bright, bold, vivid detail. What are you doing in your Dream? How does this make you feel? Who's with you on your journey? What are the benefits of making this idea a reality? Who's inspired by your Dream? How does it affect your family, your community, and the world around you? We'll be working through these answers together in Part I, "Dream."

When was the last time you took time to ponder what a miraculous and unique creation you are? When we think about the idea of superpowers, we often envision *superhero* powers, such as the ability to be invisible, read minds, cast spells, or freeze time. But you have a power that's more incredible than the abilities of Spider-Man, Wonder Woman, and Black Panther put together: it's your ability to Dream. This type of magic is tied directly to the truly miraculous essence of who we are as human creations.

Two critical traits of Dreamers are the ability to imagine what does not exist and the ability to create. During the Dream section of The Stretch, I invite you to spend time tapping into your superpower and wandering in your imagination. What I want is for you to make reality the vision you just imagined as well as other ideas you'll begin to imagine through The Stretch journey.

In the coming weeks, I'll be sharing key lessons and strategies to apply when Dreaming, and you'll also spend time with some extraordinarily successful Dreamers. These Dreamers will talk about how they tap into their imaginations and creativity, why it is important to define your Dream and success on your own terms, and how they develop the mental habits and discipline needed to bring forth a Dream. These Dreamers discovered that there's power in "knowing thyself."

Every Dream starts within, so that's where I'll start with you. You're going to spend time getting to know thyself, the Dreamer in the Mirror. And your Stretch journey will be every bit as unique as your Dream. **The Dream section is designed to help you find the Dream path that's right**

for you, understand how to harness your imagination to Dream in color, and operate as All-Star Dreamers do.

I have exciting business exercises lined up for you in the next three weeks, including:

Week 1: Exploring Your Dreaming Nature

EXERCISE 1.1: The Dreamer's Profile Assessment
EXERCISE 1.2: Dreamer's Risk Tolerance Assessment
EXERCISE 1.3: Discovering Your Dreamer's Ancestry

Week 2: Dreaming in Color

EXERCISE 2.1: Dreaming Your Dream Environment
EXERCISE 2.2: Dreaming in Childlike Wonder
EXERCISE 2.3: Your One-Year Dream Projection
EXERCISE 2.4: Create Your 90-Day Stretch Plan
EXERCISE 2.5: Declare Your Dream

Week 3: The Dream Detox

EXERCISE 3.1: Identifying Dream Bullies
EXERCISE 3.2: Time Audit

As you work through the first three exercises, you'll discover your skills, strengths, and motivation for pursuing your Dreams. It's officially time for you to dive into Week 1 of your Stretch. Get ready: your first week kicks off with Exploring Your Dreaming Nature.

CHAPTER ONE

EXPLORING YOUR DREAMING NATURE

Week 1

When I started training for the New York City Marathon, I ran alone. I focused on building my stamina, finding my stride, and running farther each week. It was months before I could even think about running in a group. But as the date for the marathon grew nearer, I knew I'd have to start running with other people to feel ready to run alongside 60,000 runners on the day of the race.

I reached out to my friend Esi, who originally inspired me to run the marathon and who turned out to be an excellent coach. She invited me to join a Central Park workout with her local chapter of Black Girls Run. The run for the day was a relatively short one: 7 miles. I knew I could do it because I'd already run 10 miles on my own, but this was my first run in the city, and my confidence began to crumble. I was distracted by the city sounds, the people, the traffic. And then there were the hills! Hills and more hills. As I tried to keep up with the group, I found myself abandoning all the training tools I had acquired up to that point. I'd lost sight of how to run the race my way. I knew that eventually I'd have to get comfortable running in a group, but first I had to become my own kind of runner.

I've come to understand that your Dream is as unique as you are. With that said, this first part of The Stretch is designed to help you find out what kind of Dreamer you are. You'll find your way to that answer by working through these exercises:

Week 1: Exploring Your Dreaming Nature

EXERCISE 1.1: The Dreamer's Profile Assessment

EXERCISE 1.2: Dreamer's Risk Tolerance Assessment

EXERCISE 1.3: Discovering Your Dreamer's Ancestry

Let's dive into our first exercise.

EXERCISE 1.1

THE DREAMER'S PROFILE ASSESSMENT

The Dreamer's Profile Assessment will help you discover which type of Dreamer you are. The Stretch isn't a one-size-fits-all program. Wherever you are in your journey, The Stretch will help you achieve your Dreams at a pace that fits.

Part 1: Understand the Five Different Dreamer Profiles

In this first Stretch tool, we'll meet five Dreamers: Amanda, Jeremiah, Kristina, Michelle, and Antonio. Each one has a different Stretch starting line and a different approach for executing an idea. As you read each Dreamer's story, think about which Dreamer's description most resonates with where you are now and where you want to Stretch.

THE CAREERPRENEUR

DREAMER PROFILE: Amanda

AGE: 28

LOCATION: St. Louis, Missouri

THE STRETCH STARTING LINE: Working as a lawyer at a midsize bank

THE STRETCH DREAM: Becoming a corporate attorney for a large corporation

Amanda is a rising lawyer at a prominent bank in the Midwest. She earns a high five-figure salary and is on the fast track to becoming a vice president. In just a few years after graduating from Spelman College, she's soaring beyond her peers and her own expectations. But when she urgently called me for a coffee date a few months ago, I knew that the life she was building wasn't what she was yearning for.

As soon as she sat down, I saw the sadness in her face, felt the heaviness in her spirit, and said, "I can tell you're at that tipping point. You know you have to go, right?"

She burst into tears. "Every week I'm making up excuses to skip work," she said. "I don't know how much longer I can do this."

Amanda had attended The Dream Project two years earlier, and at the time her plan was to stay with her company but gradually transition into a more challenging position that would offer greater meaning and value. She planned to tap into her passion and talents and reach for a higher salary. But after our coffee date, I knew she didn't have that kind of time. She was slowly robbing her spirit of purpose and needed to take some risks—and fast. If she didn't act on her Dream now, she might end up fired, which could hurt her professional reputation. Amanda courageously chose to leave her job, and before long she landed a new opportunity that made her feel challenged and satisfied.

Amanda is a Careerpreneur. **Dreamers like Amanda want to tap into their entrepreneurial natures while staying put in their corporate positions**. They like to initiate new ideas, new ventures, and new goals. These kinds of Dreamers don't necessarily want to be the boss, become Silicon Valley start-up gurus, or own their own companies. Careerpreneurs often find pleasure in working on teams and contributing to the greater collective vision. They want to make an impact, and they thrive in organized structures. It's very important for this kind of Dreamer to align passion with profession and to find meaning within their career.

Corporate rock stars like Bozoma St. John, chief marketing officer at Endeavor, are Careerpreneurs. Throughout her career, Bozoma has found ways to pair her gift of marketing and her love of pop culture with world-renowned companies like Pepsi, Apple, Uber, and now Endeavor. She aligns her career with her calling.

As Careerpreneurs spend more and more time building their paths within their chosen corporate environments, they find themselves hungry for challenges and projects they can feel passionate about.

THE MAKE-IT-HAPPEN DREAMER

DREAMER PROFILE: Jeremiah

AGE: 25

LOCATION: New York City

THE STRETCH STARTING LINE: Co-owner and chef of a popular food truck

THE STRETCH DREAM: Expanding his company to five food trucks within the next 18 months

Jeremiah is a Southerner who has loved making good food since his beloved New Orleans grandmother taught him to cook. By the time he was a senior in high school, he had developed his own spin on his grandmother's gumbo, fried catfish, macaroni and cheese, and peach cobbler. Jeremiah decided to expand his love for food and attend the Culinary Institute of America. After graduation, he moved to New York City, where several of his jobs at fast-paced restaurants ended in disaster. He didn't get along with any of the head chefs or fellow cooks, and he hated when he was reprimanded for adding New Orleans flair to traditional dishes. He decided to return to his roots, make the dishes he loved, and figure out how to maximize his passion for creating good food.

Six months later during a catering event, Jeremiah had a chance reunion with Marcus, a former classmate from culinary school. Marcus was looking for a partner to invest in a food truck, so they agreed to be partners. There were very few food trucks specializing in authentic New Orleans cuisine, and Jeremiah and Marcus quickly became an ideal duo; Marcus took the lead to purchase the food truck and manage the back end of the business while Jeremiah dazzled at the front with his legendary New Orleans dishes. By the time the next year's summer festivals began, their food truck was ready to serve.

Within their first year, Jeremiah and Marcus had long lines of hungry customers snaking around the truck eagerly waiting for more, so they hired three part-time short-order cooks. When I met Jeremiah at The Dream Project in 2016, he and Marcus were planning to expand to five trucks within 18 months.

Jeremiah is a Make-It-Happen Dreamer. **Dreamers like Jeremiah either have a hard time working for others or have never worked for another person.** Make-It-Happen Dreamers often feel confined by traditional jobs. They feel stifled by rules and routines. These kinds of Dreamers soar when they have the time, space, and flexibility to create their Dreams on their own terms.

Make-It-Happen Dreamers are innovators like Sean "Diddy" Combs, who turned his passion for creating music, fashion, and entertainment ventures into a hip-hop dynasty. Another Make-It-Happen guru is *Insecure* creator Issa Rae, who built her YouTube series *Awkward Black Girl* by gaining traction on social media and initiating several successful crowdfunding campaigns to eventually land a multiseason deal on HBO.

Make-It-Happen Dreamers have high risk tolerance and the willingness to figure out their Stretch journey as they go. They bet on themselves, are able to stomach the highs and lows of entrepreneurship, and live by the credo "Let's Do It *Now*!" Make-It-Happen Dreamer Magic Johnson reminds us that we're the ones in charge, that we need to be "the point guard of our dreams."

THE HOBBY DREAMER

DREAMER PROFILE: Kristina

AGE: 35

LOCATION: Chicago, Illinois

THE STRETCH STARTING LINE: Working as a financial planner

THE STRETCH DREAM: Becoming a noted food and travel blogger, increasing her social media audience, and gaining consistent advertising partners

By day, Kristina is a successful financial planner who earns an impressive salary at a global investment firm. By night, she's a well-known blogger with her finger on the pulse of Chicago's food scene. While Kristina's job affords her the cash and the means to travel the globe, she couldn't get enough vacation time from her firm to fully explore her passion as a food lover and travel enthusiast.

I kept in touch with Kristina over the years after she attended The Dream Project. Whenever we crossed paths, she told the same story: "My job isn't my passion, but it pays enough for me to enjoy my lifestyle and play in my passion spaces."

Kristina greatly enjoys the financial perks and travel opportunities from her job, and she has no intention of leaving. Having passion within the workplace isn't a requirement for her, but she needed to learn how to incorporate her hobby into her everyday life.

Kristina is a Hobby Dreamer. **A Dreamer like Kristina has a career and may simply want to explore creating or expanding a hobby for more personal fulfillment or to create an additional income stream**. Hobby Dreamers are people like Christina Totton, a popular Chicago lifestyle blogger with over 40,000 followers. She's monetized her blog, but her full-time job is as a financial planner at Adam Partners. Another Hobby Dreamer, Tia Mowry-Hardrict is an actress who also hosts a popular web series, *Tia Mowry's Quick Fix*, which showcases her love of cooking, home decor, and self-care.

Hobby Dreamers use their Dreams to satisfy a passion that may not be fulfilled in their 9-to-5 careers. They may also volunteer to find this fulfillment.

THE CEO DREAMER

DREAMER PROFILE: Michelle

AGE: Early fifties

LOCATION: New York City

THE STRETCH STARTING LINE: Senior VP for a global cosmetics marketing firm

THE STRETCH DREAM: Becoming the CEO of a private marketing firm

Michelle had an enviable career that includes more than 20 years as a leader in her company's global cosmetics marketing division, a beautiful corner office facing Madison Avenue, and a generous benefits package that gave her the financial freedom to send all three of her children to their chosen colleges.

When I met Michelle at The Dream Project in 2016, she was doing some heavy soul-searching. She wanted to figure out what would be the right fit for the next act of her life. She said, "Teneshia, I want to talk about The Stretch."

I replied, "I'm going to be honest with you. I believe your Stretch is going to look like the opposite of what got you to this point. You've gone as high as you can go in your company, and you're going to have to be true to yourself now."

Michelle's Stretch began with her coming to terms with leaving a secure career in a field where she was highly respected. And she did it. She quit. She took a few months to decompress with her family, and then she began drafting plans to follow her heart's true passion: to launch her own marketing firm.

Michelle is a CEO Dreamer. **A Dreamer like Michelle knows in her heart that she's reaching for BYOB—Be Your Own Boss**! A CEO Dreamer has worked within the walls of a traditional environment, developed multiple skill sets, and wants to chart an entrepreneurial course.

This Dreamer can be a seasoned professional like Sheila Johnson, CEO of Salamander Hotels and part owner of the NHL's Washington Capitals, the NBA's Washington Wizards, and the WNBA's Washington Mystics. She founded her company as an ambitious second act after founding BET Networks with her former husband in the early 1980s. Regardless of age or experience in business, these Dreamers are ready to make the transition from a traditional career path to entrepreneurship. They're not afraid to take a calculated risk, and they have the time, energy, and finances to go full throttle toward making their ventures into realities.

THE ACTIVIST DREAMER

DREAMER PROFILE: Antonio

AGE: 40

LOCATION: Philadelphia, Pennsylvania

THE STRETCH STARTING LINE: High school English teacher and founder of an after-school boys' book club

THE STRETCH DREAM: Creating more funding, recruiting more volunteers, and expanding the program to more schools before the next school year

Antonio has been a high school English teacher in Philadelphia for the past 10 years. During his third year, he realized that many of the boys in his classes were falling significantly behind the girls in their reading levels and their interest in the required books included in the curriculum.

Antonio decided to create a safe space for his male students by creating a boys-only after-school book club. As incentives, he offered the boys free snacks, extra credit, and the option to attend the book club as an alternative to detention. To keep them engaged, Antonio chose modern-day books with relatable teen heroes. He encouraged the boys to discuss the books—and anything else on their minds—freely.

The book club began with 15 members, and Antonio was able to build momentum after his department chair and vice principal saw impressive increases in the boys' grades and test scores and decreases in their behavioral problems.

By the third year, Antonio had created solid partnerships with businesses in the community that provided free books for each student, donated snacks, and sponsored visits from local authors. Now in its seventh year, the boys' book club has become so popular that Antonio had to cap participation to 50 boys per semester, and he's been asked by other schools and community organizations to introduce the book club to their after-school programs in the city. When Antonio arrived at The Dream Project in 2017, he knew that he couldn't expand his passion to reach more boys without a larger budget, more volunteers, and another creative mind to stretch his vision to the next level.

Antonio is an Activist Dreamer. **Dreamers like Antonio have a calling to address community challenges, local and global issues, and social injustices, often with a small team of volunteers and a shoestring budget.** These people are movement starters, nonprofit founders, and proactive disruptors. These kinds of Dreamers affect the world by creating award-winning schools like principal Tim King, who founded Urban Prep Academy in Chicago; by spearheading the #MeToo movement like activist Tarana Burke; or by taking a stand to stop child trafficking like bestselling author, speaker, and activist Christine Caine. Activist Dreamers see the problem and want to be the solution.

Do you see yourself in any of these Dreamer profiles? Are you a combination of one or more of these Dreamers? What can you learn from these Dreamers as you create your Stretch?

The Dreamer's Profile Assessment, Part 2, below will help you get a clearer picture of what type of Stretch journey is right for you. Beneath each Dreamer type I've listed elements common to that kind of Dreamer's work environment and risk tolerance. I also include what I think are important considerations characteristic of that type of Dreamer's work and life experience. Read the description of each type of Dreamer, and think about the degree to which you are or would be comfortable with this element in your professional or creative life.

Part 2: Dreamer, Know Thyself

Read through the Dreamer profiles below and take time to consider which of each type of Dreamer's most distinctive characteristics describe you.

Careerpreneur Dreamer

Work Environment

- You work well within structured environments.
- You enjoy working on teams and contributing to a greater vision.
- You're gratified by working within a corporate structure.
- You enjoy the security of stable working environments.
- You like the idea of building a long-standing career within a company.
- You enjoy being required to find solutions to "big business" problems.
- You like routine, schedules, and predictability.

Money Issues and Risk Tolerance

- You need income certainty; you don't do well if you can't count on consistent monthly income.
- You like being able to predict outcomes of financial ventures.

Considerations and Direction

- You do well in careers that offer structure, routine, reliable income, and teamwork.
- Look for careers that let you satisfy your personal purpose within your profession.

- Find work that you feel passionate about.
- Look for employers who welcome an entrepreneurial spirit, who are likely to give you the freedom to spearhead new projects or initiatives that allow you to pioneer and make a difference.

Make-It-Happen Dreamer

Work Environment

- You enjoy working on new concepts and enjoy facing unfamiliar challenges.
- You don't like being confined by structure and expectation.
- You've always wanted to chart your own course.
- You prefer to work for yourself and be your own boss.
- You're not a fan of doing the same tasks every day.

Money Issues and Risk Tolerance

- You can endure the challenges, sacrifices, and sometimes even struggles that come with working for yourself.
- You like to hustle and find ways to make money with business ideas.
- Your risk tolerance is high.
- You're not afraid of an inconsistent income.

Considerations and Direction

- Identify a path that gives you a chance to start your own business and explore an entrepreneurial route.
- Identify opportunities that allow you to express your purpose through your business.
- Ensure that your life's responsibilities can withstand the roller coaster of entrepreneurship.
- Try to keep overhead costs minimal relative to earnings of your Make-It-Happen Dream.

Hobby Dreamer

Work Environment

- Your job doesn't need to be your primary source of fulfillment.
- You have passions and hobbies that you'd like to monetize but that won't necessarily provide steady income.
- You find great fulfillment nurturing your hobby, and you're happy when you can dedicate a lot of time to it.
- You have a strong desire to follow your curiosity and express your passion.
- You want to launch new ideas but may not want to go financially or professionally "all in" on the idea.

Money Issues and Risk Tolerance

- You're willing to invest money in your passion but not willing to risk the disruption of your lifestyle.
- You have responsibilities and commitments for which you depend on your full-time salary.
- You enjoy the security of a stable and consistent job and would find it stressful to depend completely on your passion or hobby for money.
- You think that depending on your passion or hobby fully might take the joy out of the hobby.
- You don't mind investing in a Dream or hobby, but you're not willing to risk it all on a passion just yet.

Considerations and Direction

- Find ways to launch and nurture projects that align with your hobby or passion.
- Work to create balance between your need to keep your career healthy and your need to pursue your passion projects.
- Remember that you're in your hobby for the joy and passion and that this idea doesn't have to develop into a means of support.

CEO Dreamer

Work Environment

- You've worked in corporate environments and have acquired multiple skill sets.
- You've reached a height in a corporate setting, and you're ready to transition to running your own venture.
- Corporate structure no longer offers enough challenge or fulfillment.
- You want to be your own boss.
- You know how to use your skills to make money.
- You enjoy routines, schedule, and predictability.

Money Issues and Risk Tolerance

- Your risk tolerance may not be as high as that of a Make-It-Happen Dreamer.
- You might feel more daring after certain personal responsibilities have resolved, such as your kids graduating from college.
- You have access to a comfortable amount of savings, and you're willing to invest it as a bet on yourself in this new venture.
- You have access to people who will give you capital to start this venture.

Considerations and Direction

- This CEO may blossom later in a career, after personal responsibilities have subsided, such as kids graduating from college.
- Start planning your corporate career exit transition in advance.
- Start researching and taking other necessary steps to establish your business structure while still working at your current job.
- Work to develop the courage to leave job security for a riskier environment.
- Begin to map your exit strategy.
- Conduct Dream checkups to determine if your time to transition is now.

- When you leave, make sure that mentors, supporters, and other members of your network know your plans so they can offer support.
- Consider how your corporate skills will support your entrepreneurial venture, and draft a plan to transition those skills to your new business and monetize accordingly.
- You might have to be willing to use savings to support your lifestyle as you transition.
- Be prepared—you might have to downsize.

Activist Dreamer

Work Environment

- It's important to you that your work is about fighting a social injustice or improving some aspect of the world.
- You are often pained by the realities of the world.
- You see injustice or a need and feel moved to do something about it.
- You feel aware and called on to improve the world.
- You need to be a part of an organization or company that has solid principles and stands for something important.
- You need to feel that your time on earth is about making a positive impact.
- You don't wait for other people to create change; you're willing to work and fight for positive change.
- You like routines, schedule, and predictability.

Money Issues and Risk Tolerance

- Driven primarily by the cause; money is not a primary motivator.
- Might be willing to accept accept a lower salary if the cause is meaningful.
- Driven by purpose first, profit second.
- The more important the cause is to you, the more likely you will "risk it all" in the name of the cause.

Considerations and Direction

- Find work environments, organizations, or nonprofits that allow you to affect lives, fight against injustice, or otherwise align with causes that matter to you.
- Volunteer for organizations that fight for issues you care about.
- Research the possibilities of starting a nonprofit to tackle social causes.
- Explore how to use elements of your day job as a force for change.

Do you see yourself in these profiles? Do you identify solidly with one type? Do you possess qualities of more than one? How might you use this information as you begin your Stretch journey?

THE DREAMER'S RISK TOLERANCE

Next, let's explore risk tolerance. The Stretch isn't a program designed to flip your life upside down. I'm here to make sure that you Stretch into your Dream responsibly.

If you view the journey of a Dreamer only from the vantage point of what you see on social media, you might start believing that people all are quitting their 9-to-5 jobs and risking it all to become entrepreneurs. I was ecstatic to leave the parking lot on my last day at IBM, but I wouldn't offer my path as a one-size-fits-all Dream solution for everyone. Your current financial responsibilities might include supporting a spouse, children, and elderly parents. Maybe you have a long-term rental agreement or mortgage, student loans, and other financial obligations that prevent your being able to say goodbye to a steady paycheck and benefits. There's no shame in beginning to pursue your Dream as a side hustle or part-time venture while keeping your full-time job. If you've established seniority, credibility, and flexibility within your current career, your Stretch could be about monetizing your side hustle. Perhaps within your current work environment you'll find future potential business partners or connections who will one day support your next Dream.

Popular blogger, speaker, and *New York Times* bestselling author Luvvie Ajayi notes that fulfilling your Dream doesn't mean jumping into irrational decisions. She says, "There's nothing wrong with collecting a check from somebody else, because that check can actually help you build your dreams. It's not about leaping blindly. Going after our dreams doesn't stop bills from being there and doesn't stop you from having to pay your rent, so make sound decisions for what's best for your own life based on where you are."

Now, if you're "traveling light" as I was when I left Minneapolis—that is, with no significant other, no dependents, and no substantial real estate investments—you might be in a great position to Stretch into creating your exit plan, building up your savings account, and actively researching your field of interest.

Although we've all heard the stories of people who "risked it all" and scored big, that's not a mandate to pursue your goal while teetering on the edge of poverty or otherwise taking on massive stress or anxiety. As minister and author Michael Bernard Beckwith once said, "You can't be the light of the world if you're worried about your light bill." Throughout this book, you're going to read about people with wide-ranging risk tolerance, from low jumpers who figured out how to turn their passions into a steady income stream while working 9-to-5 jobs to high leapers who put all their money on the line to go after their Dreams. The Dreamer's Risk Tolerance Assessment is designed to help you understand your risk tolerance.

EXERCISE 1.2

DREAMER'S RISK TOLERANCE ASSESSMENT

Before you jump into the assessment, it's important to accurately define the risk you'll be taking, because your risk tolerance is an important consideration when determining how you'll Stretch toward your goal. So go ahead, take some time, and think through the following questions about your specific situation and the risk you're considering.

Define the Risk

1. What risk are you taking?
2. What makes it a risk?
3. What will be your potential reward for taking this risk?

The Risk Tolerance Continuum

To fully understand how comfortable you are with risk, we need a clear picture of where you fall on the Risk Tolerance Continuum (Figure 1.1).

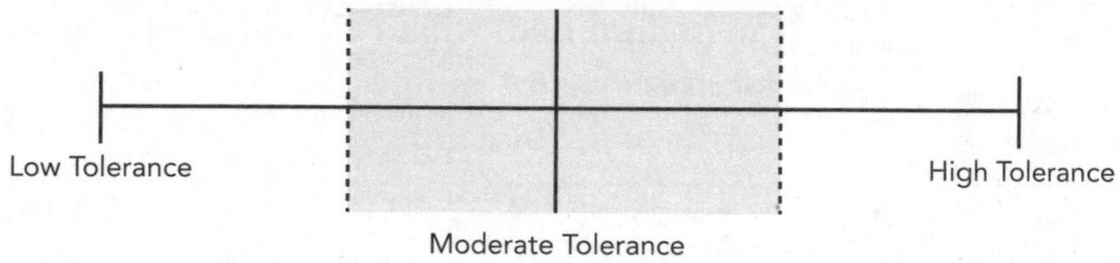

Figure 1.1 Risk Tolerance Continuum

To determine your position on the continuum, complete the following **Risk Audit** and **Risk Assessment**.

STEP 1: Risk Audit

To effectively determine your risk tolerance, let's start with an honest assessment of your current situation. What outcome do you desire most from pursuing this goal? What are your current responsibilities? Who depends on you? What are your motivations and concerns? Take some time to think through these questions and write your answers.

These answers and others will help determine not only the likelihood that you'll complete your Stretch, but the extent to which your life can tolerate risks within your Stretch process. If you have many responsibilities (and people who depend on you for their livelihood), you may be able to take only low-risk steps toward your Stretch, but if you have fewer responsibilities, you may be ready to take bigger steps. You need to identify a path that works for your current stage of life.

Directions

Using the five-category worksheet, think about your life in regard to your current Obligations, Fears, Needs, Roles, and Threats. As you complete the risk audit exercise, consider the financial, psychological, emotional, physical, spiritual, and societal factors that influence your decision to take a risk, or make The Stretch. Read through the Sample Risk Assessing worksheet first and then complete yours afterward.

Sample Risk Assessing Worksheet

Category	Category Definition	Examples of Key Factors
Obligations	Responsibility or duty for which you are primarily (or partially) accountable	Household bills Mortgage College tuition Primary caregiver for parents
Fears	Things (real or imagined) that you are afraid may happen now or in the future.	Failure Decisions' ability to negatively impact your current lifestyle Lose monetary savings Lose position in society, giving up your current working title
Needs	Things that are essential or necessary to live, survive, and thrive Not having them would cause an adverse consequence	Transportation Assurance (the need for a guarantee) Healthcare coverage Stability (consistent income and benefits)
Roles	Function or part you play in your life or someone else's life	Caregiver Primary earner
Threats	Things that are not in your control that can cause damage or harm to you, your family, or your profession	Lose money Saturated market Damage relationships Time constraints (lack of free time does not allow for you to work on Dream)

Now Complete the Form

The Sample Risk Assessing worksheet offered hypothetical responses. Now, you can complete the template below with your personal answers.

Your Risk Assessing Worksheet

Category	Category Definition	Key Factors
Obligations	What are your commitments?	
Fears	What are your apprehensions?	
Needs	What are your nonnegotiables?	
Roles	What are your primary roles?	
Threats	What is happening in the current environment that could negatively affect your Stretch?	

STEP 2: Risk Assessing

1. Prioritize the factors within each category.
2. Circle one factor per category that you believe is the most influential barrier to your willingness to go after your goal.
3. Fill in these five barriers in your notebook or the Risk Assessing worksheet.
4. Identify and fill in one or two ways to overcome each of them or lessen their impact.

Look at the example below for inspiration before you get started.

Sample Risk Assessing Worksheet

Category	Barrier to Dream Progress	Ways to Overcome
Obligations	Household bills	Decrease your overall expenses to reduce risk Create a budget that will yield a 12-month reserve for expenses
Fears	Significant decrease of life savings	Don't depend 100% on this endeavor to support your needs Create a second savings account that you can tap into, in case of emergencies
Needs	Healthcare coverage	If possible, get coverage from your partner's health insurance plan Research and select an alternative healthcare plan (freelancer's insurance, healthcare exchange)
Roles	Caregiver	Hire additional support to assist you with the role Tap your resources: invite friends and relatives to share the responsibilities Research organizations within your area that provide volunteer caregiver services
Threats	Time constraints (e.g., not enough time to work on Dream)	Conduct a time audit to assess which of your current activities can be allotted less time or eliminated Brainstorm household chore time-savers; i.e., order groceries online, use a laundry service

Now it's your turn. Complete the Risk Assessing worksheet.

Your Risk Assessing Worksheet

Category	Barrier to Dream Progress	Ways to Overcome
Obligations		
Fears		
Needs		
Roles		
Threats		

STEP 3: Risk Tolerance Assessment

Now that you have an idea of your current situation and what factors may help you either lean into your Stretch or keep you frozen in position, let's revisit the Risk Tolerance Continuum (Figure 1.1).

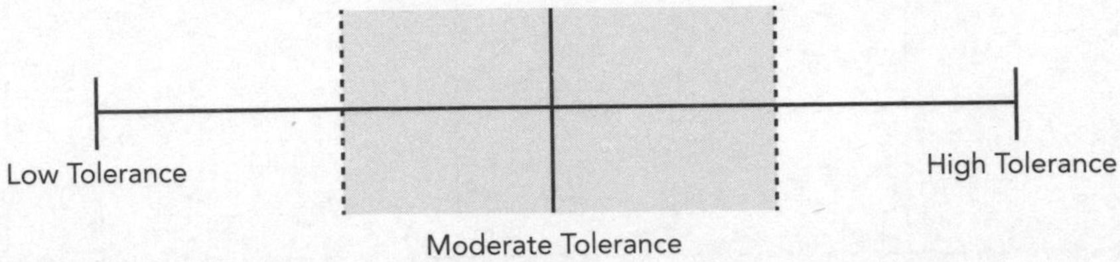

Figure 1.1 Risk Tolerance Continuum

Using the following 10 statements, assess your risk tolerance, determine where you fall on the Risk Tolerance Continuum, and decide how that position affects your ability to fully Stretch.

First, read each statement and check the box with the number that describes you.

After writing your answer for each statement, add the total points for each column in the "Totals" row. Finally, add the column totals together. This final number will be between 10 and 50 and will serve as your Risk Tolerance, or RT.

Your RT# determines where you fall on the Risk Tolerance Continuum and will indicate the recommended actions to be taken based upon your risk tolerance level.

Risk Tolerance Assessment

Statement	1 Does not describe me at all	2	3	4	5 Describes me fully
I am comfortable with failure.					
I am the first to try new things.					
It is important for me to maintain my current lifestyle.					
I am willing to sacrifice for my Dreams or goals.					
I have a strong network of people around me for support.					
I am often labeled as creative or innovative.					
I am considered resilient by others.					
I enjoy new challenges.					
I am responsible for myself and no one else.					
I value stability over change.					
Totals (Add each column.)					
Risk Tolerance Score (RT) (Add totals from above.)					

Write your RT# __________

Low RT#

If your RT# is **between 10 and 24**, you have a **low tolerance** for risk.

Because your tolerance is low, you should:

1. Evaluate which barrier is the biggest impediment to your Stretch.
2. Determine the right timing of the Stretch with the understanding that the "perfect" timing may never exist.
3. Break the Stretch into small pieces that are conducive to your lifestyle (as outlined in the Risk Audit) and your risk tolerance level.

Remember, Stretching isn't always going to be comfortable, but you must push beyond your comfort zone to experience progress. It's important that you take time to assess your current life holistically, which includes who you are, your obligations, your tolerance for risk, and most important, your desired goals.

Moderate RT#

If your RT# is **between 25 and 35**, you have a **moderate tolerance** for risk.

You should determine where you have room to Stretch further and where you should pause. Because you have a moderate risk tolerance, feel free to move past your comfort zone. You may conceive your best ideas when you allow yourself to leave what is comfortable to you.

High RT#

If your RT# is **between 36 and 50**, you have a **high tolerance** for risk.

Given your high tolerance, you need to be a bit more mindful than average about how you Stretch and how your actions affect your lifestyle. While you may be mentally or emotionally prepared to lean into your Stretch, you also need to remember to slow down and evaluate the situation fully. Based on how you completed the Risk Audit, you might discover that there are areas in your life that are not conducive to Stretching at this point. Instead of blindly taking leaps, be sure to fully evaluate the decision and have a specific plan for how you will overcome potential barriers.

Remember, often our best ideas and experiences come from stepping outside of our comfort zones and walking in uncharted territory. But always balance exploration with wisdom.

DISCOVERING YOUR DREAMER'S ANCESTRY

As you explore your Dreamer's DNA, it can be surprisingly helpful to examine your Dreamer's Family Tree. Just as your biological family tree offers insight into your family's geography and history of marriages, births, and deaths, your Dreamer's Family Tree will provide insight into the thoughts, beliefs, motivations, and execution of Dreams within your family.

What you discover in your Dreamer's Family Tree will neither catapult nor halt your success, but it's helpful to know how Dreams are valued within your family. Was Dreaming encouraged? Were Dreamers shunned and shamed? As a child, were you encouraged to imagine your future? Were you taught to believe that Dreaming was connected to your purpose? Was learning how to survive valued over reaching for goals?

Far too often our capacity for Dreaming is defined by the belief systems we're given as children. Particularly for people who grew up in hardship, when survival and harsh economic realities ring loud in your immediate environment, there often isn't room to think very far beyond what you can see today. But exploring our familial beliefs puts us in a better position to define our own destinies.

Although my great-grandparents were hardworking farmers who raised their children with dignity and honor, my mother's parents had a Dream to succeed financially beyond their upbringing. Eventually, my grandparents' drive and hard work helped them secure good jobs with benefits at the Florida State Hospital. These jobs paid for my mother's college education and our first home, which remains in our family even today. My grandparents' hard work played a role in shaping my work ethic as I began to build my career.

Growing up in the small town of Greenwood, Florida, my mother was on track to become a big Dreamer. In high school, she was a cheerleader, pianist, debater, and honor student. But her Dreams took a big turn when she became a mother at 15. After giving birth to me before her junior year, she had to adjust her Dreams and focus on making me her top priority. Despite the challenge of becoming a mother earlier than expected, my mother graduated as her high school's valedictorian, earned her degree from Florida State University, and landed stable jobs that allowed her to raise me and provide for the two of us.

My father was a Renaissance man who lived out multiple Dreams. He was a computer scientist for the U.S. Navy for more than 30 years, a basketball coach for teams throughout his community, a mechanic who could fix anything, and a full-time farmer. He was a super Dreamer who tapped into many abilities and eventually inspired all five of my siblings and me to become entrepreneurs.

While I've always had these great examples in my Dreamer's Family Tree, I wasn't always aware of them. There weren't many discussions in my family about finding and pursuing a passion, so I wound up not pursuing the entrepreneurial lifestyle, but I did find myself on a high-achieving track at IBM instead—at first. But I was miserable in the process, so I needed a new course that included strong doses of purpose and passion.

There are countless interesting and even fascinating stories among the branches of family trees. I had the pleasure of interviewing Dreamer Brandice Daniel, founder and CEO of Harlem's Fashion Row, about how her background influenced the professional she grew to become. She shared a vivid awareness of how much of what she learned from her family stayed with her as she climbed corporate ladders, starting with a father who never took rejection personally. When her father was told "no thanks," she says, "He didn't absorb it. It was like it rolled off his back or he didn't even hear it. Watching him [is why] I think I have a high tolerance for rejection. I just really don't take it personally." Her mother's tireless support of her father's Dreams also left a big impression on Brandice. She recalls, "I watched her never say anything bad about my dad and what we were doing in supporting his dreams. It was like his dream was *our* dream. I didn't even realize that that was something incredible until I became an adult with my own dream."

Make-It-Happen Dreamer Daymond John, investor on ABC's *Shark Tank*, thanks his hardworking parents for modeling a very serious worth ethic. Daymond was 10 years old when his parents divorced, at which point he felt it was time to become "the man of the house." That meant taking on several jobs to try to earn as much money as possible. And he recalls that his parents made clear that education was his ticket to success. He says, "They always taught me to work hard and that my day job wouldn't make me rich. It would be my homework that made me rich." The hard work ethic and drive that was instilled in him as a child heavily influenced him in becoming a successful entrepreneur.

DeVon Franklin, award-winning film and TV producer, bestselling author, and pastor, had a different kind of reaction to his Dreamer's ancestry. It would be an understatement to say that his family didn't support his desire to follow the path that would lead him to become one of Hollywood's "Who's Who." But DeVon wouldn't be dissuaded. After his 36-year-old father suffered a fatal heart attack, 9-year-old DeVon found comfort in the escape offered by film and television. He says that he knew then what his calling was: "There was always something in me that said, 'I need to go to Hollywood and make content—film and television.'"

But his relatives would have no part of it. They went as far as to tell him, "Hollywood's in the devil's playground. If you go there, God's not going to be able to keep you." Imagine that kind of pressure on the psyche of a nine-year-old Dreamer. But DeVon knew where he was headed.

It was later that he realized that his family's attempts to discourage him were based in their own value systems and aversion to things that scared them. His family members were not the kind that lived out their Dreams. He recalls, "I found out that it's very hard to encourage someone to follow their dreams if you've given up on yours." Firmly grounded in his belief that he was following the right path, DeVon wasn't going to be dissuaded by the feelings of others. Family or not, he wasn't going to let others dictate his future, especially if their direction was based in a lack of information. He told his family, "Look, I love y'all. I respect you. But you're giving me an opinion about Hollywood based on your secondhand account of what somebody told you *they* think it is." With love, he made his intentions clear and set off for success under the bright lights.

Regardless of which way the apples from your family tree fall, having awareness of your Dreamer's Family Tree can be valuable.

EXERCISE 1.3

DISCOVERING YOUR DREAMER'S ANCESTRY

The Discovering Your Dreamer's Ancestry Questionnaire is designed to help you discover how your family's Dreaming patterns influence your Dream potential. Answer each question as fully as possible.

1. What did the following members of your family believe about Dreams?

   Mother: ______________________________

   Father: ______________________________

   maternal Grandmother: ______________________________

   maternal Grandfather: ______________________________

   paternal Grandmother: ______________________________

   paternal Grandfather: ______________________________

   Other adults significant in your upbringing, like aunts, uncles, stepparents, or other caregivers: ______________________________

2. What Dreams did these members of your family have as children?

   Mother: ______________________________

   Father: ______________________________

   maternal Grandmother: ______________________________

   maternal Grandfather: ______________________________

   paternal Grandmother: ______________________________

   paternal Grandfather: ______________________________

   Other adults: ______________________________

3. Did the following members of your family live out their childhood Dreams? If so, what were those Dreams? If not, what did they become instead?

   Mother: ______________________________

   Father: ______________________________

   maternal Grandmother: ______________________________

   maternal Grandfather: ______________________________

   paternal Grandmother: ______________________________

   paternal Grandfather: ______________________________

   Other adults: ______________________________

4. Were the family members below resentful, disappointed, or regretful about the pursuit or the lack of pursuit of their Dreams?

   Mother: ______________________________

   Father: ______________________________

   maternal Grandmother: ______________________________

   maternal Grandfather: ______________________________

   paternal Grandmother: ______________________________

   paternal Grandfather: ______________________________

   Other adults: ______________________________

5. How did your family's beliefs about Dreaming affect your journey?

   ____

   ____

   ____

   ____

6. How did your family's beliefs about Dreaming influence your career choices?

____

____

____

____

7. How did your family's beliefs about Dreaming affect your earning capability?

____

____

____

____

8. What beliefs from your family continue to propel your Dreams forward?

____

____

____

____

9. What beliefs from your family might derail your Dreams?

____

____

____

____

Congratulations! You're almost finished with Week 1 of The Stretch! Now I'm excited to tell you about the bonus information available to you every week. At the end of each chapter, you'll see a **web address** that will link you to content from interviews with Dream All-Stars who have mastered the art of The Stretch. You may access this content by visiting **www.TheBigStretchBook.com**. Our Dream All-Stars share valuable words of wisdom, insight, and inspiration, and I know you'll enjoy reading their stories.

With great pleasure, I introduce you to your first Dream All-Star, a *Shark Tank* investor, author, public speaker, founder of FUBU, and former global Ambassador for Entrepreneurship under President Barack Obama.

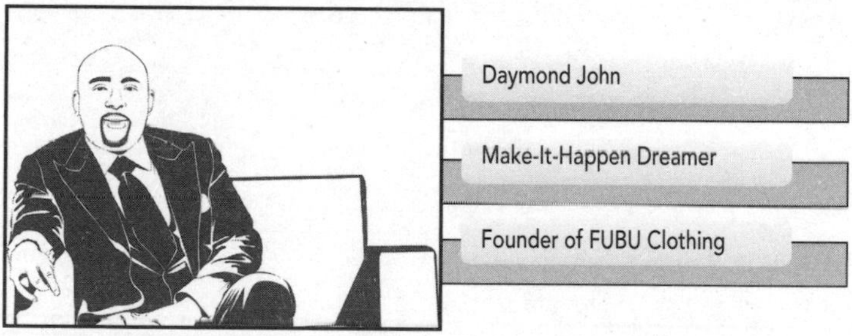

> "We're all born thinking like entrepreneurs. We say, 'I'm gonna be Superman. I'm gonna change the world. I'm gonna save the seals. I'm gonna be the richest person on the planet.' Society then says, 'You have to go and get a job,' and I think we're taught not to think like entrepreneurs. We need to teach kids to think like entrepreneurs."
>
> —Make-It-Happen Dreamer **Daymond John**

You may download this week's Dream All-Star training session at www.thebigstretchbook.com.

CHAPTER TWO

DREAMING IN COLOR

Week 2

Before I created my company, EGAMI, I Dreamed of having an all-white office. I would visualize this office, and in my imagination, I'd walk around in this space, making myself feel at home there. Years later, when I finally secured my first office in Manhattan, I shared this vision with my interior designer. "I want the walls white," I told her. "I want my team to be able to write their ideas all over the place." My desire was to give my team a white canvas to serve as a reminder that every day is an opportunity to create new possibilities, campaigns, and ideas for our clients. By providing a white canvas for my team, I was fostering and nurturing my team's creativity.

If you're the type who doesn't view yourself as creative, remember that we all have the ability to be creative to some degree. Sure, creative people tend to differ from more analytical people in that creatives are more comfortable in the art of capturing and expressing their imaginative energy, but maybe they've just had more practice. Regardless of whether you have a creative-sounding title like "visual artist" or a more traditional businesslike one like "corporate accountant," if you can imagine, you can be a Dreamer.

You might be tempted to skip over a chapter that focuses on honing your imagination, but we've already established that your imagination is your God-given superpower, so why not learn how to embrace this gift and Dream as you've never Dreamed before?

Every day, creative people are shaking up the world with breakthrough ideas and innovations—creative people like Caryn Seidman Becker, who took the hassle out of airport security checks with CLEAR, Hannah Beachler, who was the set designer for the sci-fi blockbuster film *Black Panther*, and Pat McGrath who is revolutionizing beauty with her innovative line of cosmetics, Pat McGrath Labs. These creative people began by simply tapping into their imaginations.

In the second week of The Stretch, I'm going to show you the power and benefits of dreaming in color. Together we'll work through the following Stretch exercises:

Week 2: Dreaming in Color

EXERCISE 2.1: Dreaming Your Dream Environment
EXERCISE 2.2: Dreaming in Childlike Wonder
EXERCISE 2.3: Your One-Year Dream Projection
EXERCISE 2.4: Create Your 90-Day Stretch Plan
EXERCISE 2.5: Declare Your Dream

COLORING YOUR WHITE CANVAS

As you get ready to Stretch during this next 90 days, you have a fresh white canvas on which to explore your biggest ideas. You're just like an artist who has access to every color in the largest imaginable crayon box. But before I invite you to break out your crayons with me, I want to share how some of our Dream All-Stars are using their imaginations to create extraordinary masterpieces in their lives and businesses.

CEO Dreamer, author, and digital strategist Luvvie Ajayi finds that her creativity is unleashed when she takes a look around at what other people are doing. Reading books, blogs, and even Twitter inspires her to "create dope things. Because seeing people do creative things makes me want to do creative things also, and it makes me want to step my game up." Make-It-Happen Dreamer and Grammy Award–winning rapper MC Lyte shares Luvvie's appreciation for the power of observing. She says that being open and taking in different art forms is her way of awakening the creative muse. "I unleash creativity simply by being an open vessel and listening to people talk, watching art wherever I can see it, watching a great movie, be it black and white or of this time," she told the Dream Project. "Watching stand-up comedy sometimes will hit a note for me, and they'll speak of something very quickly, but I'll take that and just elaborate on it." She acknowledges that she doesn't have a system; rather, she just lets the creativity flow in by exposing her creative eye to the work of others and letting it inspire. "My creative process isn't a process at all. It's just *to be*."

If there's a Make-It-Happen Dreamer who knows how to find the next idea, it's Earvin "Magic" Johnson, CEO and chairman of Magic Johnson Enterprises. He has a bustling life, and to find the center of his ideas, Magic likes it quiet. During his time with the Dream Project, he told fellow Dreamers, "For me it's always being able to be still first because when you're still, everything just comes to you. Those moments when I'm just sitting there chilling, whether it's on a plane, whether it's at my desk, whether it's on a treadmill, whether it's on the bike, and especially when I'm by water—my next moves always come to me."

Harriette Cole, CEO Dreamer and president of Harriette Cole Media, experienced the magical nature of the creative spirit firsthand thanks to the one and only Prince. Harriette met the musician when she was editor-in-chief of *Ebony* magazine and interviewed him for a cover story. Later, upon Prince's request, she joined his "Welcome to America" tour for a year of interviewing world-class musicians and producing a documentary based on the 21 nights that Prince played Los Angeles (and charged only $25 per ticket). Harriette was at a time of professional and creative transition, and she fondly recalls the inspiration he offered. He reminded her that the ideas are in her and that the time is now. She recalls, "What I got from Prince was, 'You can do anything you want. Anything that's good, you can do. In fact, you can do it now.' He felt that if you have a great idea, you can draw the energy to you, and it can happen."

GIVE YOURSELF TIME TO IMAGINE

One of the biggest challenges of being an adult whose life is fully loaded with a family, a career or business, and other countless responsibilities is that we don't give ourselves time and space to just think. Think about it: when was the last time you gave yourself even a solid hour to daydream possibilities for your personal life, your professional growth, or your creative Dreams? When was the last time you unplugged from all your devices, took a walk, and just wondered? If you're like most people with busy schedules, this kind of time out is rare or nonexistent. But studies have shown that the most creative people spend time each week engaging in self-development work, daydreaming, taking time for solitude, seeking new experiences, and asking big questions, like "What if . . . ?"

"What if I quit my job next month?"

"What if I didn't have any financial limitations?"

"What if I moved to a new city where no one knows me?"

"What if I could snap my fingers and be successful in any career right now; which career would I choose?"

"What if I weren't afraid of change?"

Take as much time as you can to simply let "What if" questions lead to answers loaded with possibility.

Your ideal time to create might be while you're commuting to and from your job, waiting for your child to finish basketball practice, or traveling by train or plane. One Dreamer shared with me that she uses the 30 minutes from 11:30 to midnight each night to imagine and work on her goals. Whether it's a half hour after putting your kids to bed or an unexpected five-hour delay at an airport, use this time to allow your mind to roam.

FIND YOUR CREATIVE ZONE

In order to fully tap into your imagination, you must be in tune with how you receive your inspiration. Ask yourself . . .

- At what time of day is my mind most receptive to new ideas?
- What kinds of tools do I like to use when I create? Whiteboard? Pen and paper? Laptop? Colored pencils? Bound journal?
- Where do I like to receive new ideas? At a beach house near the water? On a bench in the heart of a bustling city? In a silent bedroom at the end of a day?
- What kinds of practices do I need to incorporate into my life to hear my ideas more clearly? Meditation? Yoga? Prayer? Deep breathing?

Some of the most innovative thinkers of our time have learned to tap into their creative zones in unusual ways. Steve Jobs, the late founder of Apple, routinely sat on toilets dangling his bare feet while he came up with new ideas. Yoshiro Nakamatsu, inventor of the floppy disk, would dive deep under water until his brain was deprived of oxygen and then write his ideas on an underwater sticky pad. Jay-Z, hip-hop artist and entrepreneur, strengthened his memory by training himself to create little corners in his mind where he'd "store" his rhymes.

EXERCISE 2.1

DREAMING YOUR DREAM ENVIRONMENT

Give yourself 30 minutes this week to describe, in writing, your ideal Dream environment. Maybe you'll discover that you like Dreaming with music in the background or sketching your ideas while sitting near a dog park. Maybe you'll find yourself most excited about the idea of Dreaming while surrounded by items that reflect your Dream, like a bookstore or library, an athletic court or field, a crowded mall or farmer's market. This simple activity gives you a chance to envision the ideal space for your imagination to grow.

Some years ago, I discovered how powerful it can be to find an ideal creative environment. At the beginning of 2011, I told my mother and my close circle of friends that I "felt pregnant" with ideas that I couldn't wait to bring into the world. But in the midst of my frenetic life, I couldn't concentrate on the messages and ideas that I felt were trying to emerge. My mother suggested that I get away and change my scenery, perhaps escape to a natural environment, the kind she knows that I love. I took her advice and booked a getaway to Pine Mountain, Georgia, to give myself a few days of solitude in hope of giving birth to some new ideas.

When I arrived in Pine Mountain, I took time to pray, meditate, and walk in the relative quiet. After a few days, ideas began to flow. It was as if my ideas were saying, "Thank you! We finally have the space to come through!" I wrote, sketched, and posted my ideas on the walls around the cabin and had no fear or judgment about their content. I began to refer to these ideas as my Dream Babies.

Of course, we don't all have the luxury of dashing off to a beautiful setting and spending days alone in quiet contemplation. For me, the opportunity was a godsend, and for the discovery of this place I'm forever grateful. As creators, it is important that you become aware of the kinds of settings and scenarios that make you feel creative or inspired and do your best to spend time in those situations when you can.

RELEASE THE "HOW?" AND DREAM FREELY

Once you've discovered your creative zone and you let the Dreams start flowing, you might find yourself getting prematurely stuck in the "how?" I frequently hear aspiring Dreamers say things like, "I have the idea, but I don't know how to get started." "Am I qualified to pull this off?" "How am I going to open a new business with no capital?" "How can I move to a new city without a network?"

Now isn't the time to worry about how you're going to execute the details of this Dream. Now is the time to Dream. When you're unwilling to let your ideas flow freely, you could be killing them before they get off the ground. There will be plenty of time to explore the viability of your idea, to answer all those "How will I?" questions. But for now, all your Dream needs is the freedom to reveal itself to you. And for you to get out of its way.

A few years ago, my mother and I were creating vision boards. She had always Dreamed of visiting Paris, and she had no idea that I'd already purchased tickets for her fantasy vacation and planned to surprise her with them during our vision board session. As we created our vision boards, I placed an image of the Eiffel Tower in front of her. She said, "That shouldn't go on my board. I won't be able to get the time off work, and I can't even think about splurging on such an expensive trip."

I said, "Mom, we're just using our imaginations. Just let yourself imagine your ideal vacation."

She pushed back, "I don't want to think about a trip that I know isn't going to happen." The tickets for her Dream vacation to Paris were within inches of her, but she couldn't let go and simply imagine the outcome she wanted. She was stopped by the "how?" Talk about a Dream spoiler!

I eventually taped the tickets on her vision board and said, "Mom, you're going to Paris!" When it occurred to my mother that her Dream vacation was going to be a reality, she screamed, burst from her chair, and threw her arms around me. Only after she could actually see that her Dream was going to come true did she let herself believe it was possible.

I love my mother dearly, *dearly*. But I hope you won't follow her footsteps and get caught up in the "how?" Many of the world's best ideas are born without knowing how they'll come to be.

I'm pretty sure that when Sara Blakely had the idea to reinvent the girdle, she had no idea how to create a prototype, raise capital, and manufacture her product. She wasn't a retail guru, but she didn't let the "how?" stop her from creating Spanx, a multibillion-dollar intimate apparel company. When George Lucas imagined an alternate universe that the world came to know as the Star Wars franchise, he hadn't yet worked out how to translate the idea into cinematic reality. But that didn't stop him from becoming one of Hollywood's most iconic directors. When Oprah Winfrey decided to leave Baltimore for Chicago in the winter of 1983, she didn't know how to position her show to compete against the popular daytime talk show host Phil Donahue. But she didn't let the "how?" stop her from transforming a little talk show called *AM Chicago* into *The Oprah Winfrey Show* which would run for 25 years and grow to become the highest-syndicated daytime talk show in history. As these Dreamers have demonstrated, you simply have to let go of the "how?" and let yourself dream.

BIRTHING YOUR DREAMS IS A PROCESS

In their earliest stages, ideas that become Dreams and then become living enterprises need time to gestate. We can feel them growing, and we have to be patient as they develop while at the same time helping them through the process. And here's an exciting thought: the Dream Babies you parent will someday become teenagers! They grow beyond their original state, and you'll have to adjust to those changes. But first, remember that getting your ideas from conception to reality doesn't happen right away—regardless of how excited you might be about jumping in. It's a process. (And to any of the male Dreamers, don't be put off by the birth metaphors—think of yourselves as male seahorses, those miraculous creatures who produce the seahorse offspring!)

Remember those Dream Babies that came to be in Pine Mountain? My first of those little darlings was the idea of creating a forum to inspire other Dreamers. I could clearly picture the participants and speakers gathering to share great ideas and craft plans to change the world. That vision inspired the idea that eventually became The Dream Project, my yearly symposium of great minds that has now served thousands of Dreamers.

My second Dream Baby was to create a ceremony to salute living visionaries, organizations, and companies that positively affect multicultural communities. That ceremony eventually became EGAMI's Purpose Awards, which honor purpose-driven leaders and companies for the remarkable work they do. Some of the recipients include Disney for its Dreamers' Academy; Eunique Jones Gibson, the force behind the award-winning "Because of Them We Can" campaign that helps people of color reimagine their possibilities; and Beverly Bond, who has inspired millions of black women around the world with her groundbreaking movement Black Girls Rock.

My third Dream Baby was to cultivate a place where Dreamers could give birth to their Dreams. I could clearly see that this divine place should be an escape into the magic of the woods. It would be another six years before this vision came to life, but, finally, in the spring of 2018, I purchased a beautiful space in the Appalachian mountains of Blue Ridge, Georgia, that I lovingly named "The Dream Maker." And one of the first Dreams to emerge from the Dream Maker is this very book that you hold in your hands.

All three of these ideas required planning and patience, and yet there were times when I felt impatient with each one's gestation period. But I did my best to be patient with the process necessary for the evolution of each, and in the end, what were once ideas became real, living Dreams that I'm deeply proud of.

Dreams Need a Willing Yes to Come to Life

Bestselling author and public speaker Elizabeth Gilbert said it best when she acknowledged that we have to be a willing *yes* to our Dreams. In her book *Big Magic*, she advises, "Keep your eyes open. Listen. Follow your curiosity. Ideas are constantly trying to get your attention. Let them know you are available." I agree. I also believe in taking that idea a step further by asking, "Where do our Dreams come from?" Our Dreams are from a higher source. I choose to call this magical, never-ending source of inspiration "God." I was raised as and still am a Christian who believes in the power of God and Jesus Christ. But I'm aware that "God" can mean different things to different people, and I invite you to consider that your ideas are coming from a power greater than yourself, one that's working on your behalf to help you fulfill your destiny.

CEO Dreamer Tai Beauchamp, CEO of Tai Life Media, is a strong believer in this concept. She says that prayer and meditation lead her to be able to hear what God has in mind for her. "I have learned that to be still is one of the ways I'm able to tap into the creator within me. Faith is also another way that I do it. So constantly practice prayer and meditation because when we talk about the creator within us, it comes first from the creator that created us and planted that seed there."

Belief is key in the Dreaming process. If you can believe that something has given you this precious idea and has chosen you to be the one to bring it to life, that's powerful. This kind of thinking equips you to move ahead with the strength that comes with a sense of responsibility that developing and nurturing this Dream is your mission, and the world needs you to follow through. So what Dream is waiting for your yes?

Christine Caine, Activist Dreamer, author, and founder of the anti–human trafficking organization A21, felt that there was nothing to do but say yes when she heard the call of victims of human trafficking. In an airport in Greece, she saw posters of children and young women who were alleged victims of human trafficking, and she was both appalled and awakened. Christine knew she couldn't leave the issue alone, but she had no idea what to do about it. Despite that she didn't have a plan, Christine clearly had the motivation to say yes to the idea that was only just beginning to develop. Of the A21 organization that she founded as a result of her willingness to say yes, Christine now proudly says, "I couldn't have known then that it would become in eight years what is probably the largest anti-trafficking organization in the world. We're in 14 countries." As an inspiring Activist Dreamer, Christine is a great reminder that the person best to solve the problem, to answer the call, is you. Christine now speaks with the conviction of a true Activist Dreamer. "Don't look at what you can't do, look at where you can start. Just start from where you are."

Careerpreneur Dreamer, comedian, writer, and actress Yvonne Orji said a very big yes! to an idea that no one in her family expected. Her parents wanted her to follow a traditional career path; they expected her to be an engineer, a lawyer, or a doctor. Yvonne was walking that path as a graduate student in public health when her brother asked if she was interested in entering a beauty pageant. Although it wasn't her kind of thing, she said yes. Then she realized that the pageant was part talent competition, so another big yes! came when she chose to perform stand-up comedy. The performance was a hit, and that's when Yvonne knew that comedy needed to be part of her future. That big yes! has led to her starring in the HBO hit series *Insecure*. That's the power of yes.

SUSTAINING THE VISION FOR YOUR DREAM

I began to understand the power of visualization as I trained for the New York City Marathon. Years before I laced up my running shoes, I pictured myself running in a marathon; I created an image of myself fit, dressed to run, and crossing the finish line. I don't know where this vision came from or why it lodged itself in my mind as a goal. I wasn't even a runner! But I allowed the idea to marinate, and I knew that when the time was right, I would take action steps to bring this vision to life.

In my early training days when I was able to run only 2 miles, I regularly revisited my vision of completing all of the race's 26.2 miles. Again and again, I let myself feel the excitement of finishing the race. But as I went further into my training, I began to break the vision of completing the marathon into more manageable increments. During the early phases of training, 26.2 miles was just too great a distance for me to run, so I set myself up for little successes along the way to that goal. I did this by visualizing myself completing each run successfully and increasing my distance by 2 or 3 miles each week until I could finally complete my longest required run of 20 miles. **My grand vision was achievable because I set my sights on smaller goals along the way to it.** Although I completed the actual race on November 5, 2017, for months prior I'd visualized myself dashing across that finish line.

Because I strongly believe in imaginative Dreaming and visioning, I put these concepts into practice within my company, EGAMI Group. Once a year, I meet with my team to focus on our three-year vision. During this yearly planning session, we stop to engage in a closed-eye meditation during which we participate in a guided visualization, and from there, we determine what needs to happen during the next year to fulfill our three-year vision. Then we focus on action *now*. We visualize the path to our goals by implementing quarterly milestones—90-day goals—that we work on throughout the year. This process is similar to the journey you will undergo as you work through The Stretch.

Many of my Fortune 100 clients understand the importance of strategic, future-forward visioning. They understand that planning is key to maintaining a competitive edge, and some of them are working on ideas that won't launch for another 10 years. Through visualization, these innovators give themselves the power to travel into the future.

Envisioning for the future is powerful. So, what does that mean for you? You can use The Stretch to start imagining your biggest vision by Dreaming in Childlike Wonder, developing your One-Year Dream Projection, activating your 90-Day Stretch Plan, and Declaring Your Dream to your trusted circle of family, friends, and close advisors. There's no better time than now to walk into your future. Let's get started!

EXERCISE 2.2

DREAMING IN CHILDLIKE WONDER

Envision yourself at any age between 5 and 10. How did you use your imagination back then? Were you able to disappear into magical fantasy scenarios? Could you become a flying horse, a superhero, a tiny insect? Did your play sometimes resemble reality, as in playing teacher, surgeon, or horse trainer? Did you enjoy imaginative play without limitations?

Now, with childlike wonder, take yourself back to the beginning when your Dream first occurred to you. Can you recall the excitement you felt? Do you remember the possibilities you imagined? I welcome you to now bring those feelings forward into your mind and explore this bold, bright Dream by using your childlike wonder. Allow yourself to imagine the business, career, profession, and passion you can create. Remember to leave your adulthood worries about "how?" at the door and just daydream.

After you've given yourself time to Dream in Childlike Wonder, break out your colored markers, pencils, pens, or crayons to capture the ideas and images from this exercise. Sketch, draw, or write your Dream in your Dream Notebook.

EXERCISE 2.3

YOUR ONE-YEAR DREAM PROJECTION

Now that you have a clearer picture of your big childlike Dream, what part of it can you turn into reality within the next year? Close your eyes and imagine your life one year from now, after your Dream has become reality. What business idea have you brought to life? How much money have you earned within the last year? How many people have benefited from your idea? How many new team members are working with you to execute your Dream? What kind of impact have you made in the marketplace?

Or if you like thinking in terms of the flip side, ask yourself how you might feel if you do nothing to change your life, if you take no steps forward to make this Dream a reality. If that scenario sounds dark, think of how lucky you are: you can turn the clock right back to today and get started!

In your notebook, write your One-Year Dream Projection. Feel free to write in fragments and with bullet points, to scribble or sketch—use any format that you enjoy.

EXERCISE 2.4

CREATE YOUR 90-DAY STRETCH PLAN

Now that you have a One-Year Dream Projection, it's time to create your 90-Day Stretch Plan. Look at your notes from Exercise 2.3 and ask yourself, "How can I take action now?" Which parts of your One-Year Dream Projection can you accomplish in the next 90 days? Can you launch your first blog? Can you create a crowdfunding campaign for your business? Can you record one song for your album? Can you write the first chapter of your book? Break your 90-Day Stretch Plan down into weekly goals for the next 12 weeks. Select one or more doable parts of your Dream that you can accomplish within the next 90 days. This will be your focus for the 90-Day Stretch Plan.

Refer to the sample below and then begin creating your own 90-Day Stretch Plan. Remember that if you can measure it, you can hold yourself accountable for it.

SAMPLE EXERCISES

DREAMING IN CHILDLIKE WONDER: Become a global media expert for vegans and vegetarians

ONE-YEAR DREAM PROJECTION: Become an expert blogger for vegans and vegetarians

90-DAY STRETCH PLAN: Launch a blog focusing on recipes, lifestyle, and restaurant recommendations for new vegans and vegetarians

Sample Weekly Goals for a 90-Day Stretch Plan

Weeks 1–3	Weeks 4–6	Weeks 7–9	Weeks 10–12
Finalize blog name and purchase domain and website	Set up social media accounts and YouTube channel	Identify social media influencers	Send promotional posts to influencers
Brainstorm content for first five blog posts	Finalize first five blog posts	Build social media audience Facebook: Increase to 1,000 followers Instagram: Increase to 1,500 followers Twitter: Increase to 1,000 followers	Send out blog teasers on Facebook, Twitter, and Instagram
Create a first draft for each blog post	Identify relevant hashtags and trends	Identify relevant hashtags and trends	Launch blog on January 1

Now, as in the sample, write one action sentence each for the following:

- Your vision as you Dreamed in Childlike Wonder
- Your One-Year Dream Projection
- Your 90-Day Stretch Plan

Dreaming in Childlike Wonder:

One-Year Dream Projection:

90-Day Stretch Plan:

Next, fill in the boxes below with your corresponding goals for weeks 1 through 12.

Your Weekly Goals for a 90-Day Stretch Plan

Weeks1–3	Weeks 4–6	Weeks 7–9	Weeks 10–12

KEEP AN EYE ON YOUR 90-DAY STRETCH PLAN GOALS

Think of your getting to the end of this chapter as a kind of firing of the starting gun. You've created your 90-Day Stretch Plan, and each week, you'll want to check in with yourself (and I'll be there to remind you!) to make sure that you're hitting the goals you set. One of my dear business coaches, EOS Implementer and CEO Dreamer Dan Coleman, advises referring to management consultant George T. Doran's famous acronym, SMART, when you set goals. Make sure your goals are specific, measurable, attainable, realistic, and timely. You've created manageable steps to take on the way to realizing your big goal. Now be your own taskmaster to make sure that by the end of each week you've taken those steps and have advanced one week closer to the realization of your wonderful Dream.

EXERCISE 2.5

DECLARE YOUR DREAM

The Association for Talent Development (ATD) did a study on accountability and found that you have a 65 percent chance of completing a goal if you "officially" tell someone else that you're committing to reach that goal. Choose three people you trust to tell about your One-Year Dream Projection and your 90-Day Stretch Plan. These people don't need to offer feedback or opinions about your Dreams. Their role is simply to provide a safe space for you to Declare Your Dream and to hold you accountable for moving forward.

In your notebook, write down the name of your accountability partners and the date you Declared Your Dream to them. You can use the simple format below:

Dream Accountability Partner 1: ______________________________
Declared Dream on This Date: ______________________________

Dream Accountability Partner 2: ______________________________
Declared Dream on This Date: ______________________________

Dream Accountability Partner 3: ______________________________
Declared Dream on This Date: ______________________________

Congratulations, Dreamer! You are officially almost finished with Week 2 of The Stretch. Your Dream All-Star this week is the founder and CEO of Harlem's Fashion Row (HFR), a prestigious platform for multicultural fashion designers, and the cofounder of *Great Girlfriends*, a podcast created to offer women daily tips and solutions for living passionate lives and building thriving businesses. She went from being an industry outsider to now being called by the *Wall Street Journal*, "A Fashion Insider That Pushes for Diversity."

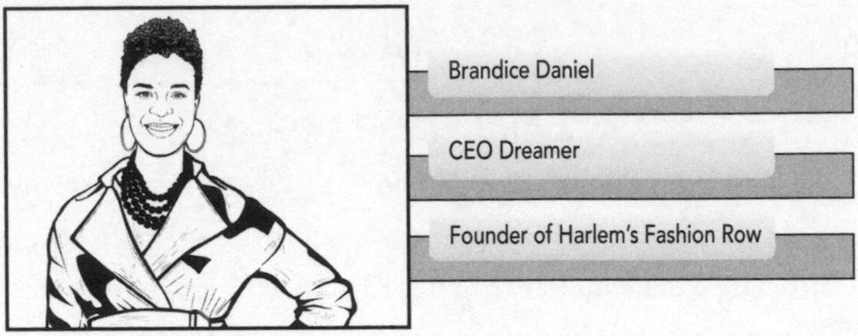

"I didn't have any experience doing a fashion show from start to finish. I didn't even know what kind of people I'd need to put it together, but I was convinced that this dream was given to me. I felt that so strongly that I didn't worry about how I was going to make it happen. I just kept going."

—CEO Dreamer **Brandice Daniel**

You may download this week's Dream All-Star training session at www.thebigstretchbook.com.

CHAPTER THREE

THE DREAM DETOX

Week 3

By now, you're starting to have a clearer picture of the Dream that you'll work toward, and I hope your heart is starting to beat faster with anticipation. You should now have your One-Year Dream Projection and 90-Day Stretch Plan ready to go. The work you've done to create this precious new idea has likely activated your imagination, and you're excited to bring the Dream to life. But will your current system of spiritual, mental, and physical habits help this new idea blossom into a fruitful reality?

In the first year of the Dream Project, I was very fortunate to host a session entitled "Exploring the Mind, Body, and Spirit" featuring some All-Star Dreamers who shared tips and tricks for getting in Dream-catching shape. This chapter will feature insights from Dreamers that will help keep your mind, body, and spirit fit as you Stretch toward your Dream for the long term. CEO Dreamer Sylvia High, life coach, author, and CEO of Aiming High, reminds us that mental toughness comes with balance and that balance is at the heart of fulfillment. "Dreaming is about living a fulfilled, full life. So many of us find ourselves living one dimension. We'll get our health part and the physical fitness really set, but we've lost our spirit. . . . Your spirit will drive you and give you the power to manage your mind because we must be the runners of our minds and not let our minds be the runners of us."

Developing mental readiness is a crucial part of The Stretch. Perhaps you've discovered that you're an Activist Dreamer and are ready to launch a platform that fights social unfairness in your community. Or maybe you're a Hobby Dreamer who feels that it's finally time for you to monetize your passions or express your underutilized talents. But are you *mentally* ready to pursue this new Dream? Are voices of doubt clanging in your head? Are the reasons to abandon this new Dream starting to sound louder than the reasons to go for it? Let me assure you that if your doubts and fears are starting to kick up during this third week of The Stretch, you're in exactly the right place.

At this point you've accepted that you're the chosen one to say "yes!" to this beautiful new vision. You've decided to have faith and jump in, and then *bam!* you lie awake at night pondering every reason your Dream won't work. Maybe you let your Dream out of the can too early or told a well-meaning but shortsighted friend about your idea, and your friend tore it to shreds. Having such doubts and fears is a very natural part of your Stretch.

You're going to have internal dialogues during which you try to talk yourself out of going through all the hassles to come. You're going to like the idea of staying in your comfort zone. You'll think about sinking back into the familiar. Even without being aware of it, you may even start to self-sabotage by thinking, *This is too much work*, or *These risks are going to add too much stress to my life*.

Activist Dreamer and founder of the #MeToo movement Tarana Burke knows about the importance of fighting negative self-talk. She recently shared with me in an interview, "One of my favorite sayings is 'feelings aren't facts.' It's hard to convince yourself that you can do something when it looks like so many other people are already doing it and doing it better. You have to really work on dealing with the negative self-doubt that says that you can't obtain your dreams. You have to actively tell yourself every day, 'This is not true.'"

There's a lot more to consider here than just your present state of mind. As I say to many of my high achievers at the Dream Project, this Dream isn't about just you. People will be inspired by your effort and tenacity, and many people will benefit from your going after this Dream. Maybe your promotional services will launch a musician's career. Maybe your food truck will provide the quick, healthy meals that an office manager has been searching for to keep her team energized. Perhaps your product or activism will reunite estranged families or even save lives. No matter what kind of Dream you're making reality for yourself, it will have an effect on others. People's lives will change. Your idea matters.

As you can see, you're vulnerable at this phase of The Stretch process. In these early stages, a high percentage of Dreamers drop out, so in this section of the book, we'll make sure that you're giving your concept the right home it needs to grow.

In this week of The Stretch we'll cover the physical, mental, and spiritual habits you'll need to develop during this journey. We will explore the importance of understanding who supports your vision versus who does not. And, finally, we will ensure that you allocate time to work toward this Dream. You will also work through the following exercises:

Week 3: The Dream Detox

EXERCISE 3.1: Identifying Dream Bullies
EXERCISE 3.2: Time Audit

GETTING READY FOR THE DETOX

In the past 15 years, every time I've had a new Dream, I've had to Stretch, and in every case a detox was necessary to keep me moving forward. Any kind of detox can cause a great shock to the body. Eliminating detriments to your creative and professional Dreams can feel as disruptive as cutting bread, pasta, and sugar from your diet. It's a jolt! But I know (and you will come to discover throughout this process) that **if you can move beyond the discomfort of letting go of what's familiar, there's greatness waiting for you**.

THE INTERRUPTION OF COMFORTABLE

I was very comfortable working as a project manager for IBM Global Services. I was quickly climbing the corporate ladder and my salary was great, but I hated the work. I would work diligently Monday through Friday, party hard on Friday and Saturday with my One Arm Up Crew, a very special group of women I've loved since college, and by Sunday night I'd be depressed because I knew that the next day I'd be returning to the unsatisfying weekday cycle. My Sunday night depression included a weekly phone call to my mother and stepfather to whine about how much I dreaded Monday morning. After five years of this routine, my mother and stepfather said, "This is officially your last Sunday night complaint call. If you don't like your job, you have to do something about it. But you can't call us to complain anymore." They delivered the wake-up I needed. This was my first interruption of comfortable.

I came to learn that such interruptions of comfortable preceded big moments of change at different stages of my life. And during my conversations with thousands of Dreamers like you, I've discovered that regardless of how scary, disruptive, and unnerving an interruption can be, such moments are a necessary entry way to real change.

CHANGING YOUR HABITS

Some of the changes you'll make to help your Dream thrive will be practical and logistical, while others will be less easy to define. Those are the ones that begin in your soul and your heart. I'm going to encourage and even push you to adopt the mind, body, and spirit of an All-Star Dreamer. Let's start by talking about your daily habits and how they affect the way you feel. Do you begin your day by checking social media? Are you spending your lunch hour engaged in office gossip? Are you crashing on your couch at the end of the day and bingeing on Netflix and Hulu? Now is the time to analyze the habits that are distracting you from your goals. There's nothing inherently wrong with scrolling through Instagram, but if your scrolling is provoking jealousy and complacency instead of motivation and inspiration, it's time to change what you're doing.

Where can these changes begin? You don't have to eliminate all your guilty pleasures at once, but maybe you can begin your detox by trading one hour of TV for an hour of listening to a business podcast. Maybe instead of engaging in office gossip, you can take a mind-clearing walk during lunch. Even small changes in your habits will open your mind and allow your Dreams to flow in. Seeing yourself making healthy changes is good for your self-esteem, and elevated self-esteem leads to greater motivation. Next, let's consider the effect of spiritual vitality on overall well-being.

FEEDING YOUR SPIRIT

On June 8, 2003, I opened a book that would change my life. Reading *Daddy Loves His Girls* by Bishop T. D. Jakes set me on a spiritual quest and deepened my connection to God. As I read, I began asking myself big questions like, "Why am I here?," "What's my true passion?," and "How can I improve the world?" I knew that pursuing the answers wasn't going to be a simple intellectual exercise, but I knew I had to find a way to make this spiritual quest a part of my everyday life. So I began engaging in spiritual practices including prayer, meditation, and spiritual reading. And I made the decision that my spiritual life would become my priority.

I've found great value in feeding my spirit through spiritual practices. Beyond attending services at a church, synagogue, or mosque, there are infinite rewards in spirit-quieting practices such as prayer, yoga, meditation, and Tai Chi. And if you're interested, consider checking out podcasts like *Woman Evolve*, *The RobCast*, and *SuperSoul Sunday* that are about keeping your spirit elevated. Make-It-Happen Dreamer AJ Johnson is a highly sought-after fitness trainer and life coach who strongly believes in *actively* pursuing spiritual health. She advises, "I don't want you to just study and read spiritual material like the Bible and share. I want you to *absorb and live* the information you're learning. Everything takes practice to become perfect. A lot of times what I'll do is wake up in the morning and before my feet even hit the ground, I'll say, 'Okay. God, I'm here. I woke up. What do you want me to work on within myself today?' I think that spiritual practice needs to be active, not passive."

During a recent interview, Careerpreneur Dreamer, EVP, and COO of Unilever's North America Beauty Esi Eggleston Bracey shared with me that she used meditation to help with her life-changing decision to change career paths. She recalled, "When I was most fearful about leaving Coty, a meditation helped me through the stress. I would repeat this mediation over and over again: 'Things are just as they are, feelings arise and pass away, all things are impermanent, and I am safe in this moment.' Whenever I felt anxiety, I would breathe and say that, 'Feelings arise and pass away. All things are impermanent. I am safe in this moment.'"

Esi also believes in just listening in order to hear the answers that are meant for us. She says, "We get signs from the universe when our path is getting blocked. My advice is to listen. Listen to where you're being called." This notion of being still to receive spiritual direction is something that I hear about a lot as I spend time with successful Dreamers.

Grammy Award winner India.Arie is a Make-It-Happen Dreamer who's very attuned to the mind/body/spirit connection. She says, "I'm actually an introvert. I recharge by spending time alone. I like things to be quiet. I love to go into nature because, in my opinion, it's a physical manifestation of God." India shared with us that when the momentum of her career began to knock her life out of balance, she chose to detox by getting back to nature. She refers to the day she pushed the "stop" button as her "breakdown" and told us, "I let go of most of my business team, and the first thing I did after that was go into nature. I went to the Pacific Northwest, outside of Seattle to the San Juan Islands. I got a little rental house and sat there for weeks and weeks." It was in that setting that she rebalanced and charted a course to start living and working her way.

Whatever your preferences, I think you'll find that creating a routine of spiritual practice that you attend to consistently will give you strength and a sense of calm that will benefit all aspects of your life and be particularly valuable as you take on The Stretch.

FORTIFY YOUR MIND

After you strengthen your spirit, you need to fortify your mind. Your thoughts can be your best friends or your worst enemies, so I must warn you that it's going to take some work to control the recordings that cycle through your mind. But there are countless experts on business and the power of the healthy mind who have blazed a miraculous trail for us. Seek their wisdom. Listen to their counsel. Buy their books and learn.

Careerpreneur Dreamer and senior editor of *Black Enterprise* magazine Alfred Edmonds is one such trailblazer who offers a relatively simple way to start thinking the positive thoughts of a successful entrepreneur. He reminds us that success starts with having a mindset for success, that you start to mentally become an entrepreneur very early in the Dreamer's process. "I always tell people that you're an entrepreneur long before you start a business. Businesses come and go, but if you want to commit to entrepreneurship, you have to want to be an entrepreneur before you ever know what kind of business you want to start. So even if you don't know what you want to build, start to hang around entrepreneurs and read books about entrepreneurs because you want to adopt the mindset." If you want to keep fortifying your mind, learn from people who have been there and want to share what they know.

A few years ago, a dear friend surprised my husband, Mike, and me with tickets to attend a motivational empowerment seminar featuring Tony Robbins. Although I didn't know much about Tony, I like to try new things, so I was excited to see what would be in store for me during this four-day experience. On the first day of the conference, 20,000 people packed the arena and shifted in their seats with anticipation while booming music blasted from enormous speakers. Then Tony bounded onto the stage like a rock star. He told the crowd to join him in vigorous dances, led us through lively group exercises, and even hyped us up to walk across fire, literally. This man is beyond vivacious, and by the end of the conference, I was both exhilarated and exhausted. During his closing remarks, he shocked the crowd by admitting that he'd been terribly sick all four days. *Wow!* What a lesson I learned that day about mental control and the power of will. Robbins gives the impression that he lets nothing stand in his way, *ever*. He models that the power of the mind is infinite, and his optimism is infectious.

What greatness can you bring forth from *your* mind? Let's work on learning to observe your thoughts and what they're telling you. During this part of the detoxification stage, observation is essential. Answer these questions without any form, structure, or thought. Just write.

- Do you find yourself more often thinking positive thoughts or negative thoughts?
- Do you tend to focus more often on the negative or the positive?
- Do your thoughts more often spark worry and anxiety, or do they inspire optimism and confidence?
- Are your thoughts helping push you toward reaching your goal?

As you walk through this observation phase, be conscious of where your unguided thinking tends to travel. Stay aware of your style of thinking, as it has the ability to create your Dream's reality.

CEO Dreamer and founder of Harlem's Fashion Row Brandice Daniel recalls how she combats her own self-doubt. "For me, so many times it's been about fighting the fear that comes up within myself. And the doubt. And making sure that I never get to a place where I start questioning if this is going to happen. I try to always have my self-talk language directed toward what I want to happen. In other words, I try to make sure that my language is following my Dream, not questioning it."

The next step in retraining your mind is to *choose* thoughts that inspire you, ignite you into action, and keep you motivated. Take time to create a working list of positive self-talk phrases that support your Dream. When you begin thinking negative thoughts, combat them by changing the channel to these positive phrases. It's easy to sink into thoughts that tell you, "I'm not enough," "I'm not qualified," or "I don't have enough resources." These kinds of fear-based thoughts can be Dream killers, so it's vital that you replace them with abundant ideas such as, "I'm enough," "I'm resourceful," "I'm creative," and "I'm capable."

Tony Robbins knows a thing or two about mindset. He teaches that the quality of your life is directed by the mental state that you choose for yourself each day. That mental state, he says, is controlled in part by where you focus your attention. According to Tony, "What happens in your life doesn't determine how you feel. How you feel is only the result of how you're using your own mind and body at any moment. No matter what happens in your life, you're in control of your own state of mind. Make sure to use that ability to put yourself in a state that's appropriate for what you want to achieve." I find this idea very compelling—that we have control of our feelings based on what we choose to focus on. That gives me a very strong sense of empowerment, and I hope you'll exercise this kind of mental power every day that you Stretch.

BUILD YOUR BODY

As you improve your mind and your spirit, also work to keep your body healthy. Great Dreamers understand that keeping your body in top physical form is essential for allowing your mind to be ready for Dreams that are vibrant, dynamic, and creative. If you don't think you have time to exercise, do your best to find the time. Make the time, even if it's only 10 minutes.

Like many of the world's leading executives, CEOs, and founders, billionaire Richard Branson, founder of Virgin Group, makes it a priority to exercise every day. He does an hour of weights and band stretches, and he changes up his routine daily. Branson understands the importance of a healthy body relative to a healthy mind and productivity and says that consistency is what's most important. He explains, "The key for everybody is sticking with it. We all know that feeling of the high we get when we do an hour of exercise. I never want to stop getting that wonderful endorphin rush, but it's easy to slip into a 'not today, I'll do it tomorrow,' mindset. You have to keep going even when you don't feel like it."

For you Dreamers who struggle with being able to give exercise its deserved place in your 24-hour day, let me emphasize the importance of not sacrificing your body for *one more hour* of work. The cumulative effect of neglecting your physical health will never be worth pushing your Dream ahead just a little faster. This applies to *everybody and every body*, even you who work long hours, go to school, and live with other time-consuming obligations. Find a way to fit exercise into the mix. If you have an assignment that's demanding extraordinary amounts of your time, maybe you can do some of the work *while* exercising, perhaps on an exercise bike, treadmill, or elliptical machine.

While writer/editor and Make-It-Happen Dreamer Jodi Fodor was a full-time grad student *and* working up to 40 hours a week as a teacher, she found herself seriously sacrificing exercise because, as she says, "I just didn't feel I could afford to take an hour away from all the required reading." But she began to feel listless and unhealthy, so she devised a creative solution. "I taught myself to read as I walked," she laughs. "I'd hold a book at about chest height and walk four miles at a time up and down the Manhattan Beach strand where there are very few places I'd encounter cars. I'd glance up now and then to make sure I wasn't about to land in a pothole. It became easy, and in that hour I'd get through 30 pages or more." Well, *that* was a creative solution!

The work that's demanding so much of your time might not involve holding a book, but you *must* exercise. Even if on some days you can do only 20 focused minutes of cardio, stretching, weights, etc., do it. Your health is the basis of everything good in your life, so do everything you can to help it thrive.

According to a *Harvard Business Review* article by psychologist and business consultant Ron Friedman, incorporating regular exercise into our routines leads to several benefits related to concentration and productivity as well as sharper memory and lower stress. He writes, "Our mental firepower is directly linked to our physical regimen. And nowhere are the implications more relevant than to our performance at work. Among the cognitive benefits resulting from regular exercise are sharper memory, faster learning, and enhanced creativity."

Dreamer AJ Johnson agrees that exercise and movement are critical to well-being. She says, "Every day I want you to do something that causes you to move. Thirty minutes. Take the stairs at work as opposed to the elevator. Park farther away from the shopping mall so you can walk the 15 minutes to the stores and back. Take a dance class. A lot of you aren't sticking to a physical fitness routine because you feel alone, you don't feel supported. Find a class where you have like-minded, like-spirited people who are after the same thing. You may only see them once a week in that class, in that dance class or that yoga class, but now you've got a tribe that's going to help support what you're after." And she says that our need to reexamine what we're eating is no joke. Sugar consumption, in particular, is serious business: "Scientifically, sugar is what helps your cells rejuvenate irregularly. Do you know what irregular cellular rejuvenation is? Cancer. Diabetes. High blood pressure. Heart disease. The beginning of a stroke. When you're eating it, it tastes so good, but you're basically committing a slow suicide. That's the truth. Try to switch over to natural sugar. Eat fruit. You're going to see a difference in 72 hours. Your body will change visibly in 72 hours if you're doing something right."

Another important part of staying healthy in order to make your Dreams a reality is getting enough sleep. Former NFL player and Careerpreneur Dreamer, Shamiel Gary, believes this wholeheartedly and explains, "When I was playing football with the Miami Dolphins, the team brought in a sleep expert. Before that, I didn't realize how important it is for us to get an adequate amount of sleep. He gave us an example of Olympic ice skaters and showed that when they got eight hours of sleep, they were able to retain more of what they did the day before, like 50 to 70 percent more. When they got only three to five hours of sleep, they weren't able to do the same movements as the day before. Sleep also helps with losing weight, focus, energy, and all that good stuff. I take my sleep seriously now."

All the business success you can dream of won't mean much if you don't take care of yourself physically. So if you're not already doing the best you can to take care of your body, learn from some of the tips that were shared by our experts and these Dreamers and start making changes. Your Dream depends on it.

ELIMINATE DREAM BULLIES

Remember when I told you that your Stretch journey includes interruptions of your comfort? These interruptions also affect the people who have been happily comfortable along with you—your friends, relatives, and coworkers, for example. What happens when you choose to change the status quo by STRETCHING into your goals? You're not only interrupting your comfortable world; you're shaking up the comfort zone of those around you. So if your favorite aunt fiercely challenges your decision to leave your safe career, it's likely that her own experiences and fears are coming to light. Strange as it may sound, your courageous leap into the unknown can often make *other* people fearful, and these people become your Dream Bullies.

When you hear the word *bully*, you probably think of a person who knowingly intends someone else harm. That's not a Dream Bully. More often than not, your Dream Bullies are people who care about you but who—sometimes unknowingly—try to derail your Dreams. Dream Bullies will often try to keep you stuck as you are, confined to *their* limited possibilities because what you're doing makes *them* uncomfortable. They say things like, "This isn't like you," or "Why would you want to go through all that?" They often treat you like a static human being and discourage you from exploring multiple versions of yourself. They're probably scared of what's going to happen when you shake it up. Be prepared: The Stretch may cost you friends, lovers, coworkers, and employees. You might have to completely restructure major elements of your life, but only you should be the one to decide if the changes are worth the costs. Even though the intentions of your Dream Bullies might be loving, you must protect your Dream from these Bullies, and that protection will take many forms.

One of my greatest heroes and inspirations is my grandmother. She is my best friend and one of the people I love most in this world. She's also my number one Dream Bully. Yes, you read that correctly. The idea of my taking professional risks gives her terrible anxiety and fear, so if I'm not careful, her issues about risk and change will seep into my Dreams, potentially stall my momentum, and maybe even derail my success. She was so pleased with and comforted by my having chosen a "secure" career path that when I decided to leave my "good, good job" as an executive at IBM Global Services, I simply chose not to tell her. I know that she'd worry herself ragged over why I was choosing the risky unknown over what appeared to be a secure career position, and I didn't want my progress or my optimism derailed by the Dream Bullying that my beloved grandmother would surely bring to my process. So I made the tough choice at that time to leave her out of my Dream circle. After I was able to secure a stable income, I shared my full professional vision with my grandmother.

Your Dream Bullies don't mean harm, nor do they want you unhappy. They simply share their concerns from *their* point of view. But you mustn't let other people's unwillingness to change or risk dictate your course.

Careerpreneur Dreamer and former White House social secretary Desirée Rogers says that to be successful, sometimes you have to be a warrior. She says, "That means that you've got to do everything you can to be successful. Some of these things include making hard decisions. You've got to get rid of the negativity." When battling cancer, Desirée had to get rid of negativity by setting an unexpected Dream Bully straight. "My mother kept saying to me, 'I remember when your father had cancer. He did this. He had that.' I said, 'Mommy, *he didn't make it*. Stop it. Otherwise you can't come back.' You've got to command your space. Sometimes that means you can't be around people close to you right then—unless they change their behavior. You've got to be a warrior."

Yvonne Orji, one of the stars of HBO's hit *Insecure* and the yes! comedian I mentioned in Chapter Two, was raised by parents who taught her that accomplishment meant things like straight A's and traditional career choices. There was no chance that her parents were going to support her choosing a career in comedy, so, lucky for Yvonne, she heard the voice of God guiding her to be strong and stand up to the Dream Bullies in her family. "I was raised by Nigerian parents whose only reason to come to this country was for us to get a good education," Yvonne recalls. "I'm their only girl. I was the straight-A student. I did everything right. And then God was like, 'Cool, cool, cool. Let me holler at you for a second.' He steered me in a totally different direction, and it literally felt like I was standing between two different directions: African parents and Jesus." She chose comedy, and with that choice came the truth that she needed to create some boundaries to protect her Dream from those who would squash it. It wasn't easy to protect her Dream from Dream Bullies, but she did, and because of that her Dream is alive and thriving today.

EXERCISE 3.1

IDENTIFYING DREAM BULLIES

Consider your closest circle of relatives, friends, and colleagues. Now think about your most recent interactions with them, and ask yourself the following questions:

1. Does this person believe in me?
2. Does this person support my vision or Dream?
3. Does this person speak affirmative words about my life?
4. Can I trust this person to support my vision even if it's beyond his or her understanding?
5. When I leave this person's presence, do I feel better or worse?
6. Do I enjoy the activities that I typically share with this person?
7. Has this person introduced me to other influential people who can advance my vision?
8. Will this relationship be a good fit for who I want to be six months from now? A year from now? Five years from now?
9. Is this person open to challenging his or her perspectives and trying new experiences?
10. Does this person bring new ideas and thoughts to the conversation?
11. Would I trust this person to make essential life choices on my behalf?

This exercise is designed to help you build your awareness. By being more mindful of the feelings and communication styles of the people in your close circle, you'll be able to see who will help or hurt your Dream. Dream Supporters are those you'll want to reach to for support and advice. Dream Bullies will resist and even try to sabotage you. And there are some neutral observers too.

Knowing who's who will show you where to draw boundary lines when it comes to your goals. These boundaries aren't about causing catastrophic change to your relationships; they're about being the protector of this Dream Baby of yours and making sure it has the chance to grow and thrive. If it takes a village, make sure that you're the one to decide who lives there.

Time Busters

As you move through this detoxification process, it is also important to pay attention to how you're spending your time. In my early days of The Stretch, I had a weakness for bingeing on seasons of *Sex and the City*. It was lots of fun, but was this activity moving me closer to my vision? No. So when I moved to New York, I made the radical decision not to have a television in my apartment. At first, I felt withdrawal. Those first two months without that familiar TV friend were rough! But I wanted to start being honest with myself, so I'd ask myself questions like, "How can you productively use the time that you used to spend watching reality shows?" and "Sarah Jessica Parker has already manifested her dreams; who's working on yours?"

Without the TV lineup to turn to, I began to read business and inspirational books. I took in as much information as I could about building a successful business, strengthening my mind, feeding my spirit, and developing the kind of relationships that would help me reach my goals. I also made the choice to stop going to clubs. My mother used to joke that I went clubbing like it was a second job. Yes, club life was a lot of fun, but the morning after a big night out, what did I have to show for my time? During this same period, I also chose to give up alcohol. Before I knew it,

I'd gone almost three years without those activities in my life, and I didn't miss them.

I'm not suggesting that you give up all social activities or even all your vices, but during that phase in my life, I saw a correlation between my detoxing from those elements and the explosive results I began to experience in my career. Within a year of my starting at RUSH Communications, a leading entertainment, media, and lifestyle company, I went from the position of unpaid apprentice to general manager of a global company. In corporate work, that kind of leap is almost unheard of. It was during this climb I learned that discipline, work, focus, and efficient use of time are what deliver remarkable results.

But before you overhaul any portion of your life, let's do a Time Audit to examine how you currently spend your time.

Reclaiming Your Time

When Treasury Secretary Steven Mnuchin avoided House Representative Maxine Waters's question by lobbing compliments her way, she interrupted him with the now infamous statement, "I'm reclaiming my time." You, too, have the right—and probably the need—to reclaim your time.

I want you to monitor how you spend all your waking and sleeping hours for the next seven days and enter the data into the table in Exercise 3.2. Include everything you do: eating meals, working, commuting, exercising, resting, watching television, talking on the phone, surfing the Internet—everything. Each part of this table is divided into half-hour sections so you can clearly see how you're spending your minutes and hours. When you can observe a week of your time as a whole, you'll be able to see where your time can be better spent toward the goals of your Stretch.

EXERCISE 3.2

TIME AUDIT

WEEK OF:

TIME	SUN	MON	TUES	WED	THURS	FRI	SAT
12 a.m.							
1 a.m.							
2 a.m.							
3 a.m.							
4 a.m.							
5 a.m.							
6 a.m.							

TIME	SUN	MON	TUES	WED	THURS	FRI	SAT
7 a.m.							
8 a.m.							
9 a.m.							
10 a.m.							
11 a.m.							
12 p.m.							
1 p.m.							
2 p.m.							
3 p.m.							

TIME	SUN	MON	TUES	WED	THURS	FRI	SAT
4 p.m.							
5 p.m.							
6 p.m.							
7 p.m.							
8 p.m.							
9 p.m.							
10 p.m.							
11 p.m.							

After a week of logging your time, take a few moments to observe your Time Audit and consider the following questions:

1. What changes can you make that might lead to greater productivity?
2. Are there any products or services (e.g., grocery delivery, housecleaning) that you could delegate so you can have more time to work on your Dream?
3. Can you name some activities that you could spend less time doing or completely eliminate from your schedule for a while?
4. Can you think of anyone who might be able to take some time busters off your hands or with whom you might share tasks, like watching each other's kids or taking each other's shopping lists to a grocery store?
5. When in your day can you designate time to work only on your Dream?

The important thing to remember as you begin the detox phase of your journey is that you don't have to change every aspect of your life at once. If you're a Career Dreamer focusing on moving into a more fulfilling position, you may want to work on creating time for networking and connecting with great mentors first. If you're a Hobby Dreamer, consider whether you can find more time to pursue your passion and boost the marketing and promotional side of your Dream.

We all have the same 24 hours each day. The question is, how are you using those hours to Stretch toward your Dreams?

YOUR 90-DAY STRETCH PLAN GOAL CRUSH REMINDER

Last week, you completed a 90-Day Stretch Plan and created goals you must achieve each week. From this point forward, make it an exercise to revisit your 90-Day Stretch Plan weekly so that you remain consistently focused on achieving the goals that you set. This is extremely important, so going forward, I will remind you at the end of every week. So this is your first official 90-Day Stretch Plan Goal Crush Reminder!

Congratulations for finishing Week 3. You're nearing the end of Part I of your Stretch, and I hope that means you're Dreaming in bright, vivid colors and feeling more clarity and courage. This week, I'm very excited to share the thoughts and words of a Grammy Award–winning musician, singer, and songwriter who has sold more than 3.3 million records in the United States and more than 10 million worldwide. She's a creative musical force who over the years has inspired me and fed my spirit with powerful messages in beautiful songs.

"We're all worthy and significant, and we matter because we exist and nobody's better than anyone else. In order to go after your dreams, you must first understand that you are worthy."

—Make-It-Happen Dreamer and Grammy Award–Winning Artist **India.Arie**

You may download this week's Dream All-Star training session at www.thebigstretchbook.com.

PART II

DESIGN

Drafting Your Dream's Foundation

Congratulations! You have successfully completed the Dream phase of The Stretch. Now you understand the creative process of Dreaming. You have explored your Dreamer's DNA, and you're doing the work to create an optimal environment for your goal to thrive. You've started the process of detoxing from Dream Bullies who could hinder the life of your idea. Most important, you've learned how to Dream in color.

As we enter this second phase of The Stretch, you have a specific Dream in mind. You've spent time with this idea in your imagination. You've taken time to map your action plans for the next 90 days. Now that you have these steps in place, are you ready, Dreamer, to create a firm foundation for your Dream? I hope so, because it's time to move into the Design phase of The Stretch.

In the Design phase, you'll learn what it means to Dream with a plan, explore the purpose for your goal, understand the opportunities that will come to life because of your goal's existence, and build your ultimate network and team. My goal for you in this part of The Stretch is to help you devise a plan and develop a strong business core. Astrid Chirinos is a Careerpreneur Dreamer and chief development executive of Latin American Economic Development Corporation. She's a Dreamer but makes a clear distinction between Dreams and plans. She says, "You need to have, first of all, a plan, and then you need to have discipline, determination, and focus that you're going to follow that plan because you need to have a road map to be able to get to your destination. Everything starts with a dream, but it ends with the results."

The exercises in the Design section give you practical steps to move from idea to reality. By the end of the three chapters within "Design," you'll have worked through the following exercises to strengthen your Stretch:

Week 4: Discovering Your Purpose

EXERCISE 4.1: 10 Questions for Discovering Your Purpose from the Inside Out
EXERCISE 4.2: Writing Your Personal Purpose Statement
EXERCISE 4.3: 10 Questions to Discover Your Dream's Purpose
EXERCISE 4.4: Developing Your Dream's Mission Statement

Week 5: Stepping into the Ideal Opportunities for Your Dream

EXERCISE 5.1: Becoming the Answer for Your Dream Irritant
EXERCISE 5.2: Building Your Dream Audience
EXERCISE 5.3: Finding Your Dream's Unique Position
EXERCISE 5.4: Know Your Competition

Week 6: Building Your Dream Network and Team

EXERCISE 6.1: High-Touch Dreaming: The Art of Networking

EXERCISE 6.2: Finding Your Mentors

EXERCISE 6.3: Six Degrees Toward Your Dream

EXERCISE 6.4: Creating a Dream Culture

EXERCISE 6.5: Building a Dream Team

After you complete the Design phase, you'll have solid business principles and tools to develop a thriving plan for your Dream.

DESIGNING A NEW REALITY FOR YOUR DREAM

In the Design phase, you'll become the chief Dream architect who drafts the critical technical drawing. Remember that you signed a contract; you agreed to do what it takes to make your Dream a reality. Now that you're entering the Design phase, you're constructing the blueprint. Roll up your sleeves. But before we move forward, I must caution the overachievers who will feel the need to get it "right": there is no such thing as a perfect plan for your idea. Give yourself the space to create, revise, tear up, and develop your blueprint as many times as you need to. Each revision will let you see your Dream with new eyes.

DESIGN YOUR DREAM WITH FLEXIBILITY

As I mentioned, I've had the opportunity to speak to more than 100,000 Dreamers and showcase more than 200 world-changing All-Stars during the past six years of the Dream Project. I have yet to meet a Dreamer who has said that everything worked according to the original plan. **Most of the creative Dreamers I've worked with write their plans in pencil.**

Create your plans in such a way that you give yourself the room to change with new business developments, new technology, new competition, changing economies, changing family dynamics, and personal pivots in your life. As Dan Coleman, an esteemed business coach of mine, often reminds me, the journey is about progress, not perfection. Don't let perfection hinder your goal; rather, learn how to embrace what I call "imperfect Dreaming." That means you don't need all the answers to get going. You don't want to become so fixed in your plan that you'll be unwilling to pivot when necessary. Throughout the Design phase of The Stretch, I'm going to help you strengthen your core business's muscles with exercises that will help you discover your purpose, unlock the unlimited possibilities for your concept, and build a strong network and team to support you.

Let's get started!

CHAPTER FOUR

DISCOVERING YOUR PURPOSE

Week 4

The most important part of the Design phase of The Stretch is discovering your purpose and your Dream's purpose. Your purpose is the answer to the question, "Why are you doing this?" Your Dream's purpose should be the primary driver of your vision, its reason for existence. It might be grounded in love, passion, or your desire to change the lives of others. Without a solid purpose, your vision won't withstand the challenges of a fast-changing world, and you'll be much more likely to abandon it at the first sign of obstacles. But when your idea is grounded in a purpose bigger than what you can see today, you'll attract like-minded Dreamers to your cause. Your purpose will help you build your brand. Your purpose will attract funding for limitless opportunities. Your purpose will become the core for every element of the Design phase of The Stretch. Your purpose will become the "why" for your idea.

During Week 4 of The Stretch, I'm going to guide you to explore your purpose, your Dream's purpose, and the ways that your purpose will uniquely serve others. Below is a list of exercises that we will cover this week:

Week 4: Discovering Your Purpose

EXERCISE 4.1: 10 Questions for Discovering Your Purpose from the Inside Out

EXERCISE 4.2: Writing Your Personal Purpose Statement

EXERCISE 4.3: 10 Questions to Discover Your Dream's Purpose

EXERCISE 4.4: Developing Your Dream's Mission Statement

Let's kick this week off by taking a look at one of my favorite Dream Masters, Oprah Winfrey. She's a master of turning Dreams into reality, so I'll be sharing examples from her Dream Playbook throughout The Stretch.

When you look at the various platforms, businesses, and programming that make up the Oprah Winfrey brand, you'll notice that all these ventures have the same purpose: to help people live their best lives. From the OWN Network, to *O, the Oprah Magazine*, to Weight Watchers, the core of Oprah's purpose is to enrich the lives of others by providing them with the tools, inspiration, resources, and knowledge to live their best lives. Your Dreams and business ventures may change, but the anchoring purpose that unites them remains the same. I encourage you to think of your Dream journey like a marathon; you'll need motivation, inspiration, and a solid reason (your purpose) to keep you in the race long term. Let me share with you how I found purpose in my journey of training for the New York City Marathon.

YOUR DREAM NEEDS A "WHY"

When my marathon training plan got tough, I discovered that my run needed a "why" that was bigger than me. On a hot summer day, somewhere around training week 11, I was preparing for a 10-mile run, and I knew that my body was too tired to run that distance. Even though I had a solid workout plan in place, it wasn't enough. The negative voices in my head were running wild.

Do you really think you're going to run a full marathon when you can't even run 10 miles?

You should just come up with a good excuse and stop now before you embarrass yourself.

Why would anybody run in this kind of heat?

I knew I had a big problem: my vision for running the marathon lacked a solid purpose to keep me invested. Without a clear *why*, I knew that I could far too easily abandon the whole thing. I had to be honest and do some soul-searching. Beyond having "run a marathon" on my bucket list, I knew that I needed something more to help me to make it to the finish line.

I was already passionate about inspiring Dreamers and building platforms to encourage others to move boldly toward their goals. I thought about this aspect of myself, and the light bulb flashed: there was a clear connection between my overall purpose and this Dream's purpose. Although I didn't finish my 10 miles on that hot day, the purpose for my run was clarified. From that day forward, the purpose for my run became:

- Always run toward my Dreams.
- Inspire others to take action and run toward their Dreams.

Solidifying my purpose for running the marathon didn't mean that I wouldn't miss any more training days, but it did mean that I now had a deeper motivation to help keep me pushing. I now had a *why* that was bigger than a bucket list. As you get ready to Stretch toward your Dream, you too will need a greater *why* to keep you anchored for the long term.

Lisa Price is founder of the hair and skin care company Carol's Daughter, and she serves as an excellent example of the power of passion. She lives by the idea that joy for the work is one of the most important components of success, a point she illustrated for Dream Project attendees by offering her "cheesecake example." "Suzy makes the best cheesecake anybody has ever tasted. Whenever it's somebody's birthday, they want Suzy to make a cheesecake, and she does. But Suzy doesn't actually *like* making cheesecake. She does it because people ask her to, and she wants to make them happy, but she doesn't actually enjoy the process. So even though Suzy makes the best cheesecake in the world, she can't go into business making cheesecake because she would be miserable and there wouldn't be any passion to fuel her through the times when it was difficult." Never forget that—**if you don't love making cheesecake, don't go into the business of making cheesecake.**

THE CORE OF YOUR DREAM LIES WITHIN YOUR PURPOSE

I know that defining the word *purpose* can be a cloudy exercise for some people, so let's start by exploring your passions, skills, and the impact you want to make in the world. Read the following questions, and then close your eyes as you begin exploring the answers:

- Which activities would/do I do if doing so never earned me a penny?
- What are my core values (e.g., faith, family, loyalty, trust, etc.), and how can I combine these values with my passion?
- What kind of impact do I want to make in the lives of others?

You might be well paid to do work that you're great at, but it could be that this path isn't where your purpose lies. You may have developed a brilliant idea that allowed you to become a successful entrepreneur, but if that Dream feels more like a burden than a blessing, this is a big clue that you're not reaching toward your purpose. Kevin Liles, a Make-It-Happen Dreamer and CEO of 300 Entertainment, reminds us that when your work is in line with your purpose, it doesn't feel like work. He advises, "Find something you love, something that you're willing to do for free, and monetize it."

This week, give yourself time to think about what gives you the most joy. Very often, many of us overlook the skills and talents that come naturally to us, and we don't recognize that these gifts are directly tied to our purpose. For example, you might have a natural talent for working with young adults. You might discover that your purpose is to mentor young people, and your purpose could lead to your serving as your company's liaison for summer interns. If you're great with numbers, your purpose could be to provide financial order to individuals and small businesses; this purpose could lead you to open an accounting firm.

Your purpose will always be the inspiration behind what you love to do. Over time, the scope, magnitude, and expression of your Dream may change, but the underlying motivation behind your purpose will remain the same. Your work now is to align your purpose—for example, inspiring others, bringing other people's stories to life, elevating education standards in inner cities, offering a great listening ear, improving people's health—with a Dream that will inspire you to take action.

Lisa Price discovered her purpose when she followed her longstanding passion for fragrance, creams, and lotions. When Lisa started this exploration, she was a Hobby Dreamer working a full-time job in TV production; she wasn't unhappy in her job, but she was more passionate about her hobbies. She began to develop homemade skin and hair care products that she gave as gifts. Then she began to sell her goods at flea markets and then out of her home. From there she opened a boutique, and that led to her selling her products online. In time she made her way to *The Oprah Winfrey Show* and Home Shopping Network and eventually scaled the business so large that it was acquired by global beauty industry leader L'Oréal USA. And what has driven Lisa since she filled her first baby food jar with her homemade skin cream? Passion and purpose.

Marc S. Pritchard is a Careerpreneur Dreamer who worked his way to be chief brand officer of Procter & Gamble. Holding this position with the world's largest advertiser gives Marc a lot of power, and he takes that responsibility very seriously. Marc recalls when he was struck by an epiphany that led him to understand his purpose, which he defines as to "use my skills, experience, and voice in advertising and marketing as a force for good, particularly focused on gender equality, on racial equality, on really equality of all kinds." He directs P&G advertising with this purpose in mind, but Marc understands the importance of leading with purpose in his professional and personal life. He shared with me recently in an interview, a piece of advice that was given to him and that he lives by: "Focus on being useful." Each day Marc looks for a way to serve others. He says, "I wake up every day and I ask God for the strength to be useful, to be useful to whoever I meet, to be useful in meetings I'm in and to the people I meet with. Think about what you can do to be the most useful for others. It'll lead to your days being more meaningful."

Even if you're still deep in the discovery stage of understanding your purpose, as long as you're alive and breathing, there's a divine reason that you're on the planet right now. This week your Stretch exercises will help you start to gauge how strong your talents are in different areas and help you define the purpose that calls strongly to you.

UNDERSTANDING WHAT YOUR PURPOSE IS AND WHAT IT ISN'T

As you begin to uncover your purpose, it's equally important that you understand both what it is and what it is not. I had the privilege of welcoming award-winning journalist, former CNN anchor, and CEO of Starfish Media Soledad O'Brien to the Dream Project a few years ago. She shared with our Dreamers that she began to open her eyes to her purpose during medical school. She said, "My sister and I were in med school at the same time. While she was excelling, I was struggling. I discovered that I was more passionate about the stories around the medicine than the practice of medicine itself. My sister is now a surgeon, and I became a journalist. We both took the time to understand what we were good at and what we were passionate about." Soledad was awake to what she was experiencing in her journey, and that awareness led her to understand her purpose. I think Soledad had to go through medical school to understand what her purpose was not, and that led her to see clearly what her purpose is. If you're currently doing work that makes you unhappy, don't be discouraged or think that you've wasted your time. Just view this phase as part of your "purpose process of elimination." **Knowing what *isn't* for you gets you a step closer to knowing what is.**

I experienced a vivid moment of understanding what my purpose *is not* when my company hosted a series of parties for a high-profile spirits brand during the Super Bowl and NBA All-Star Weekend. At that time, I felt very clear that EGAMI's purpose was to execute meaningful marketing campaigns and connect these campaigns with causes that impact multicultural communities. But I have to admit that in my desire to keep EGAMI relevant and profitable, I haven't always remained true to the company's core purpose. While the marketing campaigns for these events checked a lot of important boxes for us as an agency, a change in the brand's leadership shifted the focus of the campaign, and these events pivoted from being celebrations of multicultural music, art, culinary experiences, and community initiatives to being known as "the hottest parties in town." I knew that if we sponsored hot parties that were focused primarily on partying and liquor consumption, I'd be out of alignment, and I wouldn't last long in the business; yet I ignored my instincts and chose to move forward with the flashy parties. I was in survival mode and wanted to sustain my company's cash flow and secure the client, so I ignored the feeling in my gut.

As I sat in various clubs during these parties, my warning meter kept going off. I silently asked myself, "What the hell am I doing here? This isn't what my company is about!" Not only did I know we were the wrong agency for these events; I knew another marketing firm that would be perfect. The firm's CEO was so cool that he could often be found throwing parties at 10 a.m. on a weekday at the Soho House in Manhattan. He and his company were born to host this kind of event. Because I had lost sight of my purpose, I was blocking a prime opportunity for them.

I might have continued hosting those parties if not for an interruption that literally knocked me off my feet. At an NBA All-Star Party, an installation that included a life-sized mock liquor bottle came crashing down on my head. The pain was so intense that people could hear my screams above the party music. As I lay sprawled on the floor with a crowd around me, I could practically hear my soul ask, "Girl, how many more signs do you need?" Curled up on the floor, writhing in pain, I decided that being knocked out almost cold was enough of a warning. It was the last event we hosted for that company. A few days later, I gave my client the number for the firm that hosts the hot midmorning weekday parties.

It's dangerous to stray from your purpose. The further you wander, the greater the chance you'll decrease your value, compromise your level of excellence, and accept projects outside your skill set. Over time, the quality and reputation of your brand, your product, your service, and your Dream will be diminished. The decrease in quality will lead to a lack of trust from your audience and eventually a huge hit to your bottom line.

When you lose sight of your purpose, you might also block other people from accessing their greatest opportunities and operating in their sweet spots. You could be unconsciously taking time, money, and resources from someone who is an excellent fit for the opportunity that you're hoarding. Don't become a Dream blocker!

Once you know what your purpose *isn't*, how do you tap into what it *is*? A great way to start is to focus on what makes you want to jump out of bed in the morning. But what if, despite your great desire to go after something with passion, you don't know what you're passionate about? This is a very common scenario, one that Make-It-Happen Dreamer Lara Hodgson knows about.

Before cofounding NOWaccount Network Corporation (NOW Corp), Lara was frustrated from constantly hearing the advice that she should focus on something she was passionate about. Then she realized that **what matters isn't the "what" of an endeavor but the "so what," which refers to all those wonderful things made possible by the existence of your Dream**. The "so what" speaks to the reasons you're going after this goal and the effects it will have on people's lives. It's where the meaning of it all lies. During a session at the Dream Project, she told the audience, "When I was younger, people used to always tell me you have to do what you're passionate about, and that drove me crazy, not because I didn't have anything I was interested in. I had *too many* things. I finally realized that if what you were passionate about is the 'what' you're doing, then you miss out on too many opportunities because you're not listening. Your passion should be in the impact you're having, not on what you're doing. My 'so what' is helping people create jobs and grow the economy, so that we can all live a better life. That's my goal. NOWAccount is just a 'what.' Nobody buys a 'what' from you. They buy a 'so what.' Customers aren't buying what you're selling; they're buying the impact you can have on them."

CONNECTING THE DREAMER AND THE DREAM WITH PURPOSE

As I shared in Chapter One, I began making the connection between me as a Dreamer and my Dream itself when I took a deep breath and walked away from the comfort of a corporate job at IBM. However, I had one problem: I had no idea what my purpose was. Up until that point, earning an impressive salary was one of my only motivators. Discovering my purpose and what I was passionate about was a new challenge, and I started by asking myself the following simple questions:

- "What are my gifts?"
- "What am I most passionate about?"
- "What am I most curious about?"
- "What issues and causes do I care about?"
- "Why am I interested in these issues?"
- "What ideas keep me up at night?"

I didn't wake up with the answers to these questions. It was a process to discover the heart of my curiosity, passion, and interests. But in my exploration, I discovered that I'm creative. I learned that I love to explore new things. I found out that I'm organized, that I love entertainment and pop culture, and that I care about issues that affect people of color. I also like people and want to help others lead authentic lives.

As I continued to peel back the layers, I began thinking, "What would I see in my reflection if I could see who I am on the inside?" I started sketching and wrote the word "IMAGE" backward and read "EGAMI."

This brand-new word kicked off my journey to uncover my personal and professional purpose and would eventually become the name of my agency. **If you could see the inside of your psyche, if you could look inside and "see" your purpose, what do you think you'd see?**

Developing clarity about my gifts, skills, and passions helped to focus my efforts and create new opportunities in the world of entertainment. I eventually landed an internship, an apprenticeship, and an extraordinary career opportunity at RUSH Communications where I worked alongside the company's CEO/chairman.

One of the first opportunities I had at RUSH was to be part of a youth empowerment/voter registration campaign entitled "Vote or Die." RUSH partnered with Sean "Diddy" Combs to create a campaign to register millions of young voters and educate them about the importance of voting. By the end of the campaign, we had registered thousands of voters and sparked a new generation to exercise their right to vote. I distinctly remember how I felt at the end of this campaign: fulfilled. I had used my skills and talents to accomplish something that mattered to me and to the world, and I brought passion to the project. This is the kind of opportunity that helps you identify your purpose. So this week as you map out your purpose, begin to examine how fulfilled you are by your work and whether you feel that your skills and gifts are making a contribution that matters.

Once I became clear about my purpose, more and more opportunities presented themselves. That's how it works: as you become clear about who you really are and what you should be doing, the world begins to open. During The Stretch this week, begin thinking about where you can use your talents within your industry, company, or community. If you're an Activist Dreamer, your love for community could lead you to discover that your purpose is tied to community organizing. If you're a Make-It-Happen Dreamer, your talent for developing business ventures could help you uncover that your purpose is tied to teaching other entrepreneurs how to build their own businesses. If you're a Hobby Dreamer who loves, say, woodworking, this passion might lead you to build a successful online custom furniture business on Etsy and other online platforms.

The deliberate exploration of my purpose has become my way of life for over 15 years now. As a Dreamer, I've learned that being clear about my purpose ensures that my Dreams will always have a vehicle to bring them to life. I want this kind of clarity for you.

GREAT DREAMERS HAVE PURPOSE, AND SO DO YOU!

Iconic Dreamers like former first lady Michelle Obama; bestselling author and entrepreneur Tim Ferriss; and basketball superstar Steph Curry have passions and senses of purpose that are easy to identify: (1) bringing America together, (2) mastering the four-hour workweek, and (3) leveraging an athlete's skills to lead winning teams. As you begin to solidify your purpose and connect that purpose with your Dream, others should be able to easily connect you with your purpose in the world.

Right now, your idea could be to empower young people with inspiring summer programs. Five years from now, that idea could expand to include providing college scholarships for high school seniors. As your Dream grows, your purpose of "Providing rich opportunities for young people" will become what you're known for. **Creating a solid purpose for your Dream will help shape your idea or business, guide your investments, grow your team, and attract and retain loyal customers.**

When you enter a room, what do you want to be known for before you utter a word? Your purpose should be like a neon sign that radiates from your chest. I recently recruited Cheryl Overton to lead EGAMI as our new president. She's known throughout our industry for her creativity and big ideas. When she walks in a room, you think "Here comes creativity." As I draft this book, I'm working with Jodi Fodor, who I'm discovering is a talented editor whose purpose is grounded in storytelling and a love of words. I haven't known Jodi long, but I can see her purpose shine brightly in her attention to sentence after sentence. My friend and business colleague Elyse Kroll of Elyse Kroll Interiors has a purpose grounded in visual arts. She doesn't have to tell others what her purpose is—it's a mark that remains in every place she's made beautiful.

In my role as CEO of EGAMI, I've been fortunate to work with some of the nation's largest brands, including Target, Verizon, and HBO. These are iconic companies that serve millions of customers, and they all have one thing in common: they're companies with a strong purpose. To help their decision makers lead with purpose, we ask them the following questions:

- Why does your brand exist?
- How does your brand uniquely serve others?
- What becomes possible in the lives of others because your brand exists?

We use these simple questions when we work with huge brands, some more than 100 years old, to help anchor them with their audiences, guide them into new innovations, and lead them into new territories where they can deliver their brands with purpose. But these questions can be used by newer and smaller companies as well. And you can consider these questions to clarify your Dream's purpose.

Below are a few samples of iconic brands and their purposes. Read each purpose to help clarify and inspire your vision for your Dream.

- **Bounty** exists to improve the lives of consumers via clean environments.
- **Verizon** exists to serve as a technology partner with consumers to keep them more connected in their personal lives and more efficient in their professional lives.
- **Procter & Gamble's "My Black Is Beautiful" campaign** exists to celebrate African American women and what makes them beautiful.
- **TOMS** exists to give necessities like shoes, eyeglasses, and clean drinking water to those in need.

By having a solid purpose, these brands have an anchor that guides all they do—including overall vision, strategic plans, staffing, product development, product delivery, research, promotion, and more. P&G's CMO Marc Pritchard advises all brands to "ensure that that purpose is tied directly to the core benefit of that product or service in some way and reflects the values of that brand."

We've covered a lot of ground in Chapter Four to help you get a clearer picture of what your purpose is and how to use it to bring your company, new idea, or great invention to life. Now let's dig into the exercises for this week's Stretch to find your purpose and begin connecting it to your biggest Dreams.

EXERCISE 4.1

10 QUESTIONS FOR DISCOVERING YOUR PURPOSE FROM THE INSIDE OUT

It's time to roll up your sleeves and dig into the underlying qualities that define your purpose. In this exercise, answer the following 10 questions as fully as possible in your Dream Notebook. Your answers may relate to your current position, but they may also come from entirely different areas of your life. It's important that you be honest. You're assessing your interests and your ability to make big changes in your professional and personal life, so you need to be straight with yourself.

1. What brings you your greatest joy?
2. What are you most curious about?
3. Who are the people that light you up and bring you the most joy?
4. What gifts, talents, and skills come to you naturally?
5. What are your weaknesses?
6. What are your strengths?
7. What inspires you?
8. What annoys you?
9. What would you do on a perfect day?
10. What would you do every day without pay?

EXERCISE 4.2

WRITING YOUR PERSONAL PURPOSE STATEMENT

Now that you've explored your purpose, I'd like you to use your answers to the questions above to create your personal purpose *statement*. Your personal purpose statement should be a simple sentence that expresses your values and what you want to share with others through your life's work. Your fellow Dreamers, ideal customers, future business partners, mentors, and colleagues should be able to easily remember your personal purpose statement. For example, the personal purpose statement of India.Arie, one of our Dream Project Dreamers, is "to spread love, healing, and peace through the power of words and music." If I had to guess, I'd say that Richard Branson's personal purpose statement is "to build brands that allow others to experience life as an adventure." I think that the musically talented Adele's purpose statement is "to reflect the world's emotion through music" and that the late Steve Jobs's personal statement was "to create a future-forward world through technologies." My own purpose statement is "to create platforms that allow people to activate their purpose and empower their Dreams."

Take a minute to consider some well-known people, past and present. Could you write a purpose statement for each of these people: Gloria Steinem, Marie Kondo, Bernie Sanders, Spike Lee, Dr. Drew Pinsky, Bill Maher, or Shonda Rhimes? What about Martin Luther King Jr., Mahatma Gandhi, Princess Diana, or Harriet Tubman? These people have a rather clear "branding," if you will. That's to say that we really know what they're about. Now create your own purpose statement. If you need help getting started, choose five words from the purpose word bank below:

serve	teach	give	provide
love	create	build	grow
future	technology	innovation	develop

Use those words to craft a personal purpose statement such as, "My purpose is to provide books in rural communities," or "My purpose is to create more learning opportunities for senior citizens." Use the following space to develop your own personal purpose statement.

Your Personal Purpose Statement

____

____

____

____

____

____

____

After you develop the first draft of your personal purpose statement, invite a fellow Dreamer or Dream Mentor to "interview" you with the following questions. Do your best to answer them as fully as possible.

1. What did you learn from exploring your purpose?
2. How are you currently using these new findings in your business, company, or venture?
3. How does your purpose connect with your Dream?
4. If you're not living your purpose now, what would you need to do to close the distance between your purpose and where you want to be?

After you answer these questions, ask your Dream Mentor for feedback about whether your personal purpose statement matches what he or she knows about you. Also, ask your mentor to suggest ways that you can demonstrate this purpose in your everyday life. Sometimes others are able to recognize gifts, talents, and skills that we don't see in ourselves.

Next, you'll work on clarifying your Dream's purpose, which is somewhat different from your personal purpose. **Again, your personal purpose is an overarching motivation that guides all the Dreams you're going to develop.** It's the backbone of what matters to you and what you want to contribute to the world, and we've distilled all that into a personal purpose statement. **Your *Dream*'s purpose is specific to one particular project—the goal, product, service, etc., that you're developing at the moment.** It's the heart of the reason that you're going after this Dream, and we're going to distill that down into a *mission* statement.

EXERCISE 4.3

10 QUESTIONS TO DISCOVER YOUR DREAM'S PURPOSE

It's time to have a heart-to-heart conversation with your Dream. Invite your idea into the room and tell it to have a seat. This idea might be a book, a new invention, a new blog, a new community, or a new movement. Speak as you would to a dear friend. Say, "Hey Dream! I'm delighted that you've chosen me and thrilled that we get to make this journey together. I know you're giving me a chance to leave a mark on the world, and I want to give you a chance to fulfill your purpose of serving others." In this exercise, you'll speak for your goal as you answer the following five questions. Be as specific as you can. Even try to provide details of a timeline or the number of people you expect will be affected. Remember, your Dream is a grand opportunity, so the more detailed a description, the more vivid the Dream will seem. Answer the following questions in your Dream Notebook:

1. Why do you want to exist?
2. Whom will you help when you get here?
3. What benefits and/or possibilities will become available to others because you will exist?
4. What problems will be solved because you exist?
5. What joy will you bring to the world?

EXERCISE 4.4

DEVELOPING YOUR DREAM'S MISSION STATEMENT

In this exercise, we'll develop your Dream's mission statement, which will guide the actions of your new company, start-up, nonprofit, or idea. Your Dream's mission statement should motivate you into action during the remaining weeks of The Stretch and help you clearly articulate the mission to your community. To help you get started, let's take a look at a mission statement from a start-up company, a Fortune 500 company, and a nonprofit organization.

Start-Up Mission Statement: DIA & Co

DIA & Co provides a clothing subscription box for plus-size women. The company's mission statement:

> Shopping for clothes should be fun and easy, no matter what your shape or size.

Fortune 100 Mission Statement: General Motors

General Motors is a Fortune 500 company that has been manufacturing and selling automobiles throughout the world for nearly 100 years. Its mission statement:

> We sell products and services of superior quality and are committed to sharing our success with our employees, business partners, and stock-holders.

Nonprofit Mission Statement: United Way

The United Way is a nonprofit organization that provides community services throughout the United States. Its mission statement:

> The United Way envisions a community where all individuals and families achieve their human potential through education, financial stability, and healthy lives.

Grab your notebook because it's your turn to develop your Dream's mission statement. It should include the core beliefs of your idea and the opportunities, services, and products you'll provide. When you're done. Write in your final statement in the space provided:

Your Dream's Mission Statement

YOUR 90-DAY STRETCH PLAN GOAL CRUSH REMINDER

Time for another Goal Crush Reminder! Have a look at your 90-Day Stretch Plan. Are you staying on track? This recurring reminder appears each week to make sure you are taking time to work on your goals.

You have officially finished your first week in the Design phase of The Stretch. This week was about discovering your purpose and the purpose of your Dream, and in the next chapters we'll explore the opportunities for this Dream. To wrap up Week 4, I'm thrilled to share with you insights from one of the world's greatest brand builders, the chief brand officer of Procter & Gamble. He knows how to develop purpose-driven brands, and he also leads with purpose in his personal life.

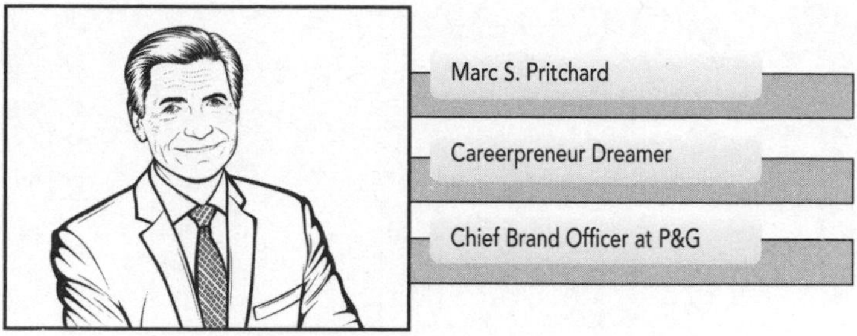

"There's one piece of advice I give to everyone, which was given to me at one point. It's to focus on being useful. It'll lead to your days being more meaningful. People who are the happiest are the people providing service and doing good things for others. And generally, people who are doing that just have better lives."

—Careerpreneur Dreamer **Marc S. Pritchard**

You may download this week's Dream All-Star training session at www.thebigstretchbook.com.

CHAPTER FIVE

THE IDEAL OPPORTUNITIES FOR YOUR DREAM

Week 5

Congratulations, Dreamer! You're approximately at the 30-day mark—one-third of the way through! Now that you understand your Dream's purpose, you've probably discovered that part of this purpose is to serve. Perhaps you have an idea to create a fashion blog. Imagine that your blog can serve the world by providing women with fashion and style advice to help them feel beautiful. Maybe you want to write and publish a children's book. Imagine that your children's book will serve by sparking a child's imagination and providing valuable life lessons through creative stories. You might have a Dream to develop an eco-friendly technology that reduces harmful air pollution. Imagine that your innovation will serve the world by preserving our environment.

I know that it might sound odd that I describe your Dream as if it's a living, breathing thing with a personality. But your concept does indeed have its own mission, and what a privilege it is that this Dream has chosen you to be its Chief Dream Architect!

Throughout this chapter, you'll have ample possibilities to step into being the Chief Dream Architect. And by the end of the chapter, you'll discover new opportunities for your ideas with the following Stretch Exercises:

Week 5: The Ideal Opportunities for Your Dream

EXERCISE 5.1: Becoming the Answer for Your Dream Irritant

EXERCISE 5.2: Building Your Dream Audience

EXERCISE 5.3: Finding Your Dream's Unique Position

EXERCISE 5.4: Know Your Competition

After you work through these exercises, you'll be able to focus on how your idea can serve the world. Bruce Wilkinson, author of *The Dream Giver*, one of our Dream All-Stars and one of my mentors, says, "[Your mission] is to achieve everything that you can with your talents for the purpose of helping as many people as possible." With this idea of service in mind, I'm now going to introduce you to a critical component of this part of your Stretch: developing the servant's mindset. People who serve solve problems and bring joy. They make life easier by giving us new possibilities. Developing a servant's mindset keeps you in touch with whom you're serving and why.

UNDERSTANDING A SERVANT'S MINDSET

After my promotion to general manager at RUSH Communications, I was excited about my new role. I was also feverishly seeking wisdom to help shape me into the type of leader I wanted to become and build the type of company I wanted to create. I took a field trip to Barnes & Noble to learn as much as I could about different leadership styles. While I was there, Larry Julian's book *God Is My CEO* got my attention. When I read the first page, I learned that to have a servant's mindset is to keep the goal of serving others at the forefront of all I do, which, of course, is possible regardless of whether one believes in God. After reading the book, I had a new outlook on how I wanted to serve the world. Throughout the book, Larry observed that when you lead with service, sales will eventually follow. *God Is My CEO* is also the first book that gave me permission to bring my spiritual principles and faith into business. I decided that God is my lead Dream Giver, and I was empowered to cocreate every part of my experience with Him.

I also loved that Larry showcased respected business leaders from companies such as General Motors, ExxonMobil, and United Healthcare who were growing their Fortune 500 and Fortune 100 companies by incorporating service into the company culture and their core business principles. Many notable brands that we have grown to love have a purpose grounded in service. For example, Mary Kay Cosmetics is committed to service by providing unlimited opportunities to women. The Walt Disney World Corporation serves the world by making people happy and sparking imaginations. Nike delivers service by making athletic gear that allows people to experience the joys of athleticism and competition. As you further design the framework for your Dream, I want you to begin thinking about how your idea or concept can serve the world.

When I was only eight years old, I discovered the power of leading with a servant's mindset. My mother had taken a job as the executive director of an adult daycare facility, and during the summer, she let me go to work with her whenever possible. I absolutely loved it. I had seen her work extremely hard as a teenage mother, and I was very excited for her to land this opportunity. I was even more thrilled that my mom's boss, Reverend Robert Jones, let her bring me to work with her. Reverend Jones owned the facility with my Uncle Rochester, which I thought was cool. This also stands out as one of my first experiences of seeing black men as entrepreneurs.

Each Friday, Rev. Jones came through the office to pass out paychecks. I wanted to figure out how *I* could receive one of those checks. Remember, I was only in third grade, so thinking about a paycheck was a big deal. As I wondered how I could make myself useful at the center, I thought about some of the things I loved to do. One activity I loved was cleaning and making spaces beautiful. I could see that the center was in dire need of a regular cleaning. This was it—I had found a way to serve! But first I had to get the courage to ask Rev. Jones to hire me. I practiced my pitch over and over. I have no idea how at that age I knew what to emphasize, but I remember repeating that hiring me to clean the office would help *him*.

During the next payday when Rev. Jones handed my mother her check, I asked to meet with him. I told him I'd noticed that the center could benefit from having a regular cleaning service. I said I'd be willing to clean the building each day to keep the facility warm and welcoming for the patients. After I finished, I held my breath in anticipation. He said, "How much do you want per week?" *Wow!* My pitch had worked! He was actually considering my idea. I said, "I could do it for $25 per week." He replied, "You've got a deal, young lady." Eight years old, and I had landed my first paying job!

The approach I used with Rev. Jones is the formula that I still use when pitching my service to Fortune 100 companies. I always begin with a servant's mindset and ask, "How can I serve you?" and "What problem can I help *you* solve today?" I've learned that when I come to the table with a servant's mindset, I reap the rewards of securing more business deals, developing stronger connections with my business partners, and growing my business even further.

WHAT DOES IT TAKE TO STRENGTHEN YOUR DREAM?

As Chief Dream Architect, your job is to design a framework with the strongest infrastructure possible. We've already established that your Dream's foundation should be anchored in your purpose. And whether it's your body or your business, core strength is critical, so as you continue your Design, you'll want to ensure that your concept has a strong core. How do you do that? You have to ensure that your Dream is built on certain core pillars of service. As you prepare to serve the world, you should know:

1. *Whom* you are serving
2. *What* you are serving
3. *When* you are serving
4. *How* you are serving

Developing a Dream with service at the core is the magic behind countless ideas that have changed the world for the better. To begin developing this core of service, you have to map the viability of your Dream and how it can thrive with your ideal audience. Now, before you get scared that I'm going to shoot your Dream before it takes flight, know that I will never deem your idea unworthy of being pursued and explored. I'm vested, and I won't let you quit. But I'll ask that you remain open to tweaking, editing, and changing your approach as you work on building your core each day. Remember that we're on this journey together. This section is simply an opportunity for you to pause and consider different approaches.

FINDING THE WHITE SPACE FOR YOUR DREAM

One of the keys to protecting your idea's viability is to ensure that you're serving the right idea at the right time to the right audience. You have to define the opportunities for this idea by understanding the unmet needs of your audience. This area is called the "white space"; it's the space where a company might have room to maneuver in a crowded playing field. It also fills in vital gaps in existing markets and product lines. The white space might also offer a lack of competition or possibilities for creating an entirely new market.

As the CEO of EGAMI, I discovered that there was a white space in my industry for delivering purpose-driven, multicultural marketing campaigns to multicultural audiences with Fortune 100 companies, and so for more than a decade, we've been helping global brands including Procter & Gamble, Toyota, and Verizon make inroads within those communities. Many of the participants in the Dream Project are world-class finders of white space. Let's take a look at how two of these experts, Myleik Teele and Lara Hodgson, identified and took advantage of white spaces.

Myleik Teele, CEO Dreamer and founder and CEO of CURLBOX, uncovered a huge white space for African American women who wear their hair naturally. With an abundance of natural hair care products in the marketplace, it can be overwhelming to know which will work best for your hair type. Enter CURLBOX, a monthly subscription box with samples of high-quality natural hair care products. If you like something you tried, you can order the full-size product. Since its inception in 2011, CURLBOX has partnered with companies like L'Oréal, Unilever, Target, Walmart, and SheaMoisture. Within its first year, CURLBOX exploded by tapping into a white space for women of color who wear their hair naturally.

Myleik was the first to market this unique offering, and within the company's first year, subscriptions increased by more than 1,900 percent, catapulting Myleik into the spotlight as an entrepreneurial superstar. When she shared with the audience of the Dream Project the story of her extraordinary journey, she said, "Our growth happened so fast. I couldn't have anticipated how high our demand was going to be. I'm glad that I have the opportunity to meet the needs of the women in this marketplace." She found a white space that proved to be fertile ground for a thriving Dream.

In Chapter Four we introduced Lara Hodgson, the Make-It-Happen Dreamer who founded NOW Corp and changed the way small businesses use money. She launched her company after first defining what she identified as a very big finance problem for small businesses. She observed that as small businesses grow, their owners often run into cash flow problems. The bigger the clients, the more aggressive the payment terms; a small business owner might have to wait net 30, 60, 90, or even 120 days to be paid, and so a long waiting period can lead to a strain on cash flow. As a small business owner herself, Lara ran into this problem again and again, and from her pain, a solution was born.

Lara told the Dream Project about the day the light went on: "I thought, *There's got to be a better way*. I was having lunch at a local sandwich shop, and mid-lunch, I started looking around and I thought, *Wait a minute. This restaurant never waits to get paid*. Right? Because everyone that goes in and out of that restaurant is going to either hand over cash or they're going to hand them a credit card. And when you hand them a credit card, they're going to get paid the next day when they settle the credit card transactions, and they pay a service charge for that. But when and if the customer pays their Visa bill or not isn't that restaurant's problem. So the restaurant doesn't have accounts receivable. My 'aha!' moment was this lunch. I thought to myself, *How do I create a solution that feels like the credit card, but a card doesn't have to be offered for business*? That was the moment that led to the creation of NOWaccount. Our solution allows for the company or small business, the people who sold the goods or service, to get paid on the NOWaccount. They get paid immediately for a flat merchant's fee. It feels exactly like a credit card for small business owners. So they haven't borrowed money; they haven't factored anything. There's no liability on their balance sheet. Meanwhile, their customer still gets the invoice, still pays when they feel like it, and still makes the check out to their vendor."

Because of her own experience with a common small business financing issue, Lara was able to clearly see the problem, which led her to solve the problem. Today, Lara's NOWaccount Network Corporation (NOW Corp) has over 40 employees, services around 400 customers across the United States, and has processed approximately $500 million in transactions.

UNDERSTANDING YOUR COMPETITION AND EXPLORING THE FIELD OF DREAMS

As you get ready to bring your idea to life, it's very important that you understand the competitive landscape. You will need to have an idea of who's in your field, what's being offered, and how this product or service compares with yours. I encourage you to research all of this with one goal in mind: to better understand your competition so you'll know what makes *your* Dream unique. Be warned—to understand your competition is not about trying to copy or *become* your competition. I made that mistake when, while training for the marathon, I tried to run like other runners. **By copying people with completely different skills from my own, I was setting myself up for failure.** Eventually I made it across the finish line because I ran the race *my way*.

Imagine yourself walking through a field of flowers where each flower represents someone else's Dream. I want you to see and appreciate these thousands of flowers for their beauty and uniqueness, but I never want you to be so in awe of them that you lose sight of what makes your flower unique, even in a crowded field. *Know* your competition; don't try to *be* your competition.

Lara Hodgson treasures a piece of advice that she received from Spanx founder Sara Blakely about studying the competition and being willing to break away from the crowd. She recalls, "One of the best pieces of advice I've ever gotten was from Sara Blakely when she first started Spanx. I remember her telling me that she had this idea for cutting the toes off of her pantyhose, and when she went to all sorts of experts in hosiery manufacturing, most of them were men who told her that was a dumb idea, and nobody would ever buy that. She said, 'But I kept thinking *I would*. I would buy it.' So the advice she gave me, which has been invaluable, was, 'Find the place to test it where you're outside of the noise.' What she meant by that was she could've gone immediately into the hosiery section, but the problem with that is there are rows and rows of hosiery with names everybody knows, and she never would have gotten any attention. So she asked herself, 'Where does somebody go *before* they need hosiery?' And so she went up to the dress section of the store and befriended the cashier and started hanging out in the dress section. As women would look at these formal dresses, she would say, 'Can I share with you this idea I have for pantyhose you can wear with sandals?' And that's what allowed her to connect directly to her customers. She broke away from the standard that was developed by the competition and carved out a unique space for herself."

Somebody who knows how to stand out from the competition is one of my favorite Dreamers, Robbie Montgomery, restauranteur, author, and star of the former OWN TV reality hit *Welcome to Sweetie Pie's*. Although she's near 80 years old, "Ms. Robbie," as she's affectionately known, has the energy of a 20-year-old, and she fired up our Dream Project audience with tales of her journey to build a restaurant empire after she ended her career as a back-up singer for the Supremes and the Ike and Tina Turner Revue. When she first left the music business, she became a dialysis technician. Before long she was laid off, but instead of wallowing in her unemployment, Ms. Robbie went back to one of her first loves, cooking.

Ms. Robbie opened her first soul food restaurant, Sweetie Pie's, in 1979. While many restaurants have taken a health-conscious approach to their menu, Ms. Robbie sticks with the soul food dishes that have earned her the loyalty of customers for more than 40 years. "I know I could be more innovative by using organic ingredients in my recipes," she says, "but that's not what people come to my restaurant for. I'm answering the call of my customers." Ms. Robbie was able to clearly see her competition, dominate her lane as a soul food expert, strategically expand her company one restaurant at a time, and thrive in a marketplace where she had eager customers waiting for her services. She believes in studying her competition because they're part of her business, and she says that she's not watching in order to copy but to learn. She says with a smile, "I'm trying to stay one step ahead of you."

WHAT KEEPS YOU UP AT NIGHT? UNCOVERING YOUR DREAM IRRITANT

Another way for you to discover the white space for your Dream is to pay attention to what pains you. I've come to learn that when an injustice or world problem tugs at your heart and you find yourself saying, "Somebody should do something about this!" that somebody is you. If the problem is keeping you up at night, don't toss around in your bed in frustration. Get up and be the solution.

I have to admit that I'm biased about this next Dreamer. Lauren Seroyer is my goddaughter and a bold Dreamer who was willing to be the solution. During her sophomore year in high school outside of Atlanta, a fellow student asked if he could have her lunch. At first, Lauren thought he was being greedy, but then she saw sincerity in his eyes. She gave him her lunch, and the student confided that he didn't have regular meals at home. This student's difficulty really bothered Lauren, and that day she went home and shared the story with her mother. Lauren wanted to know, "How can there be students who are hungry and homeless *in my school*?" She began to research, and Lauren discovered that this problem is much bigger than at her school.

She learned that when the school's counselors found out about a hungry student, that child was typically referred to the local food pantry. Then she discovered that none of the local high schools had food pantries within their buildings. Making students wait for a meal wasn't good enough for Lauren. She wanted to meet that unmet need by finding out how to give hungry students food *when they needed it*. Lauren didn't wait for anyone to give her permission to solve the problem. She acted on her Dream irritant and, along with her twin brother, Grant, created a nonprofit organization called the Community Assistance and Resource Effort (CARE) Closet. CARE Closet places food pantries in high schools, and students can anonymously take whatever they need.

In just over two years, Lauren helped to establish 15 CARE Closets in five states and has raised over $100,000 in funding. Lauren was also the winner of a $25,000 grand prize from the United Way of Greater Atlanta's "SPARK Gwinnett" Shark Tank competition. She also now has corporate partnerships with companies such as Toyota, Publix, State Farm, Ann Inc., Vital Voices, and McDonald's. Lauren has won several awards for her service including the 2016 McDonald's 365 Black Community Choice Award, the 2017 100 Black Men of America's National Youth Health & Wellness Award, the 2017 Prudential Spirit of the Community Award, and the 2018 Spirit of Anne Frank Award, just to name a few. Lauren and Grant learned that when you're courageous enough to challenge a problem that tugs at your heart, you not only find white space, but can dramatically change the lives of others.

Tarana Burke is the Activist Dreamer who has arguably changed the world with the #MeToo movement she created. Tarana has always been dedicated to social justice, so she's actively involved in several causes. She fights for fair housing, battles against predatory lending, and stands against the existence of sweatshops. She says it was "out of necessity" that she launched the #MeToo movement. Tarana is a sexual assault survivor and is acutely aware of how some communities have very few resources available to people who have experienced sexual violence. This injustice pained her, so she stepped up. She told me recently in an interview that the resource deficits were most pronounced relative to "young black and brown girls, and it became necessary to create something that would fill that gap. So in 2005 and 2006, I started trying to tackle the problem." What began as a Dream irritant has now grown into a global movement that has given millions of young girls, women, and men a voice and a vehicle to push back against all forms of sexual violence. It's a movement that started because a strong woman couldn't ignore something that pained her.

WHAT DREAM OPPORTUNITY IS CHASING YOU?

Another way to discover the white space for your Dream is to identify which ideas are chasing you. Hobby Dreamer Christina Totton is the creator of *No Special Occasion* (@nospecialoccasion), an influencer Instagram page created to explore lifestyle, fitness, travel, and fashion. Before she launched her digital platforms, Christina shared travel tips and advice with her friends. Her advice would be so detailed and organized that my husband and I would often choose where to travel after Christina explored the destination first. She was also extraordinary at recommending new health plans and training routines. Christina told me that her friends were taking her recommendations, so I encouraged her to pay attention to what people were naturally coming to her for. From there, her idea to create a platform to share her love of fashion, travel, and fitness with the world was born. Now nearly 40,000 followers are actively engaged with Christina's page each month.

Not long after the buzz around her blog began to build, influential brands, companies, and restaurants started hiring her as an influencer to review and experience their products. It certainly turned out to be profitable for Christina to discover the opportunities that were chasing her.

What's chasing you? If you still don't have an answer to that question, take a step back and ask yourself, "What do people ask me for that only I can provide?" You'll begin to see opportunities to grow your Dream when you recognize how to tap into the unmet needs of others. If you're a Career Dreamer, think about the kinds of projects you've been recommended for within your company. If you're an Activist Dreamer, think about the kinds of boards you've been invited to serve on or projects you volunteer for. If you're a Hobby Dreamer, consider whether your passions lead people to ask you for advice or service. Are people asking for your help to decorate their homes, landscape their properties, or draft e-mails? Pay attention; you might have a hobby just waiting to be monetized.

Remember AJ from Week 3, Dream Detox, the fitness trainer who believes in an active approach to spirituality? She joined me in a Dream Project session a few years ago to speak about "The Mind, Body, and Soul of a Dreamer." I invited her to talk about developing a healthy body, but I quickly discovered that she had an inspiring Stretch journey to share with our Dreamers. AJ is an actress best known for her roles in movies such as *House Party* and *Baby Boy*, and her idea began to take shape behind the scenes when she would show up on set with green juices and healthy snacks, long before this kind of food became popular. Her fellow actors and actresses were curious about why she had so much energy, and they began to ask her for tips and recipes. Before she knew it, she felt a strong pull toward a Dream to help people to live healthier lives. AJ created a company called the AJ Zone that teaches online health courses, provides online fitness videos, and sells nutritional supplements. She's also now a sought-after motivational speaker, coach, and health and fitness guru for many Hollywood stars including Sterling K. Brown, Steve Harvey, Gabrielle Union, and many more.

THE RIGHT TIMING

Stepping into the right opportunities for your Dream also means that you need to be keenly aware of knowing the right time to deliver your product or service. You have to stay current with trends and how they might affect the delivery of your product or service. You might be tempted to sit back and wait to develop your concept, but the world changes fast, so you must be courageous enough to act now.

As I began my research for this section, I did a little testing with one of my favorite Dreamers, my mother. I wanted to see what ideas and services were making a difference in her life by meeting her previously unmet needs and providing her with convenience and ease. On a Sunday afternoon, she shared some of the business innovations that were currently bringing her joy. All of the businesses that she started to rattle off were able to innovate within the marketplace by staying in tune with current times, staying abreast of trends, and constantly striving to meet consumer needs and wants.

For example, my mother loves the convenience of Netflix. She shared that she enjoyed having the freedom to watch at her leisure and binge entire seasons at once. Streaming TV services like Netflix, Hulu, Amazon Prime, and HBO GO have provided unlimited programming anytime and anywhere for their customers, and by staying aware of customer habits and trends, each company has captured a segment of this growing billion-dollar market.

My mother was also happy to share that her groceries were on the way to her house from Walmart. She hates grocery shopping, and she's now delighted to save time by ordering her food online and having groceries delivered right to her door. Walmart recognized the global trend of providing subscription and real-time delivery services for customers and followed the cue of other subscription-based services like Amazon, Blue Apron, and Hello Fresh by giving customers what they want, when they want it. These companies are on trend right now in providing the right products at the right time for the right customers.

In a look to the past, when I spoke alongside Bishop T.D. Jakes during his SOAR Tour, I had the pleasure of hearing him talk about how Kentucky Fried Chicken revolutionized the fast-food industry during the 1970s. He talked about the great wave of women entering the workforce in the 1970s and the tug they felt between wanting to work outside the home and being good mothers and wives. He said that many women during this era felt guilty that they couldn't provide home-cooked meals for their families as they had before. Enter Kentucky Fried Chicken, offering a perfect way for the working mother to give her family a warm, comforting meal. The 1970s was just the right time for KFC, but can you imagine KFC trying to enter the market today with its old menu? Timing was on its side.

WHOM ARE YOU SERVING?

If you're committed to putting service at the core of your Dream, you have to understand the audience you'll be serving. When I work with Fortune100 brands, I often remind them that one of the most critical principles of product development is to never, ever take your eyes off the person you're serving and never stop considering what the client needs. Also, you have to accept that you can't be all things to all people. Narrow your target market and tailor your Dream product, idea, or service to meet the needs of your *ideal* customer. In order to clearly define your target audience, do your research to discover who they are, what they like and dislike, what their buying habits are, and what will be possible for them because of the product or service that you're offering.

Make-It-Happen Dreamer Jennifer Fleiss is a cofounder of Rent the Runway, a business that transformed the retail industry by making designer dress and accessory rentals affordable for millions of women. She shared with the Dream Project how she was able to envision this new business model by staying in touch with the people she hoped to serve with her idea. She found that actual market testing proved to be an invaluable tool. She explains, "The first woman who rented a dress put it on and twirled around in the mirror, and she said, 'I look hot.' My cofounder and I looked to each other, and we said, "That's our concept.'" She advises not losing touch with the people you're selling to. "We're almost eight years in," she says, "and we still go back to the consumer whether it's through our customer service lines that we listen in on or focus groups that we hold every now and again. You need to have a living, breathing conversation with your consumer."

At my company, EGAMI, we talk about our core target (our ideal client) every three months. We note who our ideal clients are, where they are, how they think, what they value, and what they need. We narrowed our core target down to Fortune 100 or Fortune 500 clients that want to grow and connect with multicultural audiences. If you don't narrow your target, you might make the mistake of trying to be all things to all people. And when you cast too broad a net, you're likely to miss the best fish. So be specific about whom you want to serve, how your Dream will meet their needs, and how to best reach them.

You now have the tools you need to design a strong core for your Dream. Let's jump into the business core exercises for your opportunities.

EXERCISE 5.1

BECOMING THE ANSWER FOR YOUR DREAM IRRITANT

This is a great exercise for Activist Dreamers. Many social organizations were created from the pain of losing a loved one, a need to raise awareness about a serious illness, or a desire to provide resources for communities in need. For example, as you read earlier, the #MeToo movement was the brainchild of activist Tarana Burke after she was a victim of sexual aggression. Tarana is passionate about working to create a world in which no other young girls or women will experience that kind of suffering. The Susan G. Komen Foundation was founded in 1982 after its founder, Nancy Brinker, lost her only sister to breast cancer. Because of the organization's inception, October has officially become Breast Cancer Awareness Month, and pink ribbons can be found everywhere to continue to raise awareness about regular testing and mammograms.

Which societal issues are your Dream irritants? Are you frustrated by the lack of fresh produce for sale in urban areas? Do you want to provide safer extracurricular activities for kids in your neighborhood? In your Dream Notebook, write your Dream irritant, and begin exploring possible solutions, partners, and resources to become the change you want to see.

DREAM IRRITANT 1

Solutions: ____

Resources: ____

Partners: ____

DREAM IRRITANT 2

Solutions: ____

Resources: ____

Partners: ____

EXERCISE 5.2

BUILDING YOUR DREAM AUDIENCE

It's extremely important to understand who your key audience will be for your Dream. Knowing who and where they are helps you know how and when to deliver your product or service. First, define your ideal audience. Explore everything you can about their habits including media consumption, shopping behaviors, Internet activities, social media behavior, mobile media behavior, and where they like to connect online and in person. For example, if you're an Activist Dreamer who wants to provide an afterschool reading program for middle school students, think about where the average middle schooler enjoys hanging out in your neighborhood.

Consider their favorite smartphones, favorite apps, and favorite video games. This exercise is designed to help you better understand your ideal audience. In the space below, create vivid profiles for three of your ideal consumers who could benefit from your services. Once you have identified these three consumer types, the sample consumers will actually represent consumer groups.

For our sample Activist Dreamer, those three consumers could include 13-year-old Anna Belle who loves hanging out with her friends at the mall, posting on Instagram, and catching up on her favorite books on Goodreads; 11-year-old Michael who loves challenging his friends to games of Fortnite, hanging out with his older cousins in the park, and using his iPhone to text with his classmates; and 12-year-old Michelle who loves reading books on her Kindle, listening to music on Spotify, and playing trumpet in the high school orchestra.

Use the information below to draft three ideal Dream profiles for your service, product, or idea. Be as detailed as possible so you can begin to clearly see your ideal Dream consumer.

CONSUMER 1

Name: ______________________________

Age: ______________________________

Occupation: ______________________________

Location: ______________________________

Favorite Media: ______________________________

Favorite News Sources: ______________________________

Hopes/Dreams/Fears: ______________________________

CONSUMER 2

Name: ____

Age: ____

Occupation: _____________________________________

Location: ______________________________________

Favorite Media: __________________________________

Favorite News Sources: ______________________________

Hopes/Dreams/Fears: _______________________________

CONSUMER 3

Name: ____

Age: ____

Occupation: _____________________________________

Location: ______________________________________

Favorite Media: __________________________________

Favorite News Sources: ______________________________

Hopes/Dreams/Fears: _______________________________

EXERCISE 5.3

FINDING YOUR DREAM'S UNIQUE POSITION

This week I want you to examine what makes *your* Dream unique. This is a question that you'll need to answer over and over again. Your potential clients will want to know, "Why you?" Your investors will want to know, "What makes this concept unique?" This exercise also explores what qualifies you to deliver this Dream. Lastly, you'll explore why your idea is relevant. Answer the questions below.

Uniqueness: What Makes You or Your Dream Unique?

1. What is unique about you and your company, product, service, event, etc.?
2. What can you do that others don't do or can't do?
3. How does your product or service uniquely meet the needs of your target audience or ideal client?

Credibility: What Makes You Credible to Develop and Launch This Dream?

1. Describe your background and credentials.
2. What are your achievements and accomplishments that qualify you to develop your Dream?
3. How long have you been working on this Dream?
4. What are your greatest strengths?

Relevance: How Relevant Is This Dream?

1. Why does your target audience care about what you're offering?
2. What are the hopes and aspirations of your target audience? How does your product, service, or skill help them achieve these things?
3. How else does what you provide affect them?

Now that you have identified these answers, it is important that you are able to articulate them to vendors, clients, and partners. You must always be prepared to share what makes you and your Dream unique.

EXERCISE 5.4

KNOW YOUR COMPETITION

Let's take some time now to look specifically at some of your competitors. Who are they? What do they do? What makes you different from them? Refer to the diagram in Figure 5.1 and write your answers in your Dream Notebook.

Remember, this exercise is simply to help you understand what makes you unique. (Key messaging refers to the lead message that the brand, product or service is delivering. For example, Delta Airlines key message highlights the importance of traveling to explore the world.)

	Brand/Product/Service	Top 3 Key Messagings and Products	What Makes Them Unique
Competitor #1	• • •	• • •	• • •
Competitor #2	• • •	• • •	• • •
Competitor #3	• • •	• • •	• • •

Figure 5.1 Your Competition

YOUR 90-DAY STRETCH PLAN GOAL CRUSH REMINDER

Don't forget how critical it is that each week you dedicate time to work on your 90-Day Stretch Plan. Keep a close eye on those goals. Which actions should you have executed by the end of this week? Stay on track. Make sure you're crushing those goals every week.

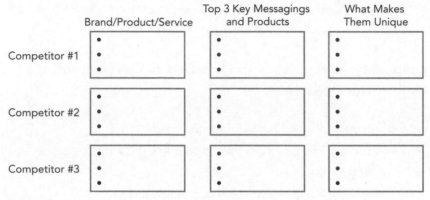

Congratulations, Dreamer! You just wrapped up your second week of Design! You now have a solid understanding of the ways in which your Dream can serve others, what makes your idea or concept unique, and how it will affect people's lives. I now welcome you to enjoy the words of a woman so quick-minded that during our interview when she spoke, I couldn't take notes fast enough. She is cofounder of Rent the Runway, a business that transformed the retail industry by making designer dress and accessory rentals convenient and accessible for millions of women. She's been recognized by a number of publications including being named to *Inc.*'s "30 Under 30," *Fortune* magazine's "40 Under 40," and *Fast Company*'s "Most Influential Women in Technology."

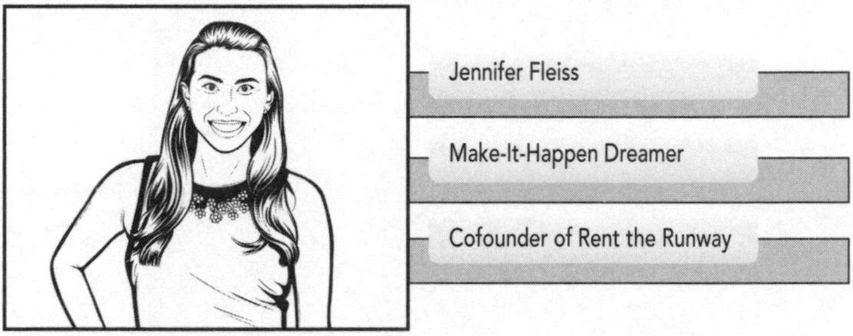

> "So, the first woman who rented a dress put it on and twirled around in the mirror, and she said, 'I look hot.' Her whole persona changed. She had better posture. She had more confidence. She didn't want to take the dress off. My cofounder and I looked to each other, and we said, 'That's our concept.'"
>
> —MAKE-IT-HAPPEN DREAMER JENNIFER FLEISS

You may download this week's Dream All-Star training session at www.thebigstretchbook.com.

CHAPTER SIX

BUILDING YOUR DREAM NETWORK AND TEAM

Week 6

Now that you're clear about your Dream's purpose and the ways it can serve, you might be overwhelmed by the prospect of the long journey ahead to bring the Dream to life. The good news is that you're not on this Stretch journey alone. As your Dream Coach, I'll be here with you step-by-step.

I also want your Stretch to be supported by two groups. First, a strong, authentic **external network** of mentors, colleagues, and connectors. Second a dynamic, diverse **internal team** of partners, collaborators, creatives, and supporters. It's critical for you to identify the best people to join your Stretch journey. Building the right network and team can make all the difference between a Dream that soars to its greatest possibilities and one that grinds to a halt before it begins.

As the Chief Dream Architect, you have the opportunity to build a strong network and team that will give you the freedom to grow your Dream. For example, if you have a Dream to become a personal fitness trainer and develop nutritional supplements to support your clients, your network could include an established trainer with a healthy roster of clients and a nutritionist who has already successfully brought nutritional supplements to the marketplace. Your team could include a virtual assistant who will handle social media, online marketing, and scheduling of clients. As your Dream evolves, people in your network could become ideal team members as business partners or support staff. And while those team members might move on as they Stretch into their own Dreams, they can remain part of your treasured network and serve as great sources of referrals and future business.

By the end of this chapter, you'll be ready to start creating your strongest network of team members and supporters by using the following exercises:

> **Week 6: Building Your Dream Network and Team**
>
> EXERCISE 6.1: High-Touch Dreaming: The Art of Networking
>
> EXERCISE 6.2: Finding Your Mentors
>
> EXERCISE 6.3: Six Degrees Toward Your Dream
>
> EXERCISE 6.4: Creating a Dream Culture
>
> EXERCISE 6.5: Building a Dream Team

Regardless of whether your Dream is still in the beginning stages of ideation or you're further along with development and execution, all Dreamers can benefit from having like-minded people within their circles.

BUILDING A STRONG NETWORK

> "A network is your professional 'family.' [It is] a community of colleagues who support you, share knowledge, request [connections with your] contacts, and help you move toward your goals over a span of decades. It is built from a myriad of connections based on commonalities of interests and shared goals."
>
> —KIM DORITY, PRESIDENT OF DORITY & ASSOCIATES AND FREQUENT PRESENTER AND WRITER ON CAREER TOPICS

Networking Rule 1: Givers Gain

One of the most important things to understand about building a strong network is that you must give to gain. If you network with the goal of gaining (such as gathering more business cards, selling your services, or adding people to your LinkedIn network), you give off a self-centered energy rather than conveying that you're here to benefit potential clients. But keeping "givers gain" in mind as you build your network is an idea similar to adopting the servant's mindset as you grow the opportunities for your venture. As you make new connections, if you prioritize the other person rather than recite your résumé or offer your services, you'll be more likely to attract authentic mentors, advisors, and colleagues into your network. Remember that one way to give is to eliminate someone else's problem.

Make-It-Happen Dreamer Jonathan Sprinkles, motivational speaker and connections coach, put an interesting spin on the "givers gain" idea when he spoke to a Dream Project audience. He said, "When networking and connecting with others, here's a quick little formula for positioning: 'What pain do you relieve?' The more you solve a problem, the less your fee becomes a problem. **Become a professional pain reliever.**" To be a pain reliever, first you have to be a listener. The importance of listening more than talking can't be overstated. Ask open-ended questions and then really listen to the answers. "What are you working on?" "What's causing you trouble right now?" "What's going on with your business that you wish were easier?" Your genuine interest will be clear and will help you create mutually beneficial, long-standing relationships.

Networking Rule 2: All Relationships Matter

One of the most important people in my network is a gentleman named DeRay, a former bellman at the Crown Plaza Hotel in downtown Minneapolis. Right after college, I moved to Minneapolis to work for IBM Global Services. On my first day in the city, my taxi pulled up to the hotel, DeRay grabbed my bags, and with his million-dollar smile flashing, he said, "Welcome to Minneapolis!" DeRay recommended restaurants, clubs, and city experiences—all perfectly chosen for a young person like me. I was grateful for DeRay's warm welcome.

A few days later, I ran into him on my way out of the hotel and told him that I'd tried to make reservations at a couple of the places he'd recommended but that they'd been booked solid. That's when I first witnessed his magic as a connector. He made a few calls, and within no time my name was added to the list for excellent restaurants, the hottest clubs, and prime tickets for sporting events in Minneapolis. These perks all came from the strength of DeRay's relationships. I thought that this was the coolest thing in the world!

Before long, DeRay became my connection for just about everything. When my dinged-up car arrived in Minneapolis, DeRay hooked me up with an excellent mechanic who let me pay for my repairs on a payment plan. When I had trouble finding an apartment because of my low post-college credit score, DeRay came through again by putting in a good word for me with the manager for a luxury high-rise apartment building. DeRay taught me many important lessons, one of which is that people do business with people they like.

One of the biggest lessons I learned from DeRay is about the power of making every relationship count, and he first presented that lesson to me when I was just about to take my first professional leap of faith and leave corporate life behind me. I was experimenting with the idea of transitioning into the entertainment industry and was interested in projects that would benefit underserved multicultural communities throughout the country. I was diligently reading business books and magazines and spending hours alone in my apartment to figure out how to design the next steps. I did as much as I could do within my own head, and then I realized that if I was going to make real progress in the next phase of my life and career, I'd need a network.

I started the process of conducting an internal relationship audit, and I began asking myself, *whom do I know*, *whom do they know*, and *whom do those people know?* DeRay was the first person I thought of. I met with DeRay to tell him about this Dream, and as we talked, he pushed me to be specific about whom I wanted to meet. He understood my vision, and he said, "Give me a call when you're ready to go." At that time I had no job, and I learned quickly that when you don't have an income safety net, networking becomes extremely important. I told DeRay that I was ready to start bringing this Dream to life *now*.

On a Friday evening a few weeks later, DeRay called to say that he had just checked in all the musicians on Jay-Z's "Roc the Mic" Tour. One of the managers gave him VIP tickets, and DeRay offered one to me so that I could begin networking within the entertainment industry. He said, "You need to come here right now and be ready to pitch yourself tonight." I got dressed and then dashed to meet DeRay at the venue. I learned another big lesson that day: **when opportunity knocks, be ready.**

DeRay's VIP tickets gave us backstage access, so I ended up right there in the middle of the managers, agents, and musicians on the tour, including Jay-Z, Snoop Dogg, and 50 Cent. This was my big chance to tell some big names in entertainment just what I planned to accomplish in their industry using my corporate experience as an asset. After two minutes backstage, I knew I wasn't in Kansas anymore. Unlike at the conferences or networking events I'd attended during my early corporate life, here nobody was interested in chitchat. I had to be bold and get straight to the point.

My first informal pitch was with Snoop Dogg. A lot of guys were standing around, many of them pressed up against women who looked like models, but Snoop looked exactly as I would have expected: true to his signature "laid-back" persona, he was half sitting, half lying on a couch smoking what appeared to be a blunt. I tried to hide my shaking hands as I described my ideas to him in the smoke-filled room. He seemed so relaxed that as I shared my ideas with him, I couldn't tell if he was interested or high as a kite, but he introduced me to his tour manager, so I consider my interaction with Snoop Dogg a genuine success. His tour manager recommended that I attend an upcoming fashion and entertainment conference, the Magic Trade Show in Las Vegas.

My next pitch was to 50 Cent, whose friendliness surprised me because I'd convinced myself that these people would have no time for me. He offered to pass my information along to anyone who might be looking for a project manager in the entertainment industry. I tried to pitch Jay-Z, but that one didn't go so well. He and his crew came walking my way, and I froze, trying to figure out how to address him. Should I call him "Jay-Z?" "Hov?" "Mr. Carter?" "Sean?" I called out "Hey, Sean," and felt the burn as he kept walking while chuckling to his friends and saying something about how I'd acted as if I'd known him forever. Ouch. It stung for a minute, but then I brushed it off.

For the rest of the evening, I made conversation with everyone I could, and I left that concert thrilled that I'd made good connections with important industry people who were willing to make further connections for me. Years later, I would find myself again in those circles, no longer an outsider. But I learned a great lesson on that night full of awkwardness: don't take rejection personally, and follow up even if the first connection doesn't click.

Per the recommendation of Snoop Dogg's tour manager, I attended the Magic Trade Show a few weeks later. The show was filled with pop culture designers and entertainment representatives from companies such as Sean John, Rocawear, and FUBU. I also met a woman named Angainein, a seasoned fashion buyer who attended the Magic Trade Show biannually. She knew the ropes and volunteered to help me get into key networking dinners and events. Angainein eventually became one of my dearest friends and greatest of Dream Champions. I also made my first connection with a person in the entertainment industry who would change the entire trajectory of my Dream—more on that *huge* connection later.

There is obvious value in riding the fast-paced river of social media and online networking, but there is even greater value in making face-to-face, personal, authentic connections with people. **Never underestimate the value of live networking and letting your new connections really get to know you.** DeRay's first lesson to me can't be overstated: people do business with people they like. Building your network online is great, but if you really want to expand your career, create a dynamic nonprofit, or build a profitable business, you must make genuine connections in the real world with real people. DeRay taught me that *all* relationships matter. And speaking of DeRay, here are a few of my favorite nuggets of business wisdom, courtesy of my favorite bellman with the million-dollar smile:

- People do business with people they like.
- Be ready to deliver your pitch anywhere at any time.

- Always lead with how you can provide value for the other person.
- Always follow up and follow through on your pitch.
- Develop a thick skin and learn to spin a no to your favor.

The Elevator Pitch Debate

I read the trades, and recently I've noticed some debate about whether or not to ditch the elevator pitch in favor of more "real" interaction. I agree that in networking it's important not to give off a sales vibe at every turn. But I'm also a firm believer that you should always have your elevator pitch ready to go. Remember that if you're lucky enough to find yourself alone in an elevator with one of the titans of your industry, you might be nervous, so preparedness will be your ally. I still cringe at the memory of the day I bumped into Oprah Winfrey at a party after a networking event that followed her New York SuperSoul session. I was so rattled that I was incapable of articulating why I was there and how my company could support her OWN network vision. And as my amused husband told me later, I also forgot to tell her my name. Oh my. I don't want another moment like that embedded in my memory, ever! Next time, I'll be ready.

If you have a great idea, don't be afraid that you're burdening someone "important" by telling them about it. Yeah, sure—they're busy, but don't fear that they're too busy to learn about something that might change their lives for the better, make them a lot of money, take their company to a new level, etc. Try an opening like this: "I've been working on an idea that I believe will (*insert fabulous outcome for their company or venture here*). Do you have 60 seconds to hear about it?" If the answer is yes, take a breath and deliver that well-rehearsed elevator pitch—while emphasizing how your idea benefits *them*. If the answer is no, smile and gracefully say, "I understand. Best of luck with your company." Who knows, maybe that "best of luck" will deliver enough nagging doubt about whether they just left a billion-dollar idea on an elevator floor that they'll turn around and say, "Okay, let's hear it."

Networking Rule 3: Add Movers and Shakers to Your Network

In Chapter Two, you met Dream All-Star Brandice Daniel who founded Harlem's Fashion Row despite the fact that she was a New York outsider with no local connections and very little experience in fashion. One of her Dream irritants was that there weren't enough designers of color featured during New York Fashion Week (NYFW), so she decided to solve that problem by creating Harlem's Fashion Row, one of the premiere fashion showcases for designers of color.

As this Dream began to thrive for Brandice, she faced several challenges, and one big one was that she didn't know anyone in the fashion industry. She remembers when she first tried to get designers and others interested in making a go of her idea. "They didn't know me. 'Harlem's Fashion Row' was a name I made up. And I'm from Memphis, so no one knew this Memphis girl living in New York."

But as is the case in the stories of many successful Dreamers, the power of Brandice's belief in her idea kept her persistent. She kept trying. She kept reaching out to new people. And eventually she built a team, her way. She recalls, "The entire fashion show in Harlem that August took place with a team of people I met as strangers. I told them about my vision, and they saw my passion and asked me what they could do. I would tell people, 'I need you to come to my house on Saturday for a meeting.' So I had probably 15 people coming to my house on Saturday. I made biscuits, eggs, and bacon, and we built this fashion show." Together, Brandice and her team researched candidates to best populate her network: fashion designers, clothing suppliers, fashion bloggers, reporters, and recent design school graduates. Brandice made a list of industry leaders and then came up with creative ways to get their attention. She didn't just send them messages on LinkedIn. Oh no. She sent each person a high-quality invitation (with flowers!) to join her for coffee so she could explain her vision for Harlem's Fashion Row. Sometimes she sent cupcakes. Although none of the industry leaders accepted her invitation to attend the first show, her efforts did lead to one industry influencer sending a representative to attend on her behalf. Brandice interpreted that interest as a win and moved forward with her plans to produce the best show possible.

After the show, she landed a coffee date with that very executive, Audrey Smaltz, CEO of Ground Crew, a backstage production company that has been a staple at NYFW for decades. Audrey listened attentively as Brandice shared her vision, and she accepted Brandice's invitation to join her Harlem's Fashion Row advisory board. Brandice knew that if she could get one fashion industry leader to say yes, more would surely follow. And, she was right. The Harlem's Fashion Row advisory board grew to include several fashion industry leaders, and Brandice remains ever conscious of how important the members of her network are to her success. Harlem's Fashion Row is now the premier destination for designers of color and has become the go-to fashion show during the biannual New York's Fashion Week.

Networking Rule 4: Make the Most of Your Mentors

When you hear the word *mentor*, you might think about a long-standing, high-touch relationship with an industry leader who will spend a lot of time with you to nurture you along your path. But that's not necessarily how mentorship works. If you've had a few mentors during your career or your entrepreneurship, you know you've been blessed. But because of the fast pace of the world we live in, potential mentors are extremely busy. As I've pursued my Dreams for my life and my companies, I've discovered that there's great power in concentrated moments with great leaders, which I like to call "Mentor Moments." I've learned that what matters more than the length of time I spend with a mentor is the impact each mentor has on my life. Some of the Mentor Moments that have made the biggest impact for me include:

- Receiving a divine e-mail from *New York Times* bestselling author and international speaker Bruce Wilkinson just as I was repositioning the Dream Project in 2016. His keen advice to expand the platform through strategic partnerships led me to increase the Dream Project from an event attended by 400 Dreamers to one attended by more than 100,000. For its inspiration and encouragement, I've reread his e-mail more times than I can count.

- Having a powerful, impromptu conversation with life coach and bestselling author Valorie Burton on a bench during a conference break in 2011. I told her that I was frustrated and felt boxed into writing dry marketing language in my first book, *Profit with Purpose*. I told her that I really wanted to write inspiring content versus just marketing content. She said, "Why don't you just do both, by writing inspiring content that will inspire marketers while also teaching them marketing best practices?" That was a huge "aha!" for me. I was able to finish my first book a few weeks later.
- Being challenged by Sylvia High, my spiritual and life coach, to look at my relationship with my father through my father's eyes. Being willing to try this exercise led to an "aha" moment that helped me see my part in the breakdown of our communication and helped heal the relationship.
- When my business coaches, Mark Hodges and Dan Coleman, pushed me to be brutally honest with myself and admit that I no longer wanted to run my company's day-to-day operations and needed to bring in new leadership that now provides me the time and breathing room for things like writing this book.

Mentors are invaluable, and as you continue moving through The Stretch, it will be important for you to add mentors to your circle of influence. Keep in mind that you'll have different mentors for different areas of interest and that your relationship with a mentor will be however the two of you define it. I have mentors for specific industries, general business, spirituality, fitness, wellness, and lifestyle. Over the years, Dream Project All-Stars have had a lot to say about mentorship. They have had mentors and have served as mentors, and one thing they have in common is that they all see value in the mentoring process.

Virtual Mentoring

My best friend Chelonnda Seroyer and I often speak of our favorite famous people as if they're our friends. Thanks to their presence on television, film, and social media and in books, we have a sense that we've known some of them for years. On a few occasions, our sense of familiarity has backfired, like the day I ran into Gayle King and felt the need to tell her that Chelonnda loved Gayle's choice of yellow as the accent color for her New York home. Short of stepping over boundaries of propriety, I encourage you to apply this "get to know you from afar" approach to mentoring. Find ways to learn from mentors without ever meeting them. Study their histories. Watch their TED Talks. Listen to their interviews. Read their books. With all the resources available, a motivated person can craft an entire curriculum! Also, don't forget the Dream All-Stars. I encourage you to continue to follow their stories, watch their moves, and add to your Dream Playbook.

As you know by now, this book is filled with iconic Dreamers that you can learn from as virtual mentors. For the full list of our featured Dreamers featured in the book, please visit wwww.bigstretchbook.com. Download The Big Stretch_Featured Dreamers List.

Mentoring Magic

Growing up in a small town in Michigan, Earvin "Magic" Johnson had a narrow view of the world and the possibilities available to him. He worked hard to develop his basketball skills, but knowing he wanted to get into the business, he was not exposed to successful minority business owners. Then he heard about Greg and Joe Ferguson, young black men from his own hometown who were creating thriving businesses. His instincts told him that getting to know these two men would be good for his future. "I asked if they'd mentor me because I didn't just want to be a good basketball player; I wanted to be a businessman as well. And they decided to do that." Magic soon began to see the merits of having mentors in his life, so he decided to build a network. He told the Dream Project, "I reached out to dozens of people and asked them to have lunch with me. Then I took a little bit from what they all said and incorporated it into my own strategy and started my business. I'm not too bashful, so I simply reached out—every chance I got."

He learned the value of cultivating mentors today but also learned that some connections develop a bit down the road. "You need to build your relationships. So many times, I met people along my journey in life, and I took their cards, and four or five years later I'm doing business with them. It's very important that you build relationships because someone you met a long time ago may now be a key executive at a Fortune 500 company. Now you can pick up the phone and say, 'Hey, you remember me? I have a business. Maybe we can do business together.'"

Make-It-Happen Dreamer Elisa Camahort Page, cofounder of BlogHer and former CCO of SheKnows Media, reminds us that mentors don't need to be all things to their mentees. Rather than trying to mentor others with a broad brush, she advocates what she calls "thin-sliced mentoring," which she says involves "looking for people to mentor you on the specific thing that they are absolutely a superhero at."

Elisa explains that dividing the mentorship experience into slices lets experts share what they really know and frees them from the time constraints of having to advise others in what might be somewhat unfamiliar categories. She recalls, "When I first got into tech back in the nineties, I had one technical mentor. He taught me about digital technology—he was a doctor from California, and he took the time. But I had a different mentor for business relationships and communications. He would let me listen in on phone calls and take me into meetings just so I could watch and learn. I don't think either one of them could have mentored me on the other aspect. But being mentored in both aspects of my job really helped my career moving forward from there."

Rent the Runway's Jennifer Fleiss adds that someone we want business advice from is probably a busy person, so it's a good idea to be clear and quick. "They've got businesses they're running, they've got stuff they're doing, and I think they're actually appreciative when you ask directly what you need help with instead of having more of an amorphous conversation."

Motivational speaker, connections coach, and Make-It-Happen Dreamer Jonathon Sprinkles offers the simple advice that when choosing mentors you should study under people who are doing what you want to do. He asked a Dream Project audience, "If you're not where you want to be, why aren't you being trained by somebody who is? If you want to be an author, why aren't you listening to an author? Why aren't you studying under an author? If you want to be a speaker, why aren't you studying under a speaker? If you want to be an expert, why aren't you studying under an expert in that field?" Good questions.

GROWING DREAMS REQUIRE GROWING TEAMS

As the saying goes, "It takes a village to raise a child." It's going to take a village to nurture your Dream. If you're serious about scaling and growing your company, moving into an executive position, or developing a grassroots nonprofit organization, your Dream will require more bodies, more brainpower, more capital, more structure, and more imagination than you alone can bring to the table. It's inevitable that you're going to find fellow Dreamers along the path who share your vision. These fellow Dreamers could become ideal business partners, assistants, financial advisors, creative partners, or simply people who listen and offer perspective. When you share a purpose with fellow Dreamers, you have a wonderful opportunity to develop purpose-inspired teams who can come together to deliver big purpose-inspired Dreams.

During the early days of building EGAMI, I wore not just many hats but nearly all the hats. I created and pitched the ideas, wrote proposals, secured the deals, developed marketing campaigns, and on and on. I was a one-woman show, and I was exhausted. Enter Allison Rhone, one of my first assistants, who became the production lead and accountant and fulfilled any other role that I needed to keep EGAMI running. Allison knew when I was about to get really hyped up during a creative project if she heard me playing "My First Song" by Jay-Z or "Juicy" by Biggie Smalls. When Biggie rapped, "It was all a Dream / I used to read *Word Up!* magazine," I would fire up! These were my anthems. They inspired me to keep it moving during those early days when I was wearing a few too many hats.

My husband, Michael, my boyfriend at the time, was one of my biggest Dream Champions. He was an executive in the music industry, and he would give me great advice on developing new ideas, acquiring new projects, and structuring deals. Known throughout the music industry as "Deal Maker Mike," Michael became my first business partner and my Dream Mate. On our first date, he asked me, "What is your dream? Whatever it is,

I want to help you build it." I don't know about you, but I didn't have many first dates during which someone asked about my Dreams. My husband is more than a soul mate; he's truly my Dream Mate, and when we joined forces, I was extremely grateful. Little by little I added more team members, and in those early days, everyone wore several hats. The more that we infused passion into our work, the more business came in.

And then one day the magic of a Dream called EGAMI stopped.

As your Dream gets bigger and bigger, your Stretch will surely include seasons of frustration and difficulty. When you get to this point in The Stretch, that's a clear sign that you need to redesign your infrastructure and include more people to help you grow. For the original EGAMI crew, our once thriving, magnetic, and fun environment began to lose its magic. As the projects became more complex, I piled more tasks onto each member's plate instead of adding more team members to share the load. I was breeding a culture of short tempers, fatigue, and burnout. As the Chief Dream Architect, you have to be vigilant about ensuring that your current structure can support the vision, growth, and development of your Dream.

As you advance in a corporation or in your own organization, it's not uncommon to spend less time doing the activities you're most passionate about. But you must do what you can to protect your passions, because venturing too far from them can have negative effects on your attitude, your motivation, and your accomplishments. My good friend Lisa Nichols, Make-It-Happen Dreamer, *New York Times* bestselling author, and motivational speaker, was a great mentor to me as I moved through this painful expansion phase with EGAMI. She said, "Teneshia, if you're in a place where you're only *visiting* your passions instead of *living* in the joy of them, it's time for you to scale, make changes, or sunset that season."

At EGAMI, we had several business experts advising us to build a new infrastructure so that we could elevate from a mom-and-pop shop to a thriving industry-standard marketing agency. During this time, I began bringing on more seasoned team members, which I thought would solve the problem of our growing pains. What I didn't expect was that as I brought in new people, the original EGAMI crew would start leaving the nest, one by one. Some left because they were no longer aligned with the expanding infrastructure and more progressive new vision. Others left because as their roles narrowed and they wore fewer hats, they felt they had lost their opportunity to grow within the company. For some who had been with the company since its early days, the sentiment was, "This isn't the EGAMI we know." And they were right. We were growing fast, and shifting from a mom-and-pop–style company to a more process-oriented business, which meant a change in the "family" culture we used to enjoy. There were fewer close-knit events like the team Christmas dinner at my apartment, and we added a dedicated human resource lead who introduced an employee handbook and operating guidelines. There was no question about it; the atmosphere was changing. Losing some of my team was painful, but I knew that if I was going to keep growing in my Stretch, I had to be brave enough to let them go to pursue their own Dreams.

I truly believe that God has a sense of humor. Just as I began writing this section of *The Big Stretch*, I got a call from the only remaining member of the original EGAMI crew telling me that she was leaving the company to take a new position elsewhere. I wish I could tell you that I've mastered the staffing element of business and can easily "let go and let God," but I cried like a baby that day. Although I was happy for her and know that she is going to soar in her career, my heart was heavy. As your Dream grows, you need the right team members to grow with you, and the team that starts with you on your journey may not be the one that carries you to the finish line. That's okay. **It's your job as Chief Dream Architect to draft your plans in pencil and use your eraser as often as you need.**

BUILDING DIVERSE TEAMS

It's important to build teams that include people who bring different perspectives to the table. All-Star Dreamer Daymond John reminds us that we should look for team members with different skill sets. He says, "When we get into businesses, we're experts at one or two things. If you think you can be an expert at warehousing, an expert manufacturer, an expert distributor, an expert advertiser, and an expert designer, you're wrong. You have to surround yourself with people and assets that can deploy these things. You can't do it alone, so be careful to build the best team you can."

Jennifer Fleiss also understands the importance of complementary relationships. In her Rent the Runway cofounder, she's found an excellent counterpart to create balance at the company's executive level. "My cofounder is very much a big, strategic thinker," she says. "She's a great salesperson who can rally teams around those ideas, and I'm the doer. I'm, 'How do we get from point A to point B?' If you have a partner, you need to look at your backgrounds and see if you have complementary skill sets. You need to make sure your personalities fit and work together."

CREATING YOUR DREAM CULTURE

The culture of your company is similar to the dynamic of a family. Think about all the inside jokes, recipes, and traditions that have been handed down through generations in your family. Likewise, the culture you create with your team now is what people will experience long after you're gone. Years ago, I was in discussions with executives at Disney, and I was also a speaker at the annual Disney Dreamer's Academy. As my meetings continued, I sensed the culture of Disney all around me—from e-mails that ended with "Have a Magical Day!" to infectious friendliness from everyone I met. I felt traces of Walt Disney's imagination everywhere, and I soon realized that the team members, wishing me a magical day wasn't a fluke—it's the energy of the Disney culture.

Chick-fil-A is known for its friendly customer service. Its team members have been trained to greet customers within three to five seconds of their arrival. The Red Door Spa has been dedicated to creating luxurious spa experiences for its customers for over 90 years. When you see Elizabeth Arden's signature red doors, you know that you're in for a day of luxury and pampering. These examples show that a company's culture can have an enormous impact on the customer's experience and therefore on public perception of the company's brand.

My business coach Dan Coleman taught me that cultures are built from core values. I believe that you must be intentional about pulling those core values through every facet of your business, including external messaging, branding, customer interactions, hiring, and even firing team members. We'll explore core values in your upcoming exercises, so start thinking about your answers to these questions:

- What core values represent you as a leader?
- What values would you like reinforced with this Dream?
- Are you ready to live these core values in all your business practices: hiring, rewarding, partnerships, firing, etc.?

We've covered a lot in this chapter! Now it's time for you to start putting this into action. Let's start building your Dream teams.

EXERCISE 6.1

HIGH-TOUCH DREAMING—THE ART OF NETWORKING

This week, I challenge you to get out from behind your desk and engage in intentional, in-person networking. High-Touch Dreaming doesn't have to be a two-hour dinner. You could have a series of short coffee dates with potential clients. You could attend a networking meeting where you can meet a variety of people across different occupations. You could find a local meetup or join an industry networking group with like-minded Dreamers. You could drop in on your local Chamber of Commerce. Remember to make your interaction about the other person. As you learned at the beginning of this chapter, givers gain, and people are more likely to do business with people they know, like, and trust.

This week is about getting you out there and comfortable connecting with new people. I want you to use the following High-Touch Dreaming Scorecard to track your in-person connections with three to five people this week. Eventually, I want you to expand this number to 10 new network contacts per month. In each square, fill out the person's name, the person's business or Dream, what kinds of opportunities he or she is looking for, and when you're going to follow up.

You can download a larger version of the blank chart from www.TheBigStretchBook.com.

Sample High-Touch Dreaming Scorecard

Name: Diane Business/Dream: Owns local dry cleaners New Opportunity: Looking for new location Follow-Up: Next Monday with real estate referral	Name: Marvin Business/Dream: College senior New Opportunity: Looking for internships in finance industry Follow-Up: E-mail recommendations by end of the week

Your High-Touch Dreaming Scorecard

Name: Business/Dream: New Opportunity: Follow-Up:	Name: Business/Dream: New Opportunity: Follow-Up

EXERCISE 6.2

FINDING YOUR MENTORS

Take time to identify the kind of mentor you'll need as you grow your project. Do you want a mentor who's good with organizational structure? Do you need one with a strong spiritual focus? Do you want a mentor who can offer you emotional support and advice? Fill in the lists below to explore the kinds of mentors you're looking for and how you might connect with them.

Top Five Qualities for My Ideal Mentor

1. ____________________
2. ____________________
3. ____________________
4. ____________________
5. ____________________

Why these qualities matter and how they might affect my Dream:

____

____

____

Top Five Leaders in My Field

1. ____________________
2. ____________________
3. ____________________
4. ____________________
5. ____________________

How I think these leaders got there and what value will come from our relationship if each becomes my mentor:

____

____

____

Five Possible Ways to Connect with Them (Coffee Date, Conference Call, Etc.)

1. ______________________________
2. ______________________________
3. ______________________________
4. ______________________________
5. ______________________________

How I'll initiate these connections, including what I'll say or write:

____

____

____

Mentors can be invaluable to you in all areas of your life. Name five people who are potential mentors for each of the nonprofessional aspects of your life and add a sentence explaining why.

You can download a larger version of the following chart from www.TheBigStretchBook.com.

Identify Your Mentor Network

Area of Life or Business
Industry Specific
1. Name:
Title:
In Network Y/N:
Ways to Reach:
2. Name:
Title:
In Network Y/N:
Ways to Reach:

3.	Name:
	Title:
	In Network Y/N:
	Ways to Reach:
4.	Name:
	Title:
	In Network Y/N:
	Ways to Reach:
5.	Name:
	Title:
	In Network Y/N:
	Ways to Reach:
General Business	
1.	Name:
	Title:
	In Network Y/N:
	Ways to Reach:
2.	Name:
	Title:
	In Network Y/N:
	Ways to Reach:
3.	Name:
	Title:
	In Network Y/N:
	Ways to Reach:
4.	Name:
	Title:
	In Network Y/N:
	Ways to Reach:
5.	Name:
	Title:
	In Network Y/N:
	Ways to Reach:

Spiritual
1. Name:
Title:
In Network Y/N:
Ways to Reach:
2. Name:
Title:
In Network Y/N:
Ways to Reach:
3. Name:
Title:
In Network Y/N:
Ways to Reach:
4. Name:
Title:
In Network Y/N:
Ways to Reach:
5. Name:
Title:
In Network Y/N:
Ways to Reach:
Physical
1. Name:
Title:
In Network Y/N:
Ways to Reach:
2. Name:
Title:
In Network Y/N:
Ways to Reach:
3. Name:
Title:
In Network Y/N:
Ways to Reach:

4.	Name:
	Title:
	In Network Y/N:
	Ways to Reach:
5.	Name:
	Title:
	In Network Y/N:
	Ways to Reach:
Lifestyle	
1.	Name:
	Title:
	In Network Y/N:
	Ways to Reach:
2.	Name:
	Title:
	In Network Y/N:
	Ways to Reach:
3.	Name:
	Title:
	In Network Y/N:
	Ways to Reach:
4.	Name:
	Title:
	In Network Y/N:
	Ways to Reach:
5.	Name:
	Title:
	In Network Y/N:
	Ways to Reach:

EXERCISE 6.3

SIX DEGREES TOWARD YOUR DREAM

We've all heard of "six degrees of separation." What if I told you that you're probably no more than six degrees away from someone who's ideal to make your Dreams come true? It's quite possible that your existing network already includes power players who will be willing to introduce you to someone who will change your life. Remember what we talked about earlier: having a servant's mindset will take you far.

Might you find a helpful connection in your house of worship? Your pastor might know the local college president—how great that will be if you're looking for recent college graduates to fill your team. A fellow congregant could have a connection with a local bank office where you might be able to secure a line of business credit. You never know who's right there, ready and willing to be helpful.

Referencing Figure 6.1, let's start your mapping. Remember, you also have the option to download a larger version of the chart at www.TheBigStretchBook.com. Write your name in the center of the chart. Then ask yourself, *whom do I know who can help me with this goal?* Write those names in adjacent spheres, and then reach out to each of those contacts to tell them about your idea. During these meetings, ask these contacts for names of people within *their* networks who might be able to support you in this venture. Add those names to your chart, then reach out to those people, and so on. You might be amazed at how a mapping exercise like this can lead you to a business mogul or other connection who will make big things happen for you. Remember, one of my most critical network chains went something like this: a doorman → Snoop Dogg → Snoop Dogg's tour manager → one of the biggest business moguls in entertainment. All along, I was only four degrees of separation away from an ultimate Dream connection that changed my life.

You can download a larger version of the following chart from www.TheBigStretchBook.com.

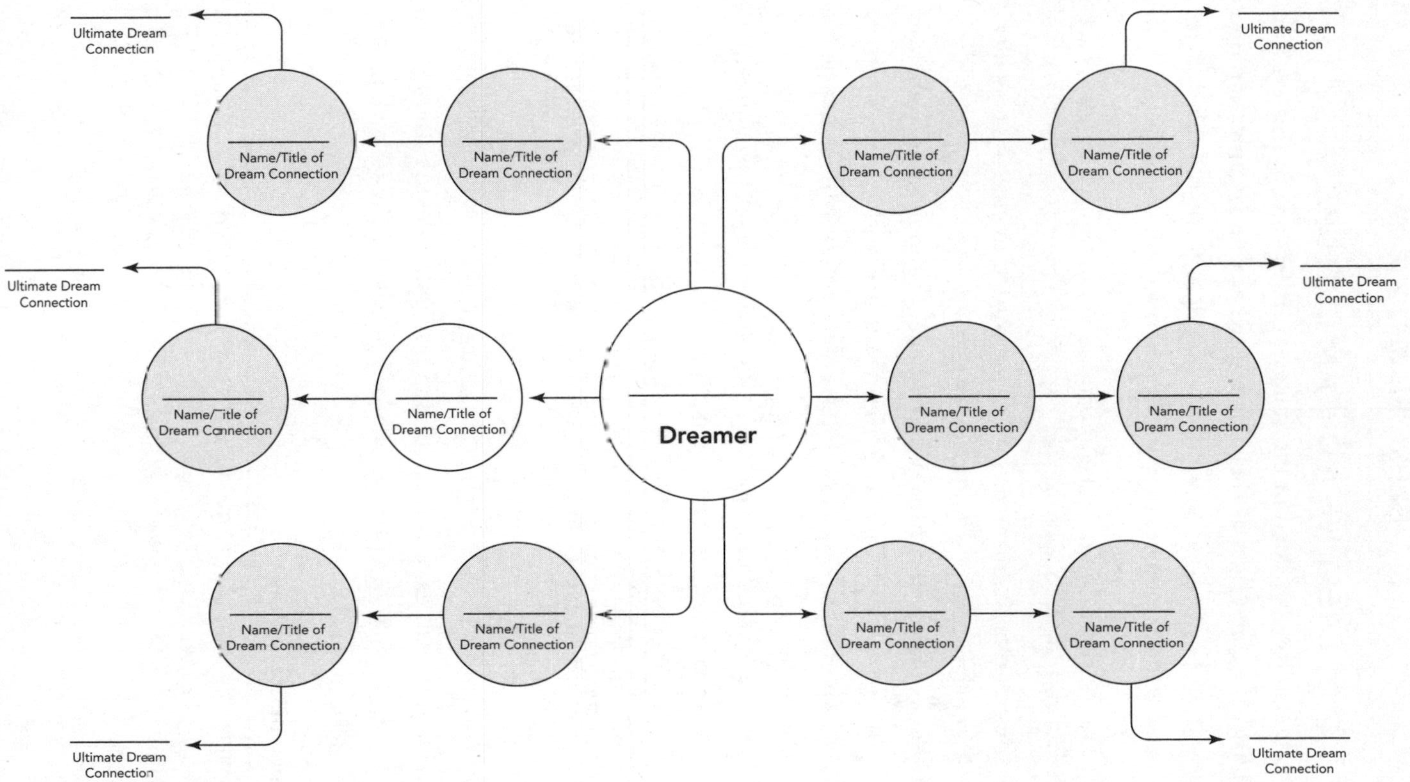

Figure 6.1 Ultimate Dream Connection

EXERCISE 6.4

CREATING A DREAM CULTURE

A Dream's culture is rooted in the values of its leaders. In this exercise, you'll list your core values as they relate to what your organization does and how it runs. A few years ago, my executive leadership did this exercise, and these are the core values that we felt described our culture:

- **Do the right thing.** As a company we're committed to always acting with the highest integrity.
- **Be creative.** As marketers we're committed to creating new ideas, campaigns, and possibilities every day.
- **Focus on relationships.** We treat clients and partners well, from paying people on time to delivering quality work. Small clients are as important as large ones, and we always start with "What can we do for you?"
- **Have a "get it done" spirit.** We are agile and scrappy and will do whatever it takes to get the job done.
- **Be humble but confident.** Work hard and stay humble, and the company will grow.
- **Commit to excellence.** No cutting corners. Underpromise and overdeliver.

What type of Dream culture do you want to create? Start by listing core values that will serve as your guiding principles. Write a list of five to eight principles that describe you and/or your vision. The following sample word list may help.

Examples of Core Values

Innovation	Fearless	Curiosity
Driving the Future	Relentless	Excellence
Creativity	Purpose Oriented	Improvement in Self
High Energy	Competitive	Unbiased
Imagination	Respectful	Dedicated

EXERCISE 6.5

BUILDING A DREAM TEAM

While you keep in mind the goal that you're currently working toward, I want you to describe the type of team you'll need to bring this venture to life. If you're a CEO or Make-It-Happen Dreamer, you'll need to think of the core functions that all businesses must address, such as marketing, operations, sales, finance, and product/service. If you're a Careerpreneur Dreamer planning to leap to another job, perhaps your team will consist of a marketing/social media expert to help you manage your online presence and assist with building your brand, a recruiter to help with staffing, and an accountant/financial advisor. Use the graph in Figure 6.2 to describe key functions that you'll need on your team. If you're in the early stages of developing your idea, you might be filling lots of the roles yourself (remember when Lisa Price told us how she wore all the hats?). However, once you outline the roles below, perhaps you can identify the top two to three functions you can have covered by gradually bringing in team members, partners, volunteers, or interns.

You can download a larger version of the following chart at www.TheBigStretchBook.com.

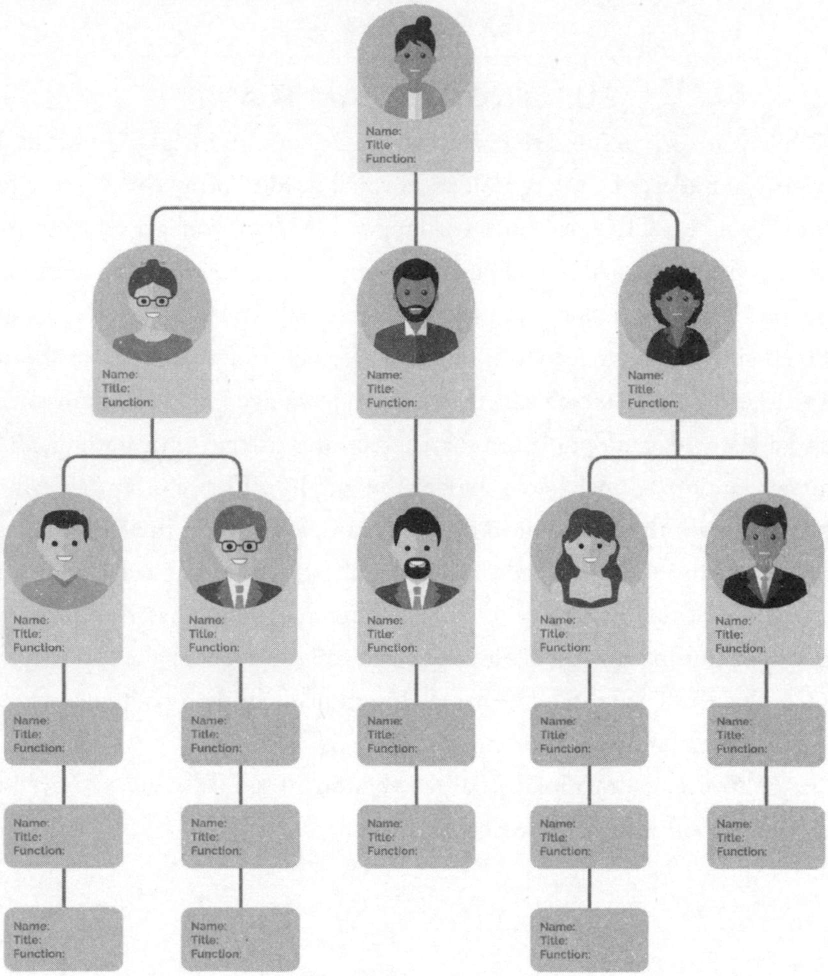

Figure 6.2 Dream Team Functions

YOUR 90-DAY STRETCH PLAN GOAL CRUSH REMINDER

It's time once again to check in with your 90-Day Stretch Plan. Have you crossed this week's actions off your list? If not, get 'em done!

Congratulations, you've completed the Design phase of The Stretch! You've explored your Dream's purpose, examined whom your Dream is serving, and assessed when and how it will be of service. You've thought about what makes your idea unique and what kinds of impact your idea will have on the lives of others. Finally, you've made sure you have a team of supporters and partners to join you along the way. Excellent! Before we move on to Part III, "Dare," let me introduce this week's Dream All-Star, a mentor and powHERful boss! She was on the founding team of BlogHer, one of the world's largest platforms for female online content creators. She's now chief strategy officer at Ellevest, an online investment platform for women.

> "BlogHer raised 20.25 million dollars in venture capital between 2007 and 2014. I am so proud of the BlogHer team because I believe we were regularly experiencing bias in our valuation by VCs, and it was so much harder than it should've been given our performance. I'm very proud of the fact that we paid all our bills and were able to exit the company the way we did. The undertold story of women in venture is that we're crushing it."
>
> —CEO Dreamer **Lisa Stone**

You may download this week's Dream All-Star training session at www.thebigstretchbook.com.

PART III

DARE

Embracing Risk and Moving Beyond Fear

You're now at the halfway mark for The Stretch—approximately 45 days along! You created a bold, colorful, vibrant Dream. You became the Chief Design Architect for this business, and you designed the purpose, opportunities, network, and team to propel your Dream to the next level. Now that you have your Dream in place and you've created a strong foundation to support its full expression, it's time to Dare.

After talking with hundreds of Dreamers, I've learned that there comes a point in The Stretch when your best-laid plans are tossed to the side, you get up from behind your desk, and you make daring moves—ready or not. As you work through the next three chapters, you'll learn how to move past thinking, wondering, and planning so you can *Dare*. Eventually you just have to take a deep breath and jump, as CEO Dreamer Vince Hunter did when he left his career in sales to start Hybrid Fitness, a training gym in Columbus, Georgia. He told a Dream Project audience that it's not likely you'll ever feel 100 percent sure that your idea is going to work. "You will never be fully assured that the journey is going to be safe," he advises. "At some point, you just have to make the decision. If you are passionate about doing, it then step out on faith and make it happen."

Activist Dreamer Christine Caine warns against waiting and waiting for the moment when all feels safe. She told the Dream Project that sometimes you just have to jump. "You're going to find 20 reasons why not, and you're going to find a different 20 reasons next week and another 20 reasons the week after," she says. "At some point you're going to have to decide that the planets haven't aligned and that they're not going to. You're never going to know until you take the risk and make that jump."

In this section, I'm going to coach the part of you that's daring, courageous, adventurous, and maybe just a little bit crazy. I challenge you in these next three weeks to explore how creative and strong you are.

After completing the Dare phase of The Stretch, you'll be empowered and challenged to go after your Dream. The following exercises will help:

Week 7: Dare Now

EXERCISE 7.1: 100 Nos and Counting
EXERCISE 7.2: The Big Ask
EXERCISE 7.3: Making Your Dream Pitch Perfect
EXERCISE 7.4: The Uncomfortable Challenge

Week 8: Going in Through the Roof

EXERCISE 8.1: The Dream Extreme Challenge
EXERCISE 8.2: First, Break All the Rules
EXERCISE 8.3: Finding the Gap
EXERCISE 8.4: Learning from Failure

Week 9: When It's Time to Level Up

EXERCISE 9.1: Checkup and Refresh

EXERCISE 9.2: Leveling Up into the Future

EXERCISE 9.3: Taking Your Dream to the Next Level

Dreamer, this is *your* moment. Now is the time to make bold, courageous moves toward fulfilling your Dream. In the next three weeks, really dig in and say, "I'm going to do this!"

Let's start the Dare phase of The Stretch!

CHAPTER SEVEN

DARE NOW

Week 7

Starting the Dare phase makes me think of one of my favorite songs, Eminem's "Lose Yourself" (the official video is on YouTube if you're not familiar with it). Eminem sings unforgettably about having a one-shot moment in which you're given the opportunity to "seize everything you ever wanted."

In this chapter I want to make sure that when "one-shot" moments are in front of you, you'll make the bold moves to seize them. You're not going to wait another day to make your business plan "perfect." You're not going to simply think about asking for the next promotion without taking action. You're not going to keep wondering if the idea for your nonprofit is good enough. This week, you're going to get out of your own way and Dare to do it. I'm going to show you how I made bold, unconventional moves to activate my Dreams. (Sometimes I blew even my own mind.) Then you're going to work through the following exercises to bring your Dream to life:

Week 7: Dare Now

EXERCISE 7.1: 100 Nos and Counting
EXERCISE 7.2: The Big Ask
EXERCISE 7.3: Making Your Dream Pitch Perfect
EXERCISE 7.4: The Uncomfortable Challenge

In this chapter, I'll share with you examples of when The Stretch required me to activate my Dare muscles. This started with one of my biggest Dares ever: standing in front of a conference crowd holding a microphone and telling the business mogul and founder of RUSH Communications and Def Jam what I wanted.

The founder and CEO was the keynote speaker for a business conference in Miami. At the time, he was widely known throughout the entertainment community as the godfather of hip-hop. By the time of this conference, I had already tried several times to get a yes to my offer to work for RUSH Communications for no fee in exchange for the chance to learn. I faxed the CEO 30 days in a row to no avail and even flew to New York where I showed up at his offices and actually ran into him as he was entering the building. He was kind enough to pass me off to one of his executives, telling the guy to "find out if she's crazy or if she has talent." That led to some polite, "keep in touch" kinds of communications, and I was close to giving up. But I decided that I'd take one last shot by flying down to Miami to make my offer one more time in person. During the post-keynote Q&A, I stepped up to the microphone and hoped that no one could see my shaking hands. The conference moderator said, "Please go forward with your question." I thought, *Okay. Ready or not, here I go!* I knew that this was my *one* shot, and I was going to seize it. I took a big breath and said, "I'd like to tell you a story of a girl with a Dream. I want you to tell me if you think she's crazy or if you believe this girl deserves a shot."

He said, "Please tell me about that young lady."

I continued, "She chose a career based on earning potential and was on a fast track in corporate America. Then she realized that wasn't enough. So she started a purpose-driven journey to explore her passions. That journey led her to find that she had a love for entertainment and pop culture. She had a chance meeting with a leader in the entertainment industry, and she offered to work for free in exchange for an opportunity to learn."

At this point, the CEO leaned forward, squinted his eyes, and said, "Oh shit! It's *that* girl again!"

I was still shaking, but I knew that now was the time to take my shot. I said, "Yes, me! I'm *that* girl! I've come all the way to Miami to make you the offer again. I'm willing to work for you for no fee in exchange for an opportunity to learn from you. You're doing deals with corporate brands every day, and I imagine you could benefit from having a team member with a corporate background, so one last time I'm offering you these skills in exchange for an opportunity to learn. What do you have to lose? It's no cost to you, and that's a win-win for both of us, if you ask me."

At this point people in the audience started rustling in their seats and murmuring to each other as they looked back and forth between him and me. I was creating a fresh blast of pure entertainment for this audience of business conference attendees, but I also sensed that their anticipation began to match mine.

The CEO was quiet for several seconds, and then he said, "Over the years I've given a lot of people chances. Sometimes they run with it, but more often they do nothing with it. Show up at my office on Monday morning. I can't wait to see which one you're going to be." The crowd erupted in cheers and applause. In the distance a few people shouted things like, "You go, girl!" I couldn't believe it. I'd done it! I flashed a huge smile and said, "You aren't going to regret this." I felt everyone's eyes on me, and I continued to shake as I set down the microphone. Overwhelmed and stunned at the same time, I felt like bursting open. You would have thought I'd scored a winning lottery ticket rather than a job that didn't pay. But I left that conference feeling immensely grateful. I had Dared greatly and was on my way to the training ground of my Dreams.

My story isn't unusual. These kinds of bold moves are part of every daring Dreamer's story. Bold Dreamers see a shot and they take it! They go all in and play full out.

There were many smaller daring moves that led to my big Dare at the mic, and by the time I got to that conference, I had Dared so much that I felt like there was nothing to lose; I had gone too far to turn back. As my cousin Chester said before my trip to this conference, "Neshia, how many bullets have you seen go back in a barrel once the shot is fired? None. You're out there now. You might as well keep going."

You see, becoming a daring Dreamer doesn't happen without practice. It's like working a muscle. Learning how to Dare—and how to Dare often—will give you the repetitions, the endurance, and the elasticity to continue in your Stretch. Just as a rubber band can't stretch without elasticity, you, my dear Dreamer, won't be able to fully Stretch without taking risks, daring to be bold, and showing courage to detour from your status quo. This week you'll work through exercises aimed at strengthening your Dare muscles.

TRUST YOUR INSTINCTS AND GO FOR THE BIG ASK

On my first day at RUSH Communications, I was the first to arrive in the office. I had no defined role, and I wouldn't be earning a dime, but I had a clean canvas to create an opportunity of a lifetime. As I walked through the company doors, I remembered some of my mother's wisdom: "Be quiet, listen more than you speak, and find ways to be of service."

I began as an intern for the vice president of operations, and for the first few weeks, I spent most of my time sitting quietly in his office, doing little more than listening. At that time, the office was booming with the Baby Phat fashion line, television and movie deals with producer Stan Lathan, and Def Jam artists coming in and out grabbing clothing for photo shoots. I was in heaven just listening and learning.

The vice president's office was a real mess, so before one of his business trips, I told him I was really good at organizing and offered to clean and organize his office. He said, "Are you sure? I don't know if you can do anything with this place." I assured him that his office would be in top shape when he returned.

I put my heart and soul into that project. I organized his contracts by clients, color-coded his folders, created a messaging system for his calls, and uploaded his documents to the company's server. After a few weeks, his office was a work of art, and when he returned from his trip, he nearly fell over in disbelief. Nothing spreads the word of your great service faster than a happy client; he started telling everyone in the office about what I'd done for him. Soon people wanted me to organize their offices, and before I knew it, I had organized most of the offices within Baby Phat, the Hip-Hop Summit Action Network, and RUSH's internal agency. After a few weeks, almost every senior-level person was happily experiencing the results of my good old cleaning and organizing skills.

After I'd finished organizing all those offices, I went back to quietly praying that another opportunity would present itself soon. Then one day I heard one of the company leaders throwing an angry fit. He was unleashing on a vice president about a troubled contract involving Verizon Wireless and the National Urban League. RUSH was supposed to be launching a program aimed at increasing literacy rates among students of color throughout the city. The goal of the program was to make reading cool for kids. As the executive continued to rant, I had that feeling again. This was my chance for a bold, daring Big Ask.

I said, "You should give me the project."

He looked surprised, responding, "I didn't know you were still working here. Why should I give you this project?"

I knew about the deal because I had learned about every contract in the company as I cleaned the offices of the senior leadership team. I told him that I was the only person in his office with corporate skills who knew the deal backward and forward, and I rattled off his project deliverables, the deadline, and the success and measurement standards for Verizon. He looked at me and then out the window for a moment. Then he said to the vice president in charge of the project, "Give her the project." My Big Ask had paid off!

The program, called The Hip-Hop Reader, launched with a star-studded event and impressive media coverage. The Hip-Hop Reader was a rewards program for New York City kids; for every book they read, they could earn points to buy things donated by record companies and cool clothing companies. After the successful launch and implementation of

The Hip-Hop Reader, the CEO called me into his office. He said, "You did a phenomenal job with The Hip-Hop Reader. I want to hire you."

I answered, "You should hire my company instead."

He replied, "I didn't know you had a company. I just know that we want to hire you. Listen, I'm going to Europe for two weeks, and when I get back, we'll do the deal."

What the CEO didn't know was that at the time there was no company! I now had two weeks to figure out how to set up a company and get ready to do my first contract. Even before EGAMI Group was started, we had a client, RUSH Communications. This was now twice that a Big Ask had changed my life.

HOW FAR ARE YOU WILLING TO GO?

Once you've decided that you're willing to make changes to your life and take risks to make this idea reality, you need to ask yourself just how far you're willing to go. At times, this pursuit of yours will ask more of you than you initially expected. Sometimes much more. Doreen Rainey, CEO Dreamer, SVP of Steve Harvey Global, and founder of Radical Success Institute, reminded a Dream Project audience that at the core of success are raw guts and a willingness to go all in. She challenged her fellow Dreamers, "Ask yourself what you're willing to put on the line. So many times, people want other people to put skin in the game, but they haven't put any of their own skin in the game. Does that mean you have to sell your house, that you have to move, that you have to quit a job that has all the benefits? What exactly are you willing to do to make it happen?" She advises that being willing to truly invest to your greatest ability will inspire other people and convince them of your commitment. Let's face it: if you're not willing to give this your all, why should anyone else believe that your Dream is going to take off? "When others see your commitment, they see your hustle," she says. "When they see the risk that you're taking, they'll come on board."

You'll recall reading in Chapter One about Yvonne Orji, the Nigerian actress/comedian who defied her parents' wishes by leaving behind a career in public health to try her hand at acting and stand-up comedy. To follow her path, she endured the emotional pain of disobeying her traditional parents and then weathered the hardships of trying to make it in Hollywood without first having a soft place to land. There were a lot of hungry days and fearful nights, and after a number of projects failed to move forward, she suffered from what she calls "a minor depression." But then the clouds began to clear. She landed the role on HBO's *Insecure* and went on to develop her original show, *First Gen*, as a half-hour sitcom with Oprah Winfrey and David Oyelowo signed on as executive producers! Yvonne Orji serves as a powerful example of the greatness that can happen when you Dare to reach high and keep fighting for what you want, no matter the obstacles.

I'm challenging you to pitch more and make bigger asks. Will great things happen for you if you *don't* make any Big Asks or daring moves this week? More than likely, your Dream will spend yet another week on the shelf. So consider which Big Asks and daring moves are just waiting for you to take action.

GETTING OUT OF YOUR COMFORT ZONE

Daring requires that you "put yourself out there" into new environments. And trust me when I tell you that it gets easier. Talking to someone "important" within your company might feel terrifying, but if you have something of value to say, say it. Think of it this way: if you have an idea that might be of use to that executive, withholding it is almost like stealing—it's letting your discomfort be the element that stands between your colleague and a potential success. The more often you do something daring, the more comfortable you'll be in those uncomfortable situations.

THE PRACTICE OF THE PITCH

If you want an activity to become easier, keep practicing it. The more you practice, the more familiar the exercise will become, and the better you'll get at the skill. One skill that you'll need to perfect is the art of the pitch, during which you'll have to be able to speak clearly and quickly about your vision and make some Big Asks. Being willing to pitch is a big part of learning to Dare. A pitch is a verbal representation of your business idea, and in most pitch settings you'll have a limited amount of time to make your case. Whether you're trying to get interest and action from potential investors, industry experts, or celebrities who might be willing to promote your product, your pitch has to be lean, clear, personal, and compelling.

Jennifer Fleiss says that it's important to remember that when you're pitching, you're selling, so entrepreneurs should never underestimate the importance of sharpening their sales skills. She advises, "If you want to be an entrepreneur, and you're not yet ready to go after your concept, do something in sales, because whether you're pitching a venture capitalist, pitching a cofounder, pitching someone to join your team, or pitching a landlord to give you space for cheap, it's really important to have that sales skill."

Tips from a Pitch Master

Before you begin this week's exercises, I want to offer you some tips on how to effectively pitch a concept, courtesy of Dream Project speaker Candace Mitchell, the Make-It-Happen Dreamer and cofounder of Techturized, who, along with her three business partners, won the Dream Project Small Business Pitch Competition and went on to be "pitch perfect" in competitions around the country. Their company uses technology to create personalized hair care regimens for women, and thanks to their powerful pitch, they raised over $500,000 to launch their Dream. Here is some of Candace's best advice on how to nail the pitch and hit one out of the park.

- **Pitching to investors.** "In a pitch to potential investors, you typically have one to five minutes to articulate your business and your vision, followed by a question and answer session. The judges will ask questions about a variety of topics: your team, your market, your financials—anything that can help them understand, "Is this a potential successful business that we should get behind?" You must effectively articulate your business model and your value composition.

- **Understand your business model.** "Show that you're serious about what you're doing and that you have the knowledge to build a great business model. Is your idea scalable? How will you make money, and what are the channels that you'll use to reach your customers to continually make money over time? Will your business grow with that model? Those are the questions you need to be able to answer. You should also know who your competition is and how this business pitch can help take your company to the next level."
- **Demonstrate that you're the expert.** "Do your research. Know everything there is to know about your industry. You never want the people you're talking to, to know more about your market and your industry than you do. It's really important that you're a subject-matter expert."
- **Tell a good story.** "Start strong and immediately grab the listener's attention. Are you entertaining? Are you including how you personally connect to your company? Also the problem and the pain that you're solving. What will people pay you money for? What pain are they experiencing that they will pay you to take away? Part of a good story is your solution. What service are you offering? What is the solution? Then you want to talk about how you're going to acquire your customers. You can have this awesome idea. You can say you're going make X millions and billions of dollars, but if you can't articulate how you're even going to get the customers, then it doesn't matter what you're saying."
- **Make the Big Ask.** "Your pitch should include your ask. What are you asking for? Are you asking for money? What do you need that money for? Is it going to help you improve your technology? Are you going to hire people with it? Is it going to help you acquire customers?"
- **Be high energy and entertaining.** "You should be confident. You should be excited. The potential investor wants to be as passion-

> ate as you are. Engage with whom you're speaking to and showcase your personality, because at the end of the day people invest in people. They might think you have a B+ idea, but you might be an A+ person, which leads to, 'I'm betting my money that this woman right here is going to pull it off, no matter what it takes.' And also going back to your story—if it's a funny story, make people laugh. If it's a painful story that made you say, 'Wow. This is what brought me to the edge, and I knew I had to start my company,' make them cry. Make people excited. That's what people want to feel as they're hearing your pitch."

Are you ready to Dare now? Let's begin this week's exercises.

EXERCISE 7.1

100 NOS AND COUNTING

As you try bolder and more daring moves, you'll hear more nos than yeses. Are you going to let that stop you? Are you going to let that be the reason you don't ask you ideal partner to join your team? Are you going to let one no stop you from going after a promotion? During this week of Dare *now*, you will learn how to develop a thick skin. You will learn how to pivot around those nos. You will learn to summon the courage to keep going until you hear the yes that will change everything.

As a budding CEO Dreamer, you might feel demoralized to hear a no for your first brilliant business idea. As an Activist Dreamer, you might feel defeated if you plan a community event for 100 people and only 20 people attend. This week's first exercise is designed to help you pivot around any no you encounter during your Stretch and keep pushing forward.

Step 1: Find four Dream Champions. A Dream Champion can be a fellow Dreamer, team member, or mentor.

Step 2: Tell your Dream Champions individually about your idea and your fears about why you think your idea won't work. Lay out the worst scenarios you can imagine. Describe small-scale embarrassments and large-scale disasters. Your Dream Champions will use these fears as objections and reasons for why things won't work out.

Step 3: Stand face-to-face with your Dream Champions and tell them about an opportunity you have for your Dream. Say, for example, that you're a Careerpreneur, and you have a chance to make a career shift to a new job in a new city. For every thought you offer that will help make your Dream work out, your Champion should fire back objections based on your fears. Your Champions can also add their own doubts and roadblocks. Tell each of your Dream Champions to be as tough as possible, even responding with replies like, "What if you find you're in over your head in the new position?" or "You hate meeting new people; how are you going to survive in a new city—at your age?" You can also tell the person to repeat your greatest excuses and fears to you so that you can really hear them. If there's someone in particular you're avoiding out of fear, have one of your Dream Champions take on the characteristics of that person.

Step 4: For every objection, pivot to create more possibilities in the conversation. In the example above, the Careerpreneur could shoot back replies like, "I'm going to take all my skills with me and apply them in this new environment," "What I don't know how to do, I'll learn," and "I'm going to network and challenge myself to meet new people each week." Maybe you have an idea for creating a new beauty product. Among your fears could be that there are too many products like it on the market and that you won't get the funding you need. Your Dream Champion might tell you that the beauty market is saturated and that your idea won't sell. A possible pivot for you is to share what makes your product different along with a proof point about why you think the product will thrive in a crowded market. You can also share the many ways you'll go after resources.

During the exercise, ask each of your Dream Champions to use the following scorecard to evaluate how many nos you pivot through before you quit. Also ask your Dream Champions to give you feedback on your body language, voice projection, quality of information, and delivery.

If you do this exercise correctly, by the end of a week you'll have heard 100 nos and will have had 100 opportunities to declare why your Dream is possible beyond the no. If your Dream Champion did a good job of imitating a tough person you'll have to face to discuss your idea, by the time you have the real conversation, you'll be prepared for any objections the person might throw your way. After reading the sample below, ask your Dream Champion to fill in the ratio of effective responses or pivots you offered after hearing a no or a reason your idea will fail and feedback about your presentation or communication style.

You can download a larger version of the scorecard from www.TheBigStretchBook.com.

Sample 100 Nos Scorecard

DREAM CHAMPION 1 MARCUS	DREAM CHAMPION 2 CHARLENE	DREAM CHAMPION 3 GERRY	DREAM CHAMPION 4 ANEKA
Date: March 8	Date: March 10	Date: March 10	Date: March 12
Number of Effective Pivots Following a No / Number of Nos 18 Pivots / 25 Nos	Pivots / Nos 17 Pivots / 25 Nos	Pivots / Nos 25 Pivots / 25 Nos	Pivots/ Nos 25 Pivots / 25 Nos
Feedback Work on direct eye contact Work on responses to questions with multiple answers	**Feedback** Tighten up answers to questions about company organization chart	**Feedback** Great pivots on financial questions Less fidgeting when you speak	**Feedback** Great eye contact Sharpen questions about company growth

Your 100 Nos Scorecard

DREAM CHAMPION 1	DREAM CHAMPION 2	DREAM CHAMPION 3	DREAM CHAMPION 4
Date:	Date:	Date:	Date:
Pivots / Nos	Pivots / Nos	Pivots / Nos	Pivots / Nos
Feedback	**Feedback**	**Feedback**	**Feedback**

EXERCISE 7.2

THE BIG ASK

Now that you know how to trust your instincts and Dare to ask for what you want, what Big Ask will you go for this week? **See the following examples and then plan your Big Asks for this week. Note and track these in the space below and/or in your Dream Notebook.**

Example Big Ask 1

DREAM: Promotion to Project Manager, Human Resources

BY WHEN: End of fourth quarter

BIG ASK: Lunch with department SVP to discuss current accomplishments and steps to achieve next promotion

RESULT: Meeting scheduled to begin negotiations for next promotion

Example Big Ask 2

DREAM: Get a corporate sponsor for Winter Supplies for the Homeless campaign

BY WHEN: October 30 for December 1 implementation

BIG ASK: Conference call with local car dealership to request $5,000

RESULT: Meeting scheduled to discuss making larger incremental donations

Your Big Ask 1

DREAM: ______________________________

BY WHEN: ______________________________

BIG ASK: ______________________________

RESULT: ______________________________

Your Big Ask 2

DREAM: ______________________________

BY WHEN: ______________________________

BIG ASK: ______________________________

RESULT: ______________________________

If you accomplish a Big Ask this week, don't stop there. Go for another one. If those two come through, ask for a third. Use this week to become more and more practiced at asking for exactly what you want.

EXERCISE 7.3

MAKING YOUR DREAM PITCH PERFECT

Daring *now* requires you to pitch your Dream to your ideal client, ideal customer, or ideal business partner—at any time. As you create your perfect pitch, be clear about what you're asking for. As a beginning entrepreneur, you may be in the ideation phase and pitching to recruit advisors. If you already have a company established, you might be creating a pitch to attract buyers or new team members. If you're working in a corporate setting, you might be pitching senior executives to promote you. Whether your ask is about a promotion, funding, or collaborations and partnership, use the following prompts to create the pitch that's best for the next phase of your Stretch.

The Ideation Pitch

If you're in the start-up phase of your Dream, your ideation pitch should include your name, the proposed name of your business, and how you would like a potential contributor to be involved. Your request might simply be to have the person spend time with you over coffee or lunch discussing your idea, and/or to get people to consider adding their support. **Write your clear, concise pitch in the space below and/or in your Dream Notebook.**

The Company Start-Up or Departmental Pitch

If you're the owner of a company or start-up or working for one, your pitch should include your name, the name of your department or business, and what you're planning to do within your company or department. Be clear about what you're asking for and how you'd like the other person to support this plan. **Write your clear, concise pitch in the space below and/or in your Dream Notebook.**

Pitching with an Ask

If you have a developed company or if you're looking for a promotion within your organization, your pitch should include a clear explanation of what you've done thus far, where you're planning to go from here, and how the other person can help you. Be clear and authentic about how you'd like the other person to support you, the time frame in which you'll need the person's support, and how you can give back to that person later. Remember that givers always gain. **Write your clear, concise pitch in the space below and/or in your Dream Notebook.**

Always create a pitch that includes exactly what you want. You might get everything you ask for.

EXERCISE 7.4

THE UNCOMFORTABLE CHALLENGE

In this exercise, I Dare you to start getting used to being uncomfortable and to learn to be okay with that discomfort all the way through this 90-day journey. Read through the challenges below, and select one challenge this week that will help you start to get comfortable with being uncomfortable.

Getting Comfortable in Bigger Spaces

You could use this week to become more comfortable being in larger rooms, in larger spaces, and on larger stages. You might make your way into rooms with people who are higher in your department. You could gain entrée into events with entrepreneurs who have businesses that are more profitable than yours. If you're a speaker or an Activist Dreamer hoping to pitch your ideas to a larger audience, you could be on a stage facing hundreds or even thousands more people than you've ever addressed before. Your work this week is to go into a new room or new meeting space and make five new contacts. **Write the name, contact info, where you met, and your follow-up action in the spaces below and/or in your Dream Notebook.**

Bigger Spaces Challenge

NAME	CONTACT INFO	WHERE WE MET	FOLLOW-UP ACTION

Making Even Bigger Asks

Your discomfort this week could also mean making even bigger asks. For some people, it's a Big Ask just to ask someone to consider buying a product or service. For you, it could be a very Big Ask to take the senior person in the department to lunch to let him or her know that you're ready to move up in the company. Make your asks bigger and bigger, and don't be afraid to get a no on the way to hearing the ultimate yes that you're after.

Identify five people to whom you want to make a Big Ask. **Write the name, contact info, and your follow-up action in the spaces below and/or in your Dream Notebook.**

Bigger Ask Challenge

NAME	CONTACT INFO	YOUR BIG ASK	FOLLOW-UP ACTION

Elevate Your Circle

Another way to Stretch this week could involve elevating your circle. That could mean networking in larger circles. It could be asking for a mentorship or creating a Mentor Moment to get more information about how to build your Dream. Elevating your circle could mean going to a conference you've never attended. It could mean going to a cocktail dinner with one of your colleagues in order to meet other people within the company. Don't be afraid to spend time with people whose positions are senior to yours and who may have more experience than you. Identify five senior-level executives or mentors with whom you want to create a genuine connection. **Write the name, contact info, and your follow-up action plans in the spaces below and/or in your Dream Notebook.**

Elevate Your Circle Challenge

NAME	CONTACT INFO	FOLLOW-UP ACTION

Be Okay with an Imperfect Pitch

I also want you to become comfortable with imperfect pitching. The first couple of times you pitch, it may not go smoothly, so practice pitching yourself three to five times per week until you feel extremely comfortable with your pitch's content and your ability to communicate it. Identify five people to whom you want to pitch your service, product, or idea. **Write the name, contact info, your pitch date, and your follow-up action in the spaces below and/or in your Dream Notebook.**

Imperfect Pitch Challenge

NAME	CONTACT INFO	PITCH DATE	FOLLOW-UP ACTION

Pitching requires courage, and practice helps you build that courage. Sometimes you have to just take that deep breath and go for it, make that pitch, ask that Big Ask, walk right into that event, grab that microphone. History favors the bold, and I want you to Dare to be bolder and bolder all the time. Sometimes you might even seem a little crazy. But I don't think that's going to bother people as they read about you in *Forbes*.

YOUR 90-DAY STRETCH PLAN GOAL CRUSH REMINDER

Goal Crush Reminder! Review your 90-Day Stretch Plan. Are you on track? Take a close look at your 90-Day Stretch Plan and at the result you desire. You're at the halfway mark. Have you done 50 percent of the tasks you laid out? If not, consider whether you need to change your strategies to get to the goal. If necessary, grab that eraser and start sketching a new route to the finish line.

As we wind down Week 7 of the Stretch, I'm very excited to share with you the words of a daring Activist Dreamer! This woman is one of the boldest, most courageous people I've ever met, a woman who refused to let a troubled past define her future. Despite being unwanted, adopted, and sexually abused for years, this warrior rose above her past and now battles human trafficking around the world. Read about how this author and founder of The A21 Campaign and Propel Women learned to embrace risks and Stretch.

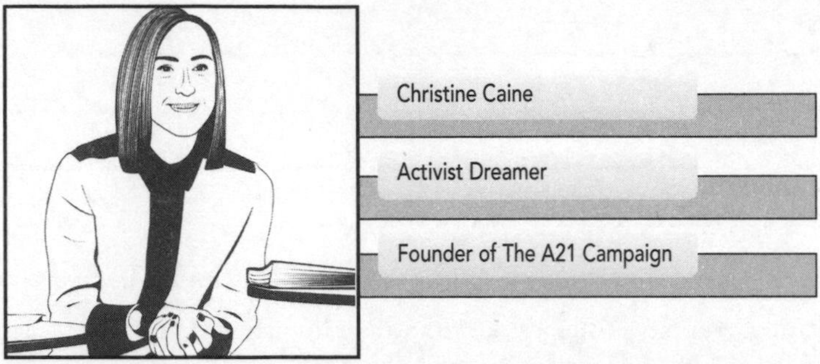

> "For anyone on the edge of launching a dream, you're going to have to jump. You're going to find 20 reasons why not, and you're going to find a different 20 reasons next week and another 20 reasons the week after. At some point you're going to have to decide that the planets haven't aligned and that they're not going to."
>
> —Activist Dreamer **Christine Caine**

You may download this week's Dream All-Star training session at www.thebigstretchbook.com.

CHAPTER EIGHT

GOING IN THROUGH THE ROOF

Week 8

Imagine that you're standing in front of a beautiful building. Inside lives your Dream. It's alive and thriving and reaching toward the future, but there's a problem: there are certain credentials and experience required for access, and you don't have them. So you're caught in a paradox: you can't get access unless you have experience, but you can't gain the experience until you get in.

That's how I felt 15 years ago when I started this Dream journey. I remember using the building analogy in a conversation with my girlfriend, Angianein Wallace, the young lady I met during the Magic Trade Show in Las Vegas who went on to become one of my biggest Dream Champions. I told her, "I want to get in that building so bad! My entertainment Dream is in that building. I know what I need to do—I need to go in through the roof!"

If I was going to work my tail off to transition to a completely new field, why enter the building like everybody else? Why work my way up floor by floor? If I could figure out a clever way to gain access to the top, wouldn't that get me to my goals much faster? "Going in through the roof" refers to entering a field by gaining access to its thought leaders, executives, and innovators. **When you start up there, your career growth tends to be expedited because you learn fast and find yourself with opportunities you'd probably miss if you'd started on the ground floor.**

In Chapter Seven, you heard about how much I wanted to get into the entertainment field. The way I landed the apprenticeship at RUSH Communications is an example of going in through the roof. At the time, the company was building thriving enterprises, leveraging hip-hop culture's appeal, and influencing numerous business categories by innovating with hip-hop culture in mind. RUSH Communications was having an impact on several industries, from banking with the prepaid RUSH Card to music with Def Jam Recordings and from philanthropic efforts with the Hip-Hop Summit Action Network to the fashion industry with Phat Fashions. My apprenticeship at RUSH gave me the chance to work alongside people who were pioneering pop culture business ventures in music, fashion, and entertainment. Because I was able to work with these leaders, things happened quickly for me.

When it was time for me to Stretch again, I decided to try another roof entrance. After working in the entertainment industry for over four years, I started to miss the corporate world. While my new entertainment environment was extremely creative, there wasn't much structure, nor were there processes in place to make the day-to-day operations of the business run efficiently. Feeling more corporate than I'd ever believed I could be (wasn't I the one who was happy to leave IBM in the rearview mirror?), I found myself regularly suggesting to leadership ways in which they could benefit from more structure. I also began to wonder if I could create an environment that would offer me some of the benefits of corporate structure but with the freedom of a creative organization. That's when I decided to create an agency that would give corporations access to fast-growing multicultural audiences. At the time, I had no idea how agencies were structured or even what they did day to day. But I wanted to learn. So, I immediately thought to myself, *why not try the "go-in-through-the-roof" method again*?

By the way, I wasn't taught the "go-in-through-the-roof" strategy in undergrad, nor did I learn this while working on my MBA. This is a Tenacious T idea that has worked for me more than once, so now I'm sharing it with you. Say you're a Hobby Dreamer and you want to work in interior design; what if you could land an apprenticeship with a seasoned interior designer? Maybe you're an Activist Dreamer and you want to have an impact in the area of women's rights. What if you could volunteer with a women's movement organizer? The go-in-through-the-roof strategy requires that you look for unconventional opportunities to learn from the leaders in your area of interest.

This chapter includes the following exercises to help you strategize how to go in through the roof right now:

> **Week 8: Going in Through the Roof**
>
> EXERCISE 8.1: The Dream Extreme Challenge
> EXERCISE 8.2: First, Break All the Rules
> EXERCISE 8.3: Finding the Gap
> EXERCISE 8.4: Learning from Failure

There is one more thing to note about going in through the roof: it may require that you do things that others may deem crazy. I call these "Dream Extreme" moments. Let's get started in this part of The Stretch by helping you to Dream Extreme.

LET'S GO CRAZY!

Are you ready to Dream Extreme? It means that you're willing to go to any lengths for your Stretch journey including taking emotional risks, trying things that make you uncomfortable, asking for things you'd never Dreamed of asking for, and daring beyond previous boundaries. During one of my Dream Extreme adventures, I left my car on the side of an interstate highway, climbed over a median, and ran into a building all in the name of trying to land a new client. Sound crazy? It was, but I had an opportunity to submit new ideas to an agency that was working on a pitch for McDonald's, so I had to go to extremes!

This was a one-shot moment, and when you Dream Extreme, you always have to be ready. I pitched our agency's ideas and left feeling confident. I felt so great that I almost forgot I'd parked my car in the middle of an interstate. As I walked out of the building, the client offered to walk me to my car." I blurted, "No! That's not necessary, but thank you so much . . ." We shook hands, and I hiked my way back to my little old Beetle, still parked in the middle of the packed freeway. That day I learned exactly how far I'll go for a goal.

ALL OR NOTHING

When you choose this Stretch journey, you *must* be willing to go all in. I'll admit that running across a highway was extreme, but when you're committed to going in through the roof, you must remove boundaries from your thinking. When I made my big announcement to friends and family that I was going to run in the New York City Marathon. I was met with raised eyebrows and instant *why nots*. "Neshia, you're not a runner," they said. "Why don't you start with a 5K and work your way up? Don't you think it's a bit ambitious much to start with a marathon?" But that's not my way. If I was going to run the race, I was going all out. Even though I hadn't run more than two miles since high school, I skipped running a 5K, a 10K, and even a half marathon and went straight for the full marathon. I decided to take on a huge goal, and I was willing to put in the work. **To Dream Extreme requires the same type of mindset—you must be willing to go all in.** I love talking about Dreaming Extreme with fellow Dreamers like Kevin Liles, a Make-It-Happen Dreamer who knows all about daring moves. In only eight years, Kevin went from being an intern at Def Jam Recordings to becoming the company's president. You don't make those kinds of leaps by staying in the safety zone.

Sometimes going all in means doing more than is expected. Kevin told a Dream Project audience about when he was first trying to break into the music industry. "The interview was at Def Jam Music in New York City, and I go up there looking like a nerd, wearing a suit. Everybody's laughing at me. People got on T-shirts and jeans, and it's like four or five people interviewing me. I'm pulling out graphs, charts, research things that I've done over the course of my time as an intern. Nobody paid me to do that; it was just how I wanted to present myself. A lot of people wait for somebody to say they need something to present themselves in a certain way, but I knew this was something nobody else would do, so I did it. I had demographic information. I put together books and charts, and they had never seen anything like this. But still, they said, 'We'll call you.'"

Sometimes it means taking a financial hit. Three months passed before Def Jam made Kevin an offer—for less than half of what he was earning at the time. "They said, 'We want to offer you $30,000 to come work for us,'" Kevin recalls. "I was making $70,000/$80,000. I was living in Baltimore, and all my family was there. I love my family, and I wanted to stay with them, but I took a big pay cut because that doesn't matter when you want something so bad. I'm not saying go broke. What I'm saying is when you want something badly, don't let your arrogance and ego get in the way. And sometimes money isn't the only factor."

To Kevin Liles, going all in means giving 100 percent every single day. "I never wanted to just be an intern; I wanted to be the president of interns. I never just wanted to be the regional marketing manager; I wanted to be the president of regional marketing managers. If I wasn't the best that day, I'd failed. I didn't want anyone to be better than me. You were not going to outwork me. You were not going to out-coffee me. You weren't going to do anything better than me because I knew instinctively that God had given me the opportunity of a lifetime. I was working on being the president from day one when I got there. So that's why they made me the president."

WORK AS HARD AS YOU CAN

I recently had the chance to interview Bravo's *Top Chef* winner, Kelsey Barnard, about her experience of going through the roof. While attending culinary school, she asked her school's president, "Which is the most difficult externship available to me?" He said, "That would be working under Chef Gavin Kaysen at Café Boulud." She accepted the chance to work in that extremely scary environment and now credits that self-challenge—and her willingness to work extremely hard—for the success she's enjoying now. Of her first days in Kaysen's kitchen, Kelsey remembers being "a young, country, blonde girl in a kitchen full of French men with the exception of Gavin, who is from Minneapolis." She says that the experience was terrifying. "I mean, it was not fun at all, but it was exactly what I wanted out of my externship, because I wanted a boot camp," she recalls. "I didn't want to coast. I didn't want to be the best in the kitchen. I wanted to be the worst and learn, which is exactly what I was." Kelsey says that she worked 120 hours per week and that thanks to throwing herself into that environment, she learned more in six months than a lot of people do in six years. Of her experience of going in through the roof, Kelsey says that while there was nothing fun about it, "it was such a challenge that now it's made me the best."

CREATING YOUR OWN RULES

Going in through the roof also lets you make your own rules. During the early years of my Stretch, I wanted to explore creating a successful marketing agency. When EGAMI Group was first formed, the only client was RUSH Communications. I knew I wanted my company to develop big campaign ideas for big clients and Fortune 100 projects. So I took the time to consider the smartest route to get to my desired goal of landing major corporate accounts *now* versus looking for clients slowly one at a time.

As I researched, I discovered that the third largest advertising firm in the world was servicing one of the largest advertisers in the world. I thought, *What if I can find a way to learn from the firm and offer my service at the same time*? I discovered that the ad agency's biggest client had announced a commitment to spend $3 billion per year to work with businesses owned by women and minorities. It wanted to ensure that its products reached and resonated with multicultural audiences, the fastest-growing demographic in the nation. Ding! My business was certified as minority and female owned, and I knew the market, so I asked a friend to introduce me to the agency's president and to set up a dinner meeting. (Remember in Chapter Six, the power of leveraging your network?)

During this dinner, I asked the president, "Did you know that your number one client has two key objectives that you are currently *not* positioned to help it meet? It wants to spend more money with women- and minority-owned businesses. It also wants to grow its target audience to reach multicultural audiences. You should have a solution ready to offer if you want to keep your seat at that table. I have ideas for you, and I'd love for our firms to collaborate on this." The underlying tone for my pitch was answering the unspoken question, "What's in this partnership for *me*?" I offered, "I will position your company to meet your client's needs. Your firm will have a dedicated diverse partner qualified to develop messaging, branding, commercials, and products that resonate with diverse audiences." (Remember in Chapter Five, when you worked through Exercise 5.3, "Finding Your Dream's Unique Position"? You listed how your skills and your business's capabilities uniquely meet the needs of others. This kind of pitch is what that exercise gets you ready for.)

My plan was mapped out, but the meeting didn't go well. I stumbled over my words. I rambled. And then there was the mix-up when I tried to pay for dinner: my fancy plastic business card felt like a credit card, and in my nervousness I handed *it* to the waiter, who soon returned to let me know that, no, my business card wasn't going to cover the tab. I was mortified, and I slunk away from the restaurant sure that I'd lost a great opportunity. But here's the good news: sometimes all God wants to see is that you're willing to get in the game. Shortly after my meeting, destiny stepped in when the agency's client asked if the agency was positioned to reach diverse audiences. The agency had been presented with a very timely opportunity that it could grab only if it were already equipped to reach diverse audiences. So I think you can guess who the agency's president called: me. He said, "Let's form a partnership, ASAP." I was ready to hit the ground running.

This specific go-in-through-the-roof example led to a five-year collaboration between my newly formed agency and the third largest communications firm in the world. Our firms won multiple industry partnership awards, including AdColor's Most Valuable Partnership for Best in Class Strategic Partnership Model. And more important than accolades, we delivered results. We connected our clients to millions of multicultural consumers, developed over $2 million in grants and scholarships that impacted multicultural communities, and increased our clients' sales.

BE STRATEGIC

The greater the height of your roof, the more challenging the climb will be, so when you go in through the roof, you have to be strategic. You should always be thinking and preparing to act on the answers to questions like, "What can I offer the pioneers in my industry?" and "What are some creative ways for me to get access to internships, volunteering opportunities, and informational interviews?"

Back when I negotiated the partnership with the advertising agency I just told you about, I kept in mind the goal of benefiting both parties. During the first round of negotiations, I was careful not to be too aggressive because I was fully aware that at this early stage in my company's life, we were getting a lot out of this deal. I knew that if I could get us to the table and learn the game now, later we'd be in a position to negotiate more favorable terms. The onset of this partnership gave EGAMI instant access to a Fortune 100 client roster and the chance to learn how to create an agency by way of this access. These were the training wheels our firm needed until we learned how to ride the bike on our own, so I negotiated accordingly. When you're going in through the roof and negotiating access, whether it involves a new partnership, a new job, an internship, or a volunteer opportunity, be mindful of who you are in the equation. Be aware of what's in it for you and what's in it for them, and negotiate accordingly. As Kevin Liles said, the greatest reward isn't always monetary; quite often it's about learning, exposure, expedited growth, and opportunities.

Speaking of opportunities, when the Internet entered our lives, it opened countless options, especially for creative people who traditionally had to wait for approval from a movie studio or music label to launch their writing or performance careers. Not anymore. If you can solve the conundrum of how to stand out from the pack, the Internet offers extraordinary opportunities for exposure that didn't exist just 25 years ago.

Issa Rae is a very successful Make-It-Happen Dreamer who shared with us at the Dream Project that after pounding and pounding on Hollywood's front doors and hearing no invitations to come on in, she chose to slip around the building and go in through a side door. Issa created a web series called *The Misadventures of Awkward Black Girl* and launched it on YouTube. As a credit to her infectious sense of humor, her content has garnered over 23 million views and over 200,000 YouTube subscribers. That got Hollywood's attention. She went on to star in HBO's *Insecure* and make such lists as *Glamour* magazine's "35 Under 35," *Forbes*'s "30 Under 30," and *Entertainment Weekly*'s "Breaking Big." She's also been nominated for a Golden Globe for *Insecure.* Stories like Issa's never cease to inspire and fascinate me. She's thriving proof that if you refuse to take no for an answer, you'll eventually get a yes, even if you have to slip through a side door to get it.

FAIL FORWARD

There's no question that I've had some extraordinary experiences because I've made some unconventional choices. Some of those choices were Dreamer missteps that left me banged up and bruised. Fortunately, I learned from those mistakes. Perhaps you, too, have forgone a traditional path in an attempt to access your Dream faster. When you choose to Stretch in an extreme way, you discover a great deal of blind spots, which are fertile ground for fumbles and costly mistakes. New business owners, for example, might choose the wrong type of business structure, as in S corp versus C corp; they might pay higher than market value for inventory; or they might fumble again and again because they don't understand how to scale a business. One of my favorite sayings about business is "entrepreneurs jump off a cliff and figure out how to build the plane on the way down." Even if you have the guts and tenacity to figure it out along the way, expect that there will be scrapes and bruises and mistakes. And even if I could write you a tidy training plan that would navigate you safely with no scratches or bruises, that would be doing you a disservice. I've yet to meet a Dreamer who hasn't learned something after sustaining an injury in pursuit of a Dream.

You will not avoid failure during your Stretch, so please, please, Dreamers, don't be hard on yourselves when you feel disappointed or feel that you've failed. As long as you're committed to getting back up, dusting yourself off, and continuing on, you'll succeed. Every failure offers another chance to turn that same failure back on its head. Careerpreneur/CEO Dreamer Soledad O'Brien shared with our Dream Project audience how she let a painful failure propel her forward but not before she considered throwing in the towel. The former CNN coanchor and founder of Starfish Media remembers, "When I started reporting on my first job in San Francisco, I was doing a story on the Giants who had just made it into the playoffs. I was sent out to interview people at a bar while they watched the game. My piece starts with 'Soledad O'Brien is joining us now from Joe's Pub with the very latest on the fans. Soledad, what are you seeing?' As I opened my mouth, literally, a drunk guy reached out and grabbed me on the butt. I stared in shock. It was a disaster. I went back to the station, and the news director actually said, 'Listen, maybe this isn't for you. Maybe you should think about Santa Barbara, a smaller market.' I called my old boss, crying, and he said, 'Whatever you do, do not quit. Make them fire you if you have to, but these are hard jobs to get. Do not quit.' And within three months, not only had I successfully navigated how to do live shots; they made me the bureau chief for the East Bay." A little good advice and a lot of tenacity helped propel Soledad into the award-winning journalist that she is today. Soledad says, "The easy thing would have been to quit. But I had to sit there and watch all my clips and try to get better, to take something that I had never done and figure out how to do it."

LIVE, LEARN, AND MOVE ON

Like Soledad O'Brien, I've had my share of incidents that felt like failures. As the owner of a small business that was growing too fast, I made mistakes almost daily. In fact, a few years into my Stretch, I had a go-in-through-the-roof scrape that went so deep it almost knocked me off my course for good. In a last-minute scramble, my firm was called in to save the day by a client that was launching a new scent campaign for a laundry detergent. The hook was that the scent "smelled so good it was music to your nose." The client had the clever idea of launching the product in a promotion during the Grammys that involved a prominent musician appearing in the commercials and also hosting a launch event during Grammy weekend. Lucky for me, the client had a bit of a fumble with its chosen celebrity spokesperson, and the original deal fell apart a few days before Christmas. This fumble opened what I thought was a perfect opportunity for our firm.

The client called and asked, "Can you help us facilitate a partnership with a celebrity musician?" I was excited to prove that our firm was up to the challenge. I said, "Yes, we can do it!" My business partner and I worked hard to secure the perfect artist, and we landed not one but all five Braxton Sisters. Securing and negotiating five deals in less than a month is on the level of a Superman–LeBron James–Black Panther power play. I was thrilled about our accomplishment, and I couldn't wait to kick off the campaign.

During this time, our office was in New York City. Our accounting firm was on Long Island, and the firm wasn't intricately involved in the details of our deals, which I would later find out was a big mistake. Without my knowledge, our accountant paid the Braxton Sisters before the campaign launched. Instead, the payments should have been delivered in increments as the singers met their deliverables, and this mistake completely threw off our agency's cash flow. (We'll address the importance of managing cash flow in Chapter Ten.) In the weeks that followed, I learned the severity and repercussions of this financial mistake. I was left with no guarantee that the talent would fulfill the terms of the contract. This mistake also kicked off other consequences as we headed into our peak execution season. Our firm needed cash on hand to pay in advance for the expenses involved with delivering high-profile events, but sometimes we had to wait 90 days to be paid. The screwup of paying the talent up front terribly imbalanced our incoming versus outgoing cash flow. Some call this "growing to your death." As all of this was going on, we took on other clients with even longer payment terms, and that further strained our cash flow. I wasn't sure that EGAMI would survive that phase. Once again, I felt banged up.

When you experience these kinds of business hits, take comfort in knowing that we've all been there and that we'll all be there again. And ease the pain by learning. When you make a mistake, one of your follow-up goals should be to examine what happened and learn from it. Some post-mistake considerations include:

- Become clear on the root cause, not the symptoms. In the example above, the accountant paying the contract out in full was a symptom. The cause: we had the wrong accounting team.
- Work to understand the consequences of the mistakes. How will this mistake affect the business, and what is the domino effect? You can't brainstorm a solution without assessing the total possible damage.
- Develop at least three to five possible solutions that will move you forward and out of the mess.
- If the person responsible for the mistake doesn't have the skill set to do the job correctly, let him or her go.
- Make a running list of things that you could have done differently. Review and keep that list so you can improve the next time.
- Reach out to your lifelines (mentors, business partners, and colleagues) for advice on navigating the mistake.

EGAMI had to do a combination of all the above. We terminated our accounting team and replaced it with an in-house chief financial officer. Then our new CFO not only played a pivotal role in saving the firm from my rookie mistakes, but also helped overhaul our financial system, hire a new financial team, negotiate favorable payment terms, and infuse structure and process into the organization. I had been guilty of letting a resource outlive its ability to serve us well. Remember, just because people start the journey with you doesn't mean they'll be with you all the way. Your most important goal during a bruise, scrape, or challenge is to stay in the game. Take time to learn and know that *this too shall pass*.

Now it's time to tap into the Extreme Dreamer in you!

EXERCISE 8.1

THE DREAM EXTREME CHALLENGE

This is not a test. This is your opportunity to Dream Extreme. You know your Dream well. You've laid its foundation. You even know how to make bigger asks and bigger pitches. Now it's time to think bigger, bolder, and brighter.

Talking with countless Dreamers over the years, I've discovered that three of the most common Extreme Dreams are moving to a new city, leaving a full-time opportunity, and starting a new venture. If you've recently done or are planning to do any of these, this exercise is for you. If none of these scenarios apply to you, feel free to skip ahead to Exercise 8.2.

After you complete the following exercise, I recommend that you evaluate your answers with the help of one of your Dream Champions.

Dream Extreme Challenge 1: Moving to a New City

DREAM CITY: ______________________________

MOVING DATE: ______________________________

1. What is the Dream that you hope to bring to life in the new city?
2. What relationships do you already have in place to help kick-start your Dream there? Make a list of these people, and reach out to let them know that you're moving and that you'd like their help in this transition.
3. Identify and book appointments for one to three housing options you can choose from in this new city.
4. Identify three to five actions you can take this week in the next 30 days to support this move, like researching living arrangements,

neighborhoods, and job opportunities. Start these efforts well in advance of moving.

5. Identify 10 things you can do (like network and join meetups) to ramp up your Dream. Prior to moving, research these organizations and make a list of steps you'll take to become involved with them.
6. Identify one to three places where you can volunteer or intern in this city. Upon arrival, select one of them and start volunteering as soon as possible. This offers a great way to acquire skills and learn from pioneers.
7. Identify and schedule 10 to 15 exploratory meetings you can have within your first 60 days there.

Dream Extreme Challenge 2: Leaving a Full-Time Job

PURPOSE FOR LEAVING: ______________________________

EXIT DATE: ______________________________

1. Who will be affected by your departure? How and when will you communicate your plans with your department or team? Tell your trusted advocates first and then others at the appropriate time.
2. How much money do you need in your savings as you make this transition? (We'll address this concept further in Dreaming Responsibly in Chapter Ten.) If possible, choose a departure date that will allow you to build enough savings first to make this a comfortable move.
3. Identify and take three to five actions you can focus on in the next 30 days to move toward this goal, like hiring a recruiter or updating your résumé.
4. Identify and reach out to three to five contacts who can assist in your transition. Let them know, specifically, what they can do to help you.
5. Remember that relationships matter, as does your reputation. What are some things you can do to ensure that you leave your current job in great standing? List these and keep them in mind each day as you begin your exit from the company.

Dream Extreme Challenge 3: Starting a New Venture

DREAM VENTURE: ______________________________

EXECUTION DATE: ______________________________

1. Why do you want to start this venture now? Write your answer as a statement that you post in your work space as a reminder of why the time is *now*.
2. Whose help do you need to get this Dream off the ground? Make a list of all the people who can help you. Let them know when you plan to launch this venture and ask for their input.
3. How can others support you in developing this new idea? Make a list, and next to each name, note how each person can help you.
4. How much money do you need to have saved to make this transition? Draft a proposed budget. You can develop this further as you work through Chapter Ten.
5. What five tasks should you focus on in the next 30 days to get this venture up and running? List these and add them to your 90-Day Goals.

EXERCISE 8.2

FIRST, BREAK ALL THE RULES

With this exercise, I challenge you to think about how to go in through the roof using nontraditional methods to stand out and gain access to industry leaders who can help you find and develop opportunities.

Do It Differently

Catching the attention of influential people in your industry may require that you leave the traditional networking path and do the opposite of the norm. You might be surprised to discover how many simple things you can do to stand out, be memorable, and get the attention of others. Do you recall from Chapter Six that Brandice Daniel, the founder of Harlem's Fashion Row, landed her first board members by simply sending handwritten notes and gifts? What about if, instead of sending an e-mail or text, you go low tech and mail a postcard or just call the person you want to connect with? And consider doing things ahead of season. If you're used to offering products at a certain time of year, instead, why not alert your potential clients and customers a few months earlier to give them a head start? You can also send a gift or communication at an unexpected time. A lot of people send cards for Christmas; what if you were to send an uplifting New Year's greeting in the middle of January rather than during the December holiday bustle? And keep in mind one of my favorite mantras: "Make yourself uncomfortable." If there's a practice commonly done in your industry, do it differently. Consider . . .

- Sending personalized gifts, notes, or invitations.
- Offering free consultations.
- Donating time in circles that will elevate your access.
- Scheduling 15-minute information interviews with industry leaders.
- Creating a "best of" representation of your work and your skill set. Share your work with industry leaders as a gift. For example, if you're a painter, send a painting to an interior designer and offer your paintings as a part of the designer's service to his or her clients.

Five Ways You'll "Do It Differently" This Week

1. ________________________________
2. ________________________________
3. ________________________________
4. ________________________________
5. ________________________________

Now, in the interest of some of that discomfort, review the five ideas you just listed and consider how you might "take it up a notch." Remember, this is about Dreaming Extreme. Maybe you listed that you would connect with three to five people. Can you up the ante by changing it to three to five CEOs? If any of your five outreach ideas are 100 percent in your comfort zone, I want you to push yourself by adding elements that make you at least slightly fearful.

Now revisit the five steps that you listed and push yourself to take it up a notch!

Become What You Say You Are

At what point in the course of learning, practicing, and executing creative and professional endeavors should we feel comfortable giving ourselves the title that goes with that pursuit? When should you be "allowed" to say, "I'm a gardener," "I'm a filmmaker," "I'm an entrepreneur"? Do you need a degree in it? Should you first be paid to do it before you can give yourself the title? I say, if you're genuinely serious about a pursuit—if you've dedicated considerable time to it and remain actively engaged in the practice of it—you should be able to comfortably say, "I'm a writer," "I'm a makeup artist," "I'm a musician." We assign a lot of value to titles, so why not be the first to title yourself? We've all heard the business cliché "Fake it 'til you make it." What bothers me about this worn-out expression is that in order to fake something, you have to believe that at your core, you don't have what it takes. I think bold Dreamers believe within their cores that they are capable. Filmmaker Tyler Perry, for example, didn't wait for film school credentials to deem him "a film producer and writer." He simply became a writer, director, and producer by writing, directing, and producing—even while he was still living out of his car! There's power in not waiting to become a certain kind of someone but rather embracing the aspects of who you want to be that are already in place.

How do you envision yourself? Do you want to become a chef, a singer, a florist, a business consultant, a CFO, an entrepreneur? In this exercise, I want you to put yourself in the mind of the person you're becoming. What are this person's habits? What does this person spend a lot of time thinking about? What thrills this person? What does this person want life to look like one year from now? Over the next week, I want you to take radical moves to start becoming that person. You might:

- Create business cards with the name and logo for your future venture.
- Showcase your products and services on social media with special offers.
- Research classes, workshops, and degrees that people in your field of interest pursue. Which of these options might be a fit for you?
- Identify leaders within this industry. Read about them. Learn from their successes and failures, and take notes.
- On the lighter side, consider having a mug or T-shirt printed with an affirming reminder of "who you are" now: "Cake Maker to the Stars," "Kids' Favorite Math Coach," "World's Greatest Financial Consultant."

Five Things You Will Do This Week in the Spirit of Who You Want to Become

1. ____
2. ____
3. ____
4. ____
5. ____

EXERCISE 8.3

FINDING THE GAP

One of the fastest ways to go in through the roof is to find the gap in the industry or service you want to work with. While working with the third largest marketing and communications company in the world, I found gaps in its services that EGAMI was able to fill. Find the gaps in the companies you want to work with and consider how you can be of service.

Some practical steps you can take:

- Make a list of industry leaders within your Dream field of interest.
- Study their businesses and become familiar with what they're doing now.
- Find areas where they can improve and where you can help them grow.
- Reach out and schedule meetings with these industry leaders.

Let's get started now!

Finding the Gap

Identify three to five organizations or people you want to work with.

1. ______________________________
2. ______________________________
3. ______________________________
4. ______________________________
5. ______________________________

Identify three to five areas where they can improve and where you can help them grow.

1. ____
2. ____
3. ____
4. ____
5. ____

List the gifts, skills, and services that you bring to the table.

1. ____
2. ____
3. ____
4. ____
5. ____

Reach out and then schedule meetings with three to five industry leaders to explore how you can be an asset or of service to them. Log those meetings here.

1. ____
2. ____
3. ____
4. ____
5. ____

EXERCISE 8.4

LEARNING FROM FAILURE

Rather than beat yourself up about your mistakes, what if you skipped ahead to learning the lessons they offer and assessing how you might handle that situation differently next time? In this exercise, I want to take you through a post-game analysis of Dreamer missteps. Today, you're a Monday morning quarterback who gets to critique from the cushy safety of the armchair. In this exercise you'll also serve as observer and advisor. Then, in the spirit of taking your own advice, after you critique this Dreamer, think about ways you can apply the lessons to your own Stretch journey.

New Business Pitch Goes Wrong

John is a new CEO Dreamer who launches a software firm that sells IT hardware to corporations. For 20 years prior, he worked with the equipment and hardware that he's now selling. He lands an opportunity to pitch his IT Tech Hardware Router solution to a major company, and when he sets up his presentation, he realizes that he didn't bring the necessary converter to use his MAC computer in a PC environment. As he stumbles to launch the conference-room presentation, executives sit and watch him for 15 idle minutes. He finally begins, and 30 minutes after the intended start time, he begins to explain the benefits of working with his firm. An executive interrupts, "John, thanks for coming in, but we all have hard stops at 30 minutes." John feels deflated as the executives say polite goodbyes and head back to their offices.

- What were John's mistakes?
- Which issues and oversights do you suspect might be behind the errors?
- How should John do things differently next time?
- What might he have done to try to salvage the meeting despite the delays?

Coach T's Advice

- Think through every detail you can imagine, well in advance.
- Develop a tech/setup pre-presentation questionnaire that you send in advance to all your potential clients so that you can plan accordingly.
- Create a presentation that should run 10 minutes shorter than the time you've been given.
- Executives are busy, so be prepared for one of them to interrupt with, "Just give us the highlights."
- The list of possible presentation surprises that can blindside you is long, but solid preparation dramatically minimizes the list.

Never-Satisfied Boss

Christal is a Careerpreneur who leaps from working as a digital e-commerce strategist for a leading retailer to working for one of its competitors because the new company promises her a chance to build a new division. For three months she works tirelessly putting together a presentation outlining the direction for the new division, the proposed staffing plan, and what she wants to accomplish over the next year. She finally has the big meeting with her boss, who waits until the end of it to tell Christal, "I'm pretty disappointed that this is the direction you've chosen. These ideas don't take into consideration our operation model. This isn't how we do things around here." Christal feels shattered. Despite trying to incorporate constructive criticism into her future presentations, each time Christal presents over the next several months, her boss says that Christal's ideas don't work with the company's vision.

- What were Christal's mistakes?
- Which issues and oversights do you suspect are behind the problem?
- How would you advise Christal to do things differently in the future?

Coach T's Advice

Develop a working collaboration with a boss from the beginning. Don't fully bake the idea and then cross your fingers that it will be well received; instead, share your ideas before fully locking them in and spending months finalizing. Also, take plenty of time to understand a new environment you enter. The company is new to you but not to those you're working for. They might have processes in place that have been successful for decades. Be aware of a business's traditions and procedures as well as the human element; people might be very comfortable with "their ways." Walk softly and spend a lot of time listening rather than bulldozing your way in.

From Big Passion to Big Problems

Lila loves to make jewelry. She works 8 to 5 as a teacher and after work makes jewelry that she sometimes gives to her fellow teachers as gifts. They love her creations and convince her to start selling her work on Etsy. They promise that they'll act as brand ambassadors to spread the word, which they do, telling all their friends who then tell their friends. Before long, Lila is receiving order after order, the details of which her business of one can't easily handle. In no time, what was a satisfying hobby for Lila becomes a headache thanks to demanding customers, fewer hours to relax and sleep, and business-based demands that aren't part of Lila's skill set. A pastime that was once all about passion is now almost all about problems. Feeling overwhelmed, Lila discontinues her Etsy business and for a long time doesn't even make jewelry for fun.

- What could Lila have done differently to prevent her big passion from becoming a big problem?

Coach T's Advice

Prior to launching a Hobby Dream, it's a good idea to be straight with yourself about which aspects of this activity you love. If you're a jewelry maker who loves creating jewelry and loves giving the gift of your work but dreads the countless elements of running a small business, you should probably remain a hobbyist, regardless of other people's aspirations for you. If you want to try turning your hobby into a business, be realistic as you assess whether you'll still feel joy after dividing your time between the actual making of the jewelry and all the other time considerations you have to meet, including your "day job." I would advise Lila to set parameters: *Here's how many jewelry pieces I can make and sell while retaining the work/life balance I want. Here's the amount I'm able to produce and still find the jewelry business joyous rather than stressful.* It's important to be clear about why you love what you love and to protect your passion.

Fail-Forward Key Questions to Ask

As we've discussed, mistakes and failures are an inevitable part of Stretching. When you realize you've made a business mistake, I want you to take a deep breath and remember that we've *all* been there. Three of the most common problematic issues in business are communicating expectations clearly, adhering to guidelines, and executing project deliverables. Tightening these three areas will help you to fail forward—that is, to be ready to use those mistakes to be more effective next time. Here are questions you can ask yourself to sort through what you could have done differently.

Communication Expectations

1. Did I have clear expectations for the project?
2. Did I clearly communicate my expectations to everyone involved (clients, vendors, volunteers, etc.)?
3. Did I fully understand my client's or customer's expectations?
4. Did I provide the client with an opportunity to give feedback along the way?
5. Was there enough communication between all stakeholders?

Adhering to Timelines

1. Did I have a clear timeline for the project's completion date?
2. Was the timeline for this project reasonable? If not, did I speak up as soon as I discovered that I needed more time?

Meeting Deliverables

1. Did I have clear milestones for each deliverable for this project?
2. Did I have all the resources and skills needed to deliver the deliverable?
3. Did I take advantage of partnerships and resources available to meet the deliverable?

General Questions for Learning

1. What are my biggest lessons here?
2. What can I improve upon for next time?
3. If I have the opportunity to work with the same people again, what can I implement differently next time?

YOUR 90-DAY STRETCH PLAN GOAL CRUSH REMINDER

Hi! It's me again. I'm just here looming over your shoulder! Have a look at your 90-Day Stretch Plan. Are you hitting your marks? If you've started to fall behind, now is the time to dig in. Arrange your schedule to allow time to go back and make up the work.

Dreamer, you've hit the 60-day mark—you're two-thirds of the way there! Now that you know how to go in through the roof, it's time to learn from someone who's mastered it. My conversation with the next Dream All-Star is one of my favorite interviewing experiences, ever. He is a delightful Dreamer who shared lots of memories and wisdom, and I didn't want the interview to end. This man played basketball for the Los Angeles Lakers for 13 seasons and later went on to become the organization's president of basketball operations. He's also an entrepreneur whose ventures include a television network, sports team ownership, a financial company, tech investments, and more.

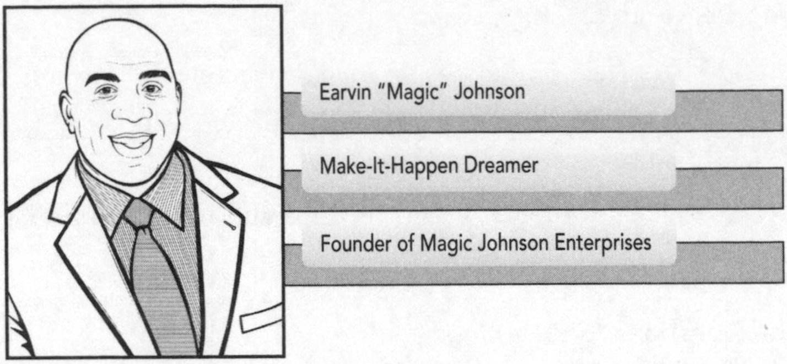

"I really wanted to bring a Starbucks to our community as a partner, but they weren't interested. Finally, Howard Schultz said, 'Okay let me come and see how you manage your business.' So he came down on a Friday night to visit my Magic AMC Theater. I'll never forget it. *Waiting to Exhale* was coming out, and I had about 5,000 black women wrapped around the corner. We went inside the theater, and every black woman in there started talking to the screen and giving their advice to Whitney Houston. Howard Schultz pulled me aside and said, 'I've never had a movie-going experience quite like this.' He said, 'You got the deal.'"

—Make-It-Happen Dreamer **Earvin "Magic" Johnson**

You may download this week's Dream All-Star training session at www.thebigstretchbook.com.

CHAPTER NINE

WHEN IT'S TIME TO LEVEL UP

Week 9

My first memory of riding a bicycle goes back to Christmas Day when I was four years old and standing in front of a shiny red bike. The bike had a wicker basket in the front, rainbow ribbons fluttering from the handlebars, and a cute little rubber ball horn. On the back of the bike were two wonderfully stabilizing training wheels. At the time, I had no idea that those training wheels would one day be removed.

I've heard a version of the "take off the training wheels" scenario enough times in my life to know that it's a relatively universal childhood memory. There's an adult pushing you and encouraging you to pedal faster. Frightened, you keep looking back for assurance that your trusted guide is still there. Then comes the moment when you're cruising, confident as can be that your support person is along for the ride, and you glance back to see the person way down the block because he or she had let go several seconds before. And all that time you've been balancing yourself! You feel the thrill of independence and pride paired with a jolt of panic because you're on your own. You're not sure you can do this.

Just as we have all had to learn to ride without training wheels, when you reach a level of mastery within The Stretch, you'll need to let go of safety in order to Stretch once again. Perhaps you've made some big, bold leaps in the past, and now you feel it's time to take it easy. Beware; the more you grow and achieve, the more susceptible you can become to resisting new challenges. But you must continually push yourself to a new level. An adult riding a child's tricycle would be a laughable sight, right? Take a moment to ask yourself if it's time to level up.

By the end of this chapter, you'll have the courage to take off your training wheels and go after your Dreams in even bigger ways—with help from the following exercises:

Week 9: When It's Time to Level Up

EXERCISE 9.1: Checkup and Refresh

EXERCISE 9.2: Leveling Up into the Future

EXERCISE 9.3: Taking Your Dream to the Next Level

IT'S TIME TO STOP PLAYING IT SAFE

In Chapter Eight, I talked about my company's partnership with a global advertising agency; during this alliance, there were disruptions to our comfort that were out of our control, disruptions that signaled the impending end of the partnership. Our client in the joint partnership cut its budgets, at which point our partner asked us to do the same amount of work for less money. Also, our partner owned several buildings in New York and often shuffled us from building to building with no apparent regard for the disruptions this instability caused EGAMI. And restructuring within the agency altered the relationship's dynamic to the degree that it became clear that it was time to walk away from the partnership. Looking back, I realize that it was clearly time to take off the training wheels and leave the comfort of the partnership, but at the time I resisted. Why?

The thought of ending the partnership was frightening. What would this mean for our small business? We had grown thanks to the partnership. We'd been supported. We'd been successful. We'd also shared resources, facilities, and team members—a huge coup for a small business. But it was time for us to level up. We were ready, but I was scared. During a conversation I had with the members of our partner agency's leadership team about dissolving the partnership, I knew they could see the fear in my eyes. The agency president put his hand on my shoulder and said, "You're ready. You can do this, Teneshia. It's time for you to go out on your own." And so we did.

EGAMI moved from our partner agency's offices to our own facilities in New York City. The office space we found was skeletal, so we hired a team to design and build out the space as we wanted it. We also had to hire support staff to replace the support we'd received during the partnership. And we had to learn how to service new accounts on our own. Every day was packed with the business of learning what had to be learned and doing what had to be done next, like buying new computers, hiring a cleaning crew, buying office furniture, and setting up payroll. The ride was wobbly, and it was another two years before we felt confident, balanced, and skilled at this level.

Are you thinking about taking off training wheels and leveling up your Dream? Maybe you're a CEO Dreamer with several years of experience in corporate settings, and you know it's time for you to leverage that skill set and jump-start a consulting firm. Maybe you're a Make-It-Happen Dreamer with a successful enterprise, and you're considering whether it's time to sell it and start a new business. Maybe you're a Careerpreneur Dreamer, and despite your excellent track record of starting new ventures within your company, you're beginning to feel that it's time to leave. Look around you. Where are you in your Stretch? Are you still riding around on training wheels of safety? This part of The Stretch will help you find out.

There are a few major signs that it's time to level up. If you know your day-to-day routine like the back of your hand, if you no longer feel challenged by your career or entrepreneurial venture, if you haven't felt any professional growth in a while—these are telltale signs that you've become complacent and need to level up. Let's examine why you might be unwilling to step up to a new level. Some of the key reasons Dreamers have reported stagnation over the years include:

- You've mastered your job, and it feels good to be an expert in your area.
- You're very financially comfortable, and you don't want to risk disrupting your lifestyle.

- You don't really like change. That includes new ideas, new settings, or new teams.
- You would be uncomfortable to no longer be the expert in the room.

HAS YOUR DREAM EXPIRED?

One of my dear friends, Jojo Brim, is a music executive whose counsel led to my first date with my husband. From the moment I met Jojo, we bonded over many things, from music to books to our optimistic outlook on life. Jojo and I have a soul connection, and our closeness came into play at a pivotal moment in his life. A few years ago, on behalf of one of EGAMI's corporate clients, I was executing a huge event at the Essence Music Festival, an annual music and empowerment experience that takes place every year in New Orleans. The event attracts more than 500,000 food-loving R&B and soul music fans for what turns into a massive, four-day party. The Essence Music Festival feels like a family reunion for these people, and each night concludes with a concert. The event is so popular that one of our Make-It-Happen Dream Project All-Stars, filmmaker Will Packer, created the popular movie *Girls Trip* centered on four friends from college who reunite at the festival.

Attending the Essence Music Festival is fun, but working it is a beast! Major brands like Coke, McDonald's, Ford, and Samsung sponsor huge interactive experiences that involve elements like musicians performing, cars on display, and complex games with prizes. EGAMI's role is to build out these interactive booth experiences. While I was dashing around the event, I caught a glimpse of my dear friend Jojo. He was working as well, managing an R&B artist who was extremely hot at the time. His artist was opening the concert later that night, and as Jojo was trying to push his client through the crowd, they were both getting mobbed in the midst of the craziness. I waved at Jojo. He smiled and waved back. But in that smile, I could see that something was wrong, something was missing. A few hours later, I saw him again in the VIP area. He should have been on top of the world. He was managing a top artist who was opening the Essence Festival, and the fans were going crazy. But there was deep fatigue in his eyes. I pushed my way through the crowd to my friend and said, "Jojo, listen to me. This Dream has expired." Right there in the middle of the Essence Music Festival, Jojo's eyes filled with tears.

THE DIFFERENCE BETWEEN A GREAT LIFE AND AN EXTRAORDINARY LIFE

Jojo would later share with me that our moment at that festival was a disruption of comfortable for him. He said he'd known that he was unfulfilled and that it was time for him to move on from that role in his life, but he'd tried to ignore the signs. Why did Jojo continue to ignore the signs? Because his life felt great.

The biggest thief of an extraordinary life is a great life. Jojo was at the top of his game in his industry, so why should he Dare to change it all? Because his great life was holding him back. Jojo was being loyal to the familiar. He'd spent over a decade grooming artists and taking them to the top of the Billboard charts, and at this point he could do the job in his sleep. Jojo's loyalty to the familiar had him trapped. He was also afraid of the unknown. Jojo dreamed of developing a curriculum to train leaders, but that was unfamiliar territory. Not having experience with leadership development, he'd have to be willing to embrace an unfamiliar Dream and learn on the job.

Are you like Jojo, living an expired Dream? I speak to groups of businesspeople all over the country, and no matter the level of success of the people in the audience, something about that question always shakes up the room. I once spoke at a conference featuring some of the nation's most successful women of color. Even Michelle Obama was in attendance and scheduled to speak. The women at this conference were living great lives, but when I asked, "Are you living in an expired Dream?" I saw tears streak down many of their faces. These women knew instinctively that their great lives were keeping them from extraordinary lives. Most people try not to rock the boat when things are going great, but courageous Dreamers reach for more. Careerpreneur Esi Eggleston Bracey is one such Dreamer.

Prior to taking over as EVP and COO of North America Beauty and Personal Care at Unilever, Esi made the daring move of walking away from what many would consider the top—she was the president of Coty Consumer: Beauty. And what made her departure even more courageous is the fact that she didn't have her next job lined up. But with an international job for which she flew approximately 400,000 miles per year and that kept her away from her two kids for weeks at a time, Esi recognized that her life had gotten out of control, so she resigned. Esi says, "I'm someone who's never quit anything in life, ever." But she allowed herself a sabbatical during which she took time to learn about other people's careers and rediscover her purpose. After a lot of listening, to herself and to others, Esi figured out what she wanted to do next. Inspired by Unilever's commitment to positive social impact and sustainable living, she signed on. Esi explains that it's thanks to networking and discovering that she found her place with a company committed to "make an impact beyond counting up the money. My purpose-driven assignment was right there." Sometimes taking the right steps into an extraordinary life calls for first taking a step back.

LEVEL UP YOUR DREAMS OVER AND OVER AGAIN

DeVon Franklin is an excellent example of leveling up. A successful CEO Dreamer and film producer, DeVon shared with the Dream Project his stories of leveling up, then up again, and then up again. His first big step up came after he worked as an assistant to Will Smith's producing partner. Six years into his tenure at Overbrook Entertainment, he wanted a promotion that didn't happen, so he decided it was time to move up elsewhere. He scored interviews with CAA, but nothing came of them. Discouraged, he attended a service by Bishop T.D. Jakes, who preached a sermon called "Turn the Page," and he remembers that on that day he had a realization. "At the end of Deuteronomy, Moses died. When you turn the page, beginning of Joshua, God says, 'Get up. Your mourning time is over.' I realized I was mourning a job that was dead." So despite advice that he was "committing career suicide," DeVon made the radical decision to quit his job before moving on to a new one.

He explained, "Monday rolled around—my first day of unemployment, and I didn't know what to do with myself. And by five o'clock that day I got a call from Tracey Edmond's company. They offered me the same executive position that I was supposed to get at Will's company. So the job was already there, but I had to be willing to have faith and leave one thing before it would manifest. That's the stretch. I couldn't stretch for the new job while holding on to the old job."

DeVon would exercise this courage once again while in the middle of great filmmaking success. For almost two decades he'd wanted his own company, and he pushed for it at a time in his career that probably surprised many. "Fast-forward, I'm working at Sony Pictures for 10 years. *Heaven Is for Real* is a movie I worked on with Bishop T.D. Jakes. We made it for $50 million and got $30 million in the first five days. Two days after the movie opened, I was in the chairman's office and I quit. I told her 'I'm gone.' I said, 'I can't keep creating value for the company that I can't actually participate in. I came to Hollywood to start my own company, and if I stay here any longer, I'm going to miss it. So not only am I quitting, but I want to start my company and I want you to fund it.'" DeVon credits his faith in God for giving him the strength to be so bold. As he puts it, "The Bible says, 'You can go before the throne boldly,' so if I can go before God boldly, why can't I go before a man or woman boldly?" The Sony executive said yes.

And then DeVon leveled up *again*. Despite the fact that things were going very well between DeVon's new company, Franklin Entertainment, and Sony Pictures, two years after the alliance began, he felt strongly that it was once again time to move on. His agent arranged meetings with Fox Studios, but making the transition was complicated, and DeVon had to jump over several corporate hurdles on his way to exiting his relationship with Sony. One of those hurdles was that Fox couldn't negotiate with him while he was still in a deal with Sony, and another was that there were

Sony executives who didn't want him to leave. Little by little, the pieces fell into place, and in 2016 Franklin Entertainment signed a multiyear production deal with 20th Century Fox. DeVon advises Dreamers who are thinking about leveling up, "When God tells you to move, don't worry about who's in your way."

Dreamers, I want to remind you of a very important point about taking risks, leveling up, and working through phases of a Stretch. When you feel yourself wanting to make these kinds of changes, what often holds you back is fear. But as Elisa Camahort Page, Make-It-Happen Dreamer and BlogHer cofounder, reminds us, fear is relative, and if we articulate our fears in concrete rather than abstract terms, they become more manageable. She offers, "Don't be afraid of failure. Perhaps your fear is that when you fail, you'll have to move back into your mother's house—into your old bedroom—and start over and get a job. When you actually articulate your fear and make it concrete, it's usually not a tragedy. It's not going to result in your death or dismemberment. That was her advice: 'If it's not going to cause your death or dismemberment, you should probably go for it.'"

Now let's assess whether it's time for you to level up. Many of you *know* that you're staying loyal to the familiar. You know that you're settling for a great life, thus preventing an extraordinary one. If you're in the middle of a successful career or a profitable venture, it might make little sense to upset your situation. But I challenge you to shake up what's familiar and be willing to wobble, fall, and skin a knee in the process. In this week's exercises, let's level up.

EXERCISE 9.1

CHECKUP AND REFRESH

I know you have big Dreams that you've been exploring and expanding throughout The Stretch. You may have executed a big Dare like asking for a promotion, pitching your company's services, or petitioning a board. Let's pause for a moment to see how you feel about the profession and/or creative life you're pursuing now. As I've said, your Dream need not necessarily be the pursuit that earns your income, but you probably spend many hours a week doing your primary job, so it's worth a checkup to gauge your feelings about the path you've chosen. Satisfaction or dissatisfaction in any areas of your life affects the other areas, so it's a wonderful goal to try to keep all areas thriving.

In this exercise, we're going to examine:

- Inspiration
- Innovation
- Execution
- Collaboration

If you discover that your career's vital signs are weak in any one of these areas, consider the recommendations that follow.

Inspiration Check

	YES	NO
1. Are you excited to wake up and pursue your venture each day?		
2. Are you inspired by the tasks that you're currently executing?		
3. Would you like to tackle new roles and challenges within your current career position?		
4. Does the idea of working in this position indefinitely sound good to you?		
5. Do you generally feel energized or content after a day of working at your job?		

If you answered no to at least two of the five questions, consider the following changes:

- Wake up 20 minutes earlier than usual to meditate, pray, or work out to jump-start your creativity.
- Create shorter to-do lists to help you feel more accomplished at the end of the day.
- Volunteer to take on a new role or task within your organization.
- Take a training course to stay fresh within your field.

Innovation Check

	YES	NO
1. Are you actively creating new ideas within your career or venture?		
2. Are you continually looking for new ways to update your business's operations?		
3. Are you curious about how to develop a new product or add new technology into your business?		
4. Are you open to learning new skills?		
5. Are you being challenged to be highly creative?		

If you answered no to at least two out of the five questions in this section, consider the following changes:

- Stay current by reading business magazines such as *Forbes*, *Fast Company*, or *Inc.* to learn about the latest trends in business. Also be sure to read the trade publications that are specific to your industry.
- Learn new technologies related to your everyday work and take refresher courses to make sure you're up to speed on the ones you already use.
- Collaborate with your team members to solve a problem from different perspectives.
- Hang out with kids! You might be surprised what you'll learn by being near their curiosity.

Execution Check

	YES	NO
1. Are you encouraged to try different roles within your organization, company, or nonprofit?		
2. Are you actively seeking new opportunities for your venture?		
3. Are you performing tasks using the newest or best methods available?		
4. Have you assembled the best team possible to support you?		
5. Are you doing the day-to-day key duties of your job, role, or business in the same way you were in the last year? Five years? Ten years?		

If you answered no to at least two out of the five questions in this section, consider the following changes:

- Take a different route to your office. A new path can inspire you to execute things in a new way.
- Be open to learning from new people. They can help you see in new ways.
- Go low tech. Sometimes writing your ideas with pen and paper can help fire up your creativity.

Collaboration Check

	YES	NO
1. Are you actively working with others to breathe new life into your company?		
2. Do you have the right people in your network or tribe of support for this phase of your career or business?		
3. Do you find ways to include others in a project?		
4. Are you using each team member's best skills to execute your goals or the team's collective goals?		
5. Do you seek the opinions of others and incorporate their ideas whenever appropriate?		

If you answered no to at least two out of the five questions in this section, consider the following changes:

- Go back to Chapter Six to evaluate whether you have the right people on board for this season of your Dream.
- Use this week to collaborate with a member of your department or team you haven't worked with in at least six months.
- Consider hiring interns or temporary staff members to support your business endeavor. Sometimes fresh minds can pump new energy into your venture.
- Strive to work in more collaborative work environments like coworking spaces or coffee shops.
- Join meetups with like-minded peers to bounce ideas off one another.

EXERCISE 9.2

LEVELING UP INTO THE FUTURE

When I was a teenager, my driver's ed instructor taught me a concept he called "driving short and long." "Short" refers to everything immediately around the driver: the elements on the dashboard, the windshield, the car directly in front of you, etc. "Long" refers to the awareness of what's happening up ahead in the distance: a congested intersection, merge signs, road construction, or maybe even an approaching ambulance. When you "drive long," you see what's coming so you're ready to make the right decisions when you get there. The most successful Dreamers master the art of driving both short and long.

Early in your Stretch you developed the 90-Day Stretch Plan that you're currently working on and your one-year plan. In this exercise, I want you to drive long—three to five years ahead—and map a plan for that growth. Steve Jobs didn't launch a new iPhone two months after he envisioned it. Instead, he mapped future generations of Apple products years in advance. How do you intend to expand your Dream in the next three to five years? For example, perhaps you're a Make-It-Happen Dreamer on track to open a bakery this year. Your three-to-five-year vision could include expanding to multiple locations, catering corporate events, and offering dessert delivery service to restaurants.

Let's work through three simple exercise steps to help prepare you for the longer term of your Dream.

Step 1: Write Specific Answers for the Following Questions

- What will your title and roles be within the organization?
- What new services or products will you deliver?
- How much revenue will your business or career generate?
- How many streams of revenue will you have?
- How many people will you employ?
- Which networks of influence will you be part of as a result of this business endeavor?

- Who will be in those networks? Name positions and specific people when you can.

Step 2: Take Time to Daydream

Now that you've thought through some specifics, allow yourself time to daydream and be creative. Create a visual representation of this future, maybe in the form of a vision board or a digital collage that you can make into a screen saver. Keep this visual creation where you can see it regularly to remind yourself where you're headed.

Step 3: Take a Field Trip

Visit where you want to go. Do you have a way to experience a location where you imagine yourself in three to five years? For example, if your Dream is to run a bed-and-breakfast in the next three to five years, plan to visit some bed-and-breakfasts to study them and refine your vision for yourself as you learn.

EXERCISE 9.3

TAKING YOUR DREAM TO THE NEXT LEVEL

You're ready. You understand that great Dreamers look for ways to level up, and it's time for you to seek such challenges. Will that mean going after a new promotion? Developing an application? Finally leaving your corporate job to open your own business? We have three weeks left in The Stretch. Use the following chart to name big, bold moves that you'll make between now and the end of the program.

Leveling Up Your Dream

	Week 10	Week 11	Week 12
What bold move will you make?			
Describe the actions that will be required for you to make this bold move.			
How will this action support you in leveling up?			

YOUR 90-DAY STRETCH PLAN GOAL CRUSH REMINDER

Once again it's time to revisit the Stretch goals you created all those chapters ago. Are you on track?

You're officially wrapping up the Dare section, but not before spending time with a daring Careerpreneur Dreamer! This week I'm very excited to share with you the words of a dynamic woman who left a huge career position as president of Beauty and Design at Coty to walk into the unknown where she wrote her story of success, purpose, and impact on her own terms. She served as my tireless marathon coach, and I'm proud to call her a dear friend. She's currently the EVP and COO of North America Beauty and Personal Care at Unilever.

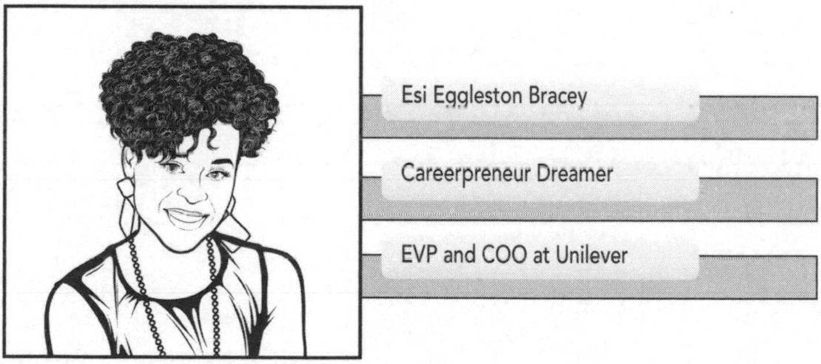

> "I didn't know what I wanted to do. So I did a training curriculum and did a purpose workshop. I also interviewed people and asked them who I was for them, not who I wanted to be. To find my true purpose, I listened to people tell me who I was to them."
>
> —Careerpreneur Dreamer **Esi Eggleston Bracey**

You may download this week's Dream All-Star training session at www.thebigstretchbook.com.

PART IV

DO

The Action, the Execution—the Doing

You're officially ready to enter the last phase of The Stretch, and at this point I want to make sure that the notion *to do* becomes second nature for you. I realize that you've been in action for the past nine weeks, and I salute you for that action. Now this section will present the tools to make sure that you are ***Do* Your Dreams** profitably, responsibly, and for the long term. I want to make sure you understand that *action* is part of the everyday life of a Dreamer.

Dreamers are creators who *do*
Dreamers are innovators who *do*
Dreamers are imagineers who *do*
Dreamers are believers who *do*
Dreamers are disrupters who *do*
Dreamers are visionaries who *do*
Dreamers are pioneers who *do*
. . . for the long term.

Doing is the difference between being a one-hit wonder and becoming a legend. Without doing, your Dream will end up just another lovely idea that might have become something fabulous if only someone had thought it was worth the effort. The difference between great and extraordinary is the extent to which you are prepared and willing to *do*.

A few years ago, I asked every speaker at the Dream Project the following question: "What is the most important element required to turn an idea into a success?" Again and again, these successful businesspeople stressed the importance of *taking action*. For CEO Dreamer Soledad O'Brien, an award-winning broadcast journalist, producer, and CEO of Starfish Media Group, part of *doing* means reviewing her work so that she can do better next time. She says, "A lot of people don't watch their clips. Every single thing I do, I watch. I go back over every interview and take notes. I came up with a system of finding three things that need work. I kept the list with me, and then I would cross off one, and then replace it with something else. So I was always working on three things."

Careerpreneur Dreamer Karmetria Burton, director of supplier diversity for Delta Airlines, has a simple formula for doing what it takes to move a Dream forward: a vision, a plan, and intention. After you've envisioned your Dream, she says, "you have to have the plan to know how you're going to do it, the steps you're going to take. And you need the intention to do it; show up *every day* to get it done."

And Sherri Daye Scott, Careerpreneur Dreamer and former director of marketing at JWT Atlanta, also says that making a Dream into a success is about making sure that you **do something every day to push the Dream forward, even if it's an action that seems somewhat insignificant in the big picture.** "It can be as small as going online and researching other businesses. It can be as easy as setting up a coffee date with somebody who's already doing that. It's a matter of doing something every day, no matter how small, that moves that dream forward."

One of my favorite quotes is by the seventeenth-century philosopher Baruch Spinoza: "All things excellent are as difficult as they are rare." I offer this quote to you, dear Dreamer, as a reminder that excellence comes from a great deal of *doing*, especially in the face of difficulty.

In this section, you'll work through the following exercises to help you move from a Dream to a Mega Dream:

Week 10: Dreaming Profitably and Responsibly

EXERCISE 10.1: Discovering Your Financial DNA

EXERCISE 10.2: Building a Strong Budget for Your Dream

EXERCISE 10.3: Creating Cash Flow That Works for Your Dream

Week 11: Dream Warriors Fight the Giants

EXERCISE 11.1: The Surrender Jar

EXERCISE 11.2: Dream Warriors Expect the Best and Prepare for the Worst

EXERCISE 11.3: Life Balance Tracker

Week 12: Leave Room for the Mega Dream

EXERCISE 12.1: Keeping Your Dream in Flight

EXERCISE 12.2: Your Mega Dream Wild Card

Your commitment to your Dream will be easily demonstrated—in your willingness to execute Nike's beautifully simple advice, *Just Do It*.

CHAPTER TEN

DREAMING PROFITABLY AND RESPONSIBLY

Week 10

I want to begin this section of The Stretch by acknowledging that, of course, earning money is extremely important. But I also want you, my Dreamers, to consider the importance of first focusing on the pursuit of your passion and true purpose—*then* turning that pursuit into a profitable venture.

For the first five years of my career, I prioritized income over everything else, which, as I've mentioned, led to great dissatisfaction. I happen to know that it's not rare for this kind of career start to be followed in time by a corrective "aha!" moment. Countless other Dreamers I've interviewed have reported similar awakenings. Lisa Price, CEO Dreamer and founder of Carol's Daughter, strongly advises to lead with passion rather than desire to make money, because if it's all about money, you won't last. She explains, "It takes too long to get money that you actually get to keep. Every time you get it, you have to give it away, because you need to grow."

When Make-It-Happen Dreamer and owner of Sweetie Pie's Robbie Montgomery decided to set off into the soul food business, it wasn't money or even outside support that motivated her. It was passion from within. In fact, she says that no one in her life was particularly excited about her opening a restaurant. "Nobody encouraged me," she says. "I was driven to have another success, as I had with my singing career, so I decided, 'Well,

I'm going to do this. I don't care if they don't encourage me.' To me, anything you love to do is your passion and worth taking a chance on."

FOR THE LOVE OF MONEY

Let's explore the connection between your passion and your earning potential.

Connecting Your Dreams to Money

Should your Dream be profitable? At what point should your Dream have the responsibility to financially take care of you and those who depend on you? All Dreamers have to consider these questions as we decide what kind of Stretch Plan will work for us and our families. In this chapter, I and other Dreamers will share what we've learned about going after our Dreams in a financially responsible way.

Now that you're in Chapter Ten of The Stretch, I encourage you to revisit the Dreamers' Risk Tolerance Assessment exercises from Chapter One and keep them in mind as we explore what it means to Dream profitably and responsibly. It will be good for you to be aware of your risk tolerance, as that also plays a role in what Dreaming responsibly may look like for you. Building upon those exercises, the following exercises from this chapter will help you understand your financial belief system and how those beliefs might influence your approach to business:

Week 10: Dreaming Profitably and Responsibly

EXERCISE 10.1: Discovering Your Financial DNA
EXERCISE 10.2: Building a Strong Budget for Your Dream
EXERCISE 10.3: Creating Cash Flow That Works for Your Dream

This part of The Stretch will give you practical tools and tips to develop a Dream that you'll not only love but be able to sustain.

Understanding Financial Limitations and Expectations

Perhaps you're a Hobby Dreamer and you love to paint. You Dream of one day showcasing your paintings at an art gallery. It would be unfair to saddle that goal with the immediate pressure of taking care of you and your family. This is not to say that you may not one day showcase your work in an art gallery or even sell it. But you should be able to do what you love just for the joy of it. I meet happy and fulfilled Hobby Dreamers every day, people who follow their passions outside of their income-earning work. I was recently in a board meeting with an executive from Sprint, Ramiro Crespo, whose eyes lit up, not when he talked about his work with Sprint, but when he talked about his adventures in the kitchen. He's such a good chef that he was chosen to compete on TV's *Iron Chef*, but he didn't saddle his hobby with the burden of supporting his life. Ramiro found a happy balance, working as an executive while always leaving time to nurture his love of cooking and taking that hobby to the highest places he can.

You might be a Make-It-Happen Dreamer who's never spent a day working for another person—a true hustler. If you are, it's important that your passions generate revenue as well. Make-It-Happen Dreamers often have a high tolerance for risk and the sacrifices that come with entrepreneurship. Bruce Wilkinson, Make-It-Happen Activist Dreamer and *New York Times* bestselling author of *The Dream Giver*, shared with the Dream Project that he was willing to risk a lot in the name of his Dream. He took an extra mortgage out on his house not once but twice. Loved ones of this kind of Dreamer often have to navigate risks as well, which Bruce illustrated when he told the Dream Project about how he and his wife proved they were all in. "Darlene and I mortgaged our house. We took all the money we had, more than once. We took all of our retirement—all the money we had—to do another Dream. Why? In my opinion, the Dream has to be more important than your security."

CEO Dreamer and BlogHer cofounder Lisa Stone weighed her willingness to take risks against her responsibilities as a single mother. With a one-year-old to support, she says, "I made calculated decisions about how to balance opportunity with my responsibilities." So for a time she "put the concept of becoming a bazillionaire to the side." As Lisa puts it, "I never sacrificed my son's education, his orthodontia, or his future."

Whichever kind of Dreamer you are, it's critical that you take an honest look at your financial needs as you strategize for your Dream. While there is more than one road to realizing Dreams, choosing one that fits your life can make the difference between a lot of joy and a lot of pain.

Understanding Your Financial Beliefs

I remember when it clicked for me that a piece of paper carries a lot of weight. When I was a child, my great-grandfather, Daddy Major, was my best friend. Growing up, we all lived in the same house, and each week when his paycheck arrived by mail, he took it to town to cash it. After his weekly trip to the bank, he returned with green folding paper, gave me one dollar, and told me to buy myself something from the store. That's when I first experienced the magic of commerce; in exchange for green paper, I could have gum, candy, and toys! In time, I learned that my great-grandfather's weekly giving ritual extended only to me, and I also learned that he wouldn't give or lend money to anyone else. These realizations began to form in me a scarcity belief about money that I would later have to reverse.

My earliest memories of money were also tied to stress. My grandfather on my mother's side, Coley Hearns, was hurt in an accidental fall that severely injured his spinal cord. We were told he would be confined to a wheelchair from then on, and although he was able to rehab and walk again, he never returned to work. It would be months before we collected disability checks, which left my entire family depending on my grandmother and mother for income. During this time, there was a lot of talk about not having enough money, and we'd get calls from bill collectors. I grew up with the fear that the next money crisis was just around the corner. For me, money was never connected to thoughts of ease or peace, and to this day I remain aware of my history when financial fear starts to creep back in. I combat fearful thoughts with positive self-talk to ensure that my decisions aren't grounded in fear. I'm careful not to design my life from a reactive position focusing on what I don't want to happen; instead, I choose to be proactive and go after what I *do* want.

Another pivotal moment that influenced my financial beliefs occurred when I was in first grade. My teacher gave our class a big assignment that further confused my already tangled feelings about money and work. She asked us to decide what we wanted to be when we grew up—she said we could be *anything*. I remember this assignment vividly, especially because my teacher told us to choose without considering whether the pursuit would make us any money. After giving the question a lot of thought, I decided that I wanted to be a maid. I loved cleaning and organizing, and I was extremely good at it, so I was thrilled to declare my plans to my grandmother. She'd been a maid, so I thought she'd be happy and proud to hear about my choice. But she yelped, "No! You cannot be a maid. You have to choose something else!" I was deflated as she explained that maids didn't earn "good" money. As young as I was, I remember thinking, *I guess it doesn't matter what you love to do as long as you make "good" money*. That was the day that I gave money the keys to drive my choices. For the next 20 years, earning potential would direct every major decision I made.

A great deal of what we learn about money and our worth is taught to us early on, either consciously or unconsciously. Remember Exercise 1.3, in which we examined your Dreamers' Ancestry? You were asked to think about the lessons you were taught about Dreams early in your life and how that affected your beliefs about following your own Dreams. This week, you'll examine how your past informed your perspective on money and finance and how that perspective is tied to your current approach to business and life.

T'S MONEY LESSONS

Coming up next, in the form of six short lessons, I'll share some of the "aha!" moments I've experienced about the relationship that money has to Dreams. I'm not a financial advisor, so I'll be including financial wisdom from some of my most trusted financial experts. Although I'm no financial wizard, I am someone who managed to turn a Dream into a profitable business entity. I'm proud that EGAMI has grown from earning a few thousand dollars in 2007 to generating millions each year. The company affords me a living and employs more than 20 other team members. The success of this Dream has also allowed our company to contribute millions in the form of grants, scholarships, and donations to other Dreamers, vendors, and communities of color. I've learned that it is indeed possible to Dream profitably and responsibly.

Lesson 1: Profit with a Purpose

I was 26 years old when I committed to living a life of purpose, and it's the best decision I've ever made. I owe great thanks to one of my professors for that shift in my thinking. While working on my MBA, I was given the assignment to examine the major driver behind my life choices, and this exercise opened my eyes to the degree to which I'd empowered money. Shortly afterward, I chose to let purpose guide my life.

In my earlier days, I wondered, if you're not prioritizing financial profit, where is the greatest profit to be found in the pursuit of a Dream? Motivational speaker, author, and Make-It-Happen Dreamer Jonathan Sprinkles says that profit is defined by what you offer someone else and that the rewards for yourself will follow. He suggests that we in business ask ourselves what customers, associates, investors, etc., would "expect to have in their life one week or one month after having done business with you. The profit or the value that you add to them will be reciprocated through them investing in your product or service. In other words, money chases value. When you add value, they in turn reward you "by doing business with you." I have to admit, of all the topics we've discussed at the Dream Project, the value of leading with purpose is easily one of my favorites.

Lesson 2: Demand Your Worth

In Chapter Three, I told you about my first job for which I was paid $25 per week to clean an adult daycare facility. That experience taught me that through service you can earn money for your work. Not long after that lesson, I learned to demand to be paid what I'm worth. My great-grandmother owned a farm, and she paid workers to do various jobs around the property. When I was nine years old, I convinced her that she should keep some of that money in the family by paying my Uncle Jerrold and me to help work the farm. She agreed, and I can easily say that that was some of the hardest work I've ever done. I tagged along with my great-grandmother, cleaning the chicken coop, picking peas, scrubbing the porches, and churning butter. Jerrold worked with my great-grandfather, plowing the fields and picking watermelons. For two weeks we did this painstaking work, and then came the big payday. I could barely wait! My great-grandmother gave us our pay in brown satchel bags, and when we got home, we sprinted through the doorway and turned the bags upside down to pour out the money. Jerrold's money fluttered out of his bag, but mine spilled out jingling. I was confused, then furious. I demanded that my mother drive me back to my great-grandmother's house. I stormed into her home screaming, "Grandma Ossie, you paid Jerrold more. Where's the rest of my money?" She turned away from the soup she was stirring on the stove and said, "Neshia, girls don't make what boys make."

"*Why*?" I demanded.

She said, "Boys have to do harder labor."

I demanded, "Put me in the field! I'll do the hard work, but I want to make the same amount of money as Jerrold."

She answered, "Neshia, I'm never going to pay you what a boy makes because the world will not pay you what a boy makes."

My next move was a bold one. With my hands planted on my hips, I stared straight into her eyes and barked, "Well, *I ain't* gonna work for you no more!" Then I turned and ran as fast as I could. My great-grandmother believed in the rod, and I would have been spanked for back talk, so I jumped into my mother's car and yelled, "Let's go! I'm never working for her again!" My mother was shocked—by my great-grandmother's words and even more so by my courage to stand up to the family matriarch. She said, "You're right. If she won't pay what you deserve, then she doesn't deserve your great work."

CEO Dreamer Harriette Cole, media strategist and founder of Dream Leapers, recalls, "When I started my business 20 years ago, a woman in the music industry said to me, 'Whatever price you're coming up with for your services, multiply it times three.'" She explains that pricing is difficult for many women because "we undervalue ourselves." Make-It-Happen Dreamer Luvvie Ajayi, *New York Times* bestselling author and digital strategist, says that pricing is difficult for any entrepreneur "because a lot of us aren't talking to each other, and everyone is operating from different frames of reference. The lack of communication means everyone's just pulling numbers out of the air. That's why it helps to have a community of people within your industry to bounce numbers off of." Remember, don't be shy. You must become your own champion, your greatest advocate. And the depth of your support for the enterprise that is you will be reflected in your willingness to demand what you're worth.

Lesson 3: As Your Dreams Grow, Your Knowledge Needs to Grow

Just as I established my worth with my great-grandmother, as my company grew, I learned to stand up for my worth as a business owner. In the first three years of my firm's existence, I was thrilled that we experienced steady growth, going from a company of one to a five-person team. Business was coming in, and the future looked promising. As a creative, I found it easy and comfortable to focus on sharpening our creative skills and creative service. But I didn't work as hard to understand the financial side of things, and, as a result, without a solid understanding of financials, I was delivering business but not profit (more on that later). I needed to put the right financial team in place to support our growing financial needs, and I needed to become much better informed about the financial aspects of my endeavors.

According to Careerpreneur Dreamer and *Black Enterprise* chief content officer Alfred Edmond Jr., seeking knowledge is a part of dreaming responsibly. He advises, "If you're not taking concrete action to gain knowledge, you're not dreaming responsibly. And you can't do that as an entrepreneur without understanding how to take care of your financial business." As you work your way up the ladder of expertise, remember that you must remain an eternally curious student.

Lesson 4: Read the Fine Print for Your Dream

Over the years, I've learned that contracts are critical in business. For most people, contracts aren't the fun part because they often cause confusion and lead to resistance. But they exist for several important reasons, including clarity and protection. They establish aspects of your agreement relative to deliverables, responsibilities, and payments. So if contracts are an issue of discomfort for you, you're going to need to make peace with this aspect of business.

Do you remember my reference in the previous chapter about EGAMI partnering with Fortune 100 brands at the Essence Music Festival each year? We learned a big lesson the first time we participated in one of those festivals. We were thrilled to work a platform with national visibility, knowing that completing this project successfully would elevate our company's portfolio and make us contenders for more of these kinds of large-scale, high-stakes projects. But in our excitement, we didn't pay close enough attention to certain elements of the contract, like the terms governing deliverables and payments. We were required to conceive, develop, and execute a concept for a four-day experience at the festival and to include big celebrities in our client's events. Work began in February and the festival was in July, but the contract's fine print stated that we would be paid around 120 days *after* the event. That's right—our company wouldn't be paid until *eight months* after we'd begun spending thousands and thousands for hotels, event execution, staffing, celebrities, flights, and more. Those kinds of expenses called for substantial liquidity. The lesson I won't forget: understand how to factor deliverables, outgoing expenses, and payment terms when structuring a deal, and negotiate based on what your business can handle.

Pay very close attention to the fine print of any agreement you're going to sign. What are you expected to deliver within the contract? When?

What will it cost you to deliver the product or service? Are you charging enough to cover the costs you'll incur? Are you charging enough to make money from the project? Do you have enough cash on hand to run your business and deliver the product before you get paid? Often, not understanding the fine print of your Dream's contract can mean the demise of a business, even a multimillion-dollar company. In your exercises this week, you'll learn some finance fundamentals and cash flow management tips to keep your Dream venture profitable.

Lesson 5: Employ the Right Financial Teams for the Right Dreams

In addition to reading the fine print, make sure that you have the right financial team on board. In Chapter Eight, I shared that I had to fire our entire accounting team. This was a difficult decision because those accountants had been with us from the beginning, but despite their desire to grow along with us, they didn't have the capacity. Our business model was project oriented, so we needed a project-based accounting team, but our accounting team at that time couldn't manage the necessary financial tracking. Realizing that I needed to replace my financial team helped me understand the importance of having a strong financial right hand. If you're not financially savvy, you need to work with someone who is in order to help you thrive and plan for growth. For EGAMI, that team member is our CFO, Cammillia Campbell. It would be impossible for me to list every important lesson I've learned from Cam, but I'd like to include two biggies here.

First, make sure you have an ethical accountant. In digging through EGAMI's finances, Cam discovered several transactions and charges that from a bookkeeping perspective were questionable and from a tax perspective bordered on unethical. Making *sure* that your accountant is both capable and honest can spare you devastating financial surprises.

Second, know the difference between accounting and finance. Cam helped us understand that there is a difference between a CPA with an accounting background and one with a finance background. Accounting professionals focus on the day-to-day flow of money in and out of the company, while finance professionals focus on all the financial aspects of the business from proposals, to contracts, to cash flow, to the financial health and wellness of the business. It took me about three years to grasp the significance of the differences in those disciplines. But I now understand the power of having accurate financial books and having a financial overseer. Together they result in a solid financial infrastructure.

Lesson 6: Financial Accountability Starts with You

If you're the founder, boss, and foundational Dreamer, the buck stops with you. That means that you not only have to be the first to sacrifice; you also need to know what's really going on within your business—no burying your head in the sand and trusting that things are being "handled." During EGAMI's expedited growth and after making a few substantial mistakes, I realized that I needed to look for the right financial partner. It wasn't until I hired Cam that I began to grasp just how little I understood about business finance.

My first couple of months with Cam were eye-opening; the more I learned, the more I understood how vulnerable we were. For example, our previous accountant cared primarily about reporting a very low number for our yearly income so we would pay the least possible in taxes. After auditing our books, Cam determined that some of his behavior was questionable, even unethical. The first change Cam made to EGAMI was to separate our business expenses from our personal expenditures. That meant that my husband, Mike, and I, the company's lead principals, needed to be on the payroll. Then she put us on an extremely strict budget. During a budget meeting, I practically laughed out loud at her proposed salaries. I said, "Cam, this salary is ridiculous. Why should I make so little?"

She said, "Teneshia, this is your reality check. This is what your small business can afford to pay you. If you want a big, plush package, you should go work for a global firm or go back to corporate work." That was an awakening, and one I needed. By not knowing enough about my own company's operations and bottom line, I'd been living with my head in the sand. No longer.

Not everyone is designed to be an entrepreneur. Not everyone is equipped to take on the level of risk associated with growing a business, nor does everyone have the discipline to budget and sacrifice for high-risk projects. If you want to live the American Dream of having a house, cars, vacations, and disposable income, that's great. But you have to be honest with yourself that going after a Dream might erase some of those material things from your picture. Mike and I dreaded the day we would transition to a small-business payroll. Our lavish dinners and shopping sprees were brought to a halt, and from that point on, a large portion of company earnings was reinvested in the business. We adapted. The financial reality of your Stretch will require you to make tough choices and select a path that works for you, your family, and your enterprise.

DREAMING FOR THE LONG GAME

In addition to mastering crucial money lessons, I also had to learn how to plan with a long-term view in mind, which includes considerations like buying health insurance, mapping a retirement plan, and contemplating exit strategies for down the road. Think of it as preparing to run a marathon. In anticipation of the pre-marathon anxiety that so many runners experience, the New York City Marathon organization sets up tents, running centers, and classes for a week before the marathon. My running mate and I went to one of the classes where a teacher spoke of the importance of choosing a mental strategy to conquer the race. We were offered two plans, and I chose the target plan, which broke the entire 26.2-mile run into the following three mental targets:

- **Mental Target 1**—10 miles: **Your training will take you through the process.** I repeated to myself, *I trained for over six months. The training will get me through it.*
- **Mental Target 2**—10 miles: **Dig in and run with your legs.** I told myself, *Dig in. Use your leg strength to push through these 10 miles.*
- **Mental Target 3**—6.2 miles: **Finish this race with all the heart in you.** I silently chanted, *Heart will get you through this. Do* ***not*** *stop.*

I knew that conquering my mind was going to be 99.9 percent of the challenge, so on race day, I kept repeating to myself, *10–10–6.2*. As we waited for the pop of the starting gun, my running mate asked, "Teneshia are you Okay? You look so serious!" I was concentrating on the first mental target. I was playing the long game.

Over the years, I've heard countless experts speak of the long game, and I took notes. Two of the commonly discussed ideas—ones that I'm ever conscious of—are to **Dream responsibly** and to **safeguard your Dream**. Each of these topics could warrant its own panel at a business conference, but for now let me share just a few thoughts on these two concepts that I consider to be exceptionally important for entrepreneurs.

Dream Responsibly

When I arrived in New York with two bags, a Bible, and a copy of *The Prayer of Jabez*, I had a few things going for me: I was young and tenacious and had few responsibilities. Today, my risk tolerance wouldn't be as great because I now have a marriage, a mortgage, and 20 full-time employees. Taking on more responsibilities will affect the details of your Stretch journey, a journey that should be mapped while taking into consideration anyone who depends on you, including your staff.

A few years ago, I attended an industry conference where the partners of one agency were hosting lavish customer dinners, giving out gifts, and popping countless bottles of French champagne. Everyone was having a blast. I remember thinking, *How in the world can we compete with that?* Fast-forward a few years—that company went under and its employees heard about it in the news. On the flip side, I can remember speaking with a high-profile executive who left his position at Target. He was very excited as he contemplated launching into his CEO Dream. After praying and talking through it, he said that although he was passionate about this direction, this wasn't the right time. His kids were heading to college soon, so he chose to accept another high-paying corporate position and tried to find one that aligned as closely as possible with his passions. He would leap at another time. So even if you have the heart of a maverick, take very seriously the responsibilities you've entered into, and if you have dependents, plan your Stretch with an eye on the quality of their lives.

Safeguard Your Dream

Over the years, I've also learned the importance of protecting this Dream that means much to me. That involves putting safeguards in place both for the present and for the long-term future. While building EGAMI, we had to make decisions about workers' compensation insurance, key person insurance, health insurance, life insurance, and liability insurance for our activations. We also needed to remain competitive while offering our employees solid benefits. We need the protection of insurance, and so do our employees.

I'll never forget the story that CEO Dreamer Shirleyann Robertson shared with the Dream Project about the importance of being covered. A financial planner for Prudential, Shirleyann was guided by a very astute mother who insisted that at the very beginning of her career Shirleyann buy health, life, and disability insurance. Then Shirleyann was in a car accident during which she was thrown from a car and after which she spent a year and a half learning how to walk and speak again. Thanks to very sound advice and protective action, the traumatic event didn't break her financially. She recalls, "Emotionally I was distraught, but financially I was un-impacted, and the reason was that I had that disability policy my mother made me get. The disability policy paid me an income which was only 80 percent of my salary. The savings account that my mother made me contribute to covered the additional 20 percent. I had a house, and I had a nurse who came to stay with me—covered because I had a long-term care policy. It gave me that time to truly heal and not to rush and try to get back to work. I could heal in a space of calm because I knew the paychecks were still coming in. That's why I always share that it's not 'if' something is going to happen, it's 'when.'"

For CEO Dreamer Lisa Price, safeguarding a business includes addressing the relatively misunderstood issue of intellectual property. Of many entrepreneurs, she says, "They've never registered the name of their company with the United States of America Trademark and Patent Office. They don't understand the difference between a patent, a trademark, a service mark, and a copyright. People think that because they own their domain name, that means that they're trademarked, and they're not. That can get you into so much trouble later. It's never an issue in the beginning when you're small. It becomes an issue as soon as you start to get notoriety, and it's very, very important." Remember, Dreamer, you don't have to be an expert in finance, law, intellectual property, accounting, or any of a list of several other specialties that affect running a business, nor will you have to manage these considerations by yourself. Enlist lawyers and advisors to help you protect your business. We don't like that we need these experts, and we don't like what they cost, but as Lisa Price reminds us, "You desperately need them because there are loopholes that only they understand. You have to get advice from them, or you could go under just from being ignorant."

So, Dreamers, with insurance, advisors, and sound decision making, I urge you to protect the precious endeavors you're giving so much of yourselves to. Let's be safe out there.

Building a Dream That Lives Beyond You

Another important consideration for entrepreneurs is whether you intend for your endeavor to go on indefinitely. Ask yourself where you see this Dream headed. Do you intend for it to outlive you? Do you have the right partners on board to continue the project after, for whatever reason, you're no longer involved? Do you have an exit strategy? Whether you intend to grow and then sell your business or intend for it to continue for generations, the early days of your Stretch should reflect these considerations. If you're clear about your intended direction from the beginning, you'll structure your business accordingly. For example, if you're growing a long-lasting enterprise that you plan to pass to the next generation, you'll want to start integrating family members into the business. If you're growing an enterprise to sell, you should stay aware of what makes the business the most valuable and when might be a good time to sell it. Different goals require different strategies for success.

For Procter & Gamble's CMO chief brand officer Marc S. Pritchard, a long-term Dream is about "significance versus success." One of Marc's priorities is to make sure that he makes a significant impact on the world and that the effects of his work outlast him. While on vacation and reading *Halftime*, by entrepreneur and author Bob Buford, Marc began to reassess what it meant to be halfway through his life, and he had an epiphany that solidified his purpose. He knew then that he wanted to focus on using his "skills, experience, and voice in advertising and marketing as a force for good, particularly focused on gender equality, on racial equality—on really equality of all kinds." Marc says that this pursuit became his "true purpose, his destiny."

In this chapter, we've covered a lot of material relative to financial planning, safeguarding, and looking forward to the future. That's because I want you to develop a solid plan that ensures your venture's financial vitality for years to come. The exercises that follow will give you the tools to develop a working budget and plan for your cash flow. Let's begin.

EXERCISE 10.1

DISCOVERING YOUR FINANCIAL DNA

In the beginning of the book, you explored your past; in particular, what you were taught about Dreaming. In this exercise, you'll explore your beliefs about finance. Discovering your underlying money-based beliefs is essential for creating a solid financial foundation for your Dream. The Financial DNA Questionnaire is designed to help you uncover your family's beliefs about money and how these beliefs continue to affect you and your Dream now. Answer each question as fully as possible. Share your thoughts and your beliefs with one of your Dream Champions.

Financial DNA Questionnaire

1. How did your family's beliefs about money affect your major life decisions, like choice of college and major, career moves, etc.?

   ____

2. How have your family's beliefs about money affected your career choices?

   ____

3. Have your family's beliefs about money led you to want to earn as much as possible?

   ____

4. Which beliefs from your family continue to inform your position relative to money, as in, were you taught to always save? To spend whatever you want now? To never lend?

   ____

5. Which beliefs from your family might derail your earning potential?

   ____

EXERCISE 10.2

BUILDING A STRONG BUDGET FOR YOUR DREAM

Learning how to develop a budget is essential for creating realistic expectations for a new business, venture, or nonprofit, regardless of which kind of Dreamer you are. As you develop your budget, it's important to keep the following considerations in mind:

Overall Factors

- Generate a budget that includes realistic expectations for your venture.
- Begin by developing a quarterly budget.
- Create room in your budget for unexpected expenses.

Income Projections

Your income projections should include the following line items:

- Income expected from existing contracts
- Income expected from projected new contract awards

Expense Projections

Your expenses could include line items such as:

- Rent or mortgage
- Utilities
- Payroll
- Federal and state taxes
- Insurance (health, facility, vehicle, disability, workers' comp)
- Dues and subscriptions
- Training and conferences
- Marketing expenses
- Office supplies

Read the sample below and then use the blank template to develop a quarterly budget for your venture. If your expenses exceed your revenue, think about ways you can balance your budget by reducing your spending for the next quarter.

Sample Quarterly Dreamer's Budget: Start-Up IT Developer

	January	February	March	Total
Client 1	$0	$7,500	$3,000	$10,500
Client 2	$2,500	$2,500	$2,500	$7,500
Client 3	$1,250	$1,250	$2,500	$5,000
Client 4	$0	$0	$5,000	$5,000
TOTAL				**$28,000**

OPERATING EXPENSES	January	February	March	Total
Coworking Space	$1,000	$1,000	$1,000	$3,000
Office Supplies	$0	$0	$500	$500
Marketing/Social Media	$200	$200	$750	$1,150
Virtual Assistant	$250	$250	$450	$950
TOTAL EXPENSES				**$5,600**
TOTAL INCOME				**$28,000**
QUARTERLY REVENUE				**$22,400**

Your Quarterly Dreamer's Budget

	January	February	March	Total
Client 1				
Client 2				
Client 3				
Client 4				
TOTAL				

OPERATING EXPENSES	January	February	March	Total
Expense 1				
Expense 2				
Expense 3				
Expense 4				
Expense 5				
Expense 6				
TOTAL EXPENSES				
TOTAL INCOME				
QUARTERLY REVENUE				

EXERCISE 10.3

CREATING CASH FLOW THAT WORKS FOR YOUR DREAM

To paraphrase finance expert Shirleyann Robertson, you need to understand, down to the penny, what it costs to run your office and what it costs to run your personal life. Complete the following Cash Flow Questionnaire. Then read the sample, and in the blank template that follows, develop your own Yearly Dreamer's Cash Flow Statement.

Dreamer's Cash Flow Questionnaire

1. How much cash do you expect to generate each month, quarter, and year?

   ____

2. What are the standard payment terms for your contracts? 30, 60, 90 days?

   ____

3. How much cash will you spend each month, quarter, or year per client?

   ____

4. How much cash will you need for labor, support staff, and contractors?

   ____

5. How much cash will you need for credit lines, loans, and investments?

   ____

Yearly Cash Flow Statement for Building Equipment Supplier

	For the Year Ending	12/31/XX
	Cash at Beginning of Year	15,700
Operations		
Cash receipts from customers		693,200
Cash paid for		
	Inventory purchases	(264,000)
	General operating and administrative expenses	(112,000)
	Wage expenses	(123,000)
	Interest	(13,500)
	Income taxes	(32,800)
Net Cash Flow from Operations		**147,900**
Investing Activities		
Cash receipts from		
	Sale of property and equipment	33,600
	Collection of principal on loans	
	Sale of investment securities	
Cash paid for		
	Purchase of property and equipment	(75,000)
	Making loans to other entities	
	Purchase of investment securities	
Net Cash Flow from Investing Activities		**(41,400)**
Financing Activities		
Cash receipts from		
	Issuance of stock	
	Borrowing	
Cash paid for		
	Repurchase of stock (treasury stock)	
	Repayment of loans	(34,000)
	Dividends	(53,000)
Net Cash Flow from Financing Activities		**(87,000)**
Net Increase in Cash		**19,500**
	Cash at End of Year	**35,200**

Yearly Cash Flow Statement for Your Dream

	For the Year Ending	
	Cash at Beginning of Year	
Operations		
Cash receipts from customers		
Cash paid for		
	Expense #1	
	Expense #2	
	Expense #3	
	Expense #4	
Net Cash Flow from Operations		
Investing Activities		
Cash receipts from		
	Expense #1	
	Expense #2	
	Expense #3	
Cash paid for		
	Expense #1	
	Expense #2	
	Expense #3	
Net Cash Flow from Investing Activities		
Financing Activities		
Cash receipts from		
	Expense #1	
	Expense #2	
Cash paid for		
	Expense #1	
	Expense #2	
	Expense #3	
Net Cash Flow from Financing Activities		
Net Increase in Cash		
	Cash at End of Year	

YOUR 90-DAY STRETCH PLAN GOAL CRUSH REMINDER

Goal Crush Reminder! Have another look through your 90-Day Stretch Plan. You probably have it memorized by now! Keep at it—hitting these goals is extremely important for the success of your venture.

Now that you've started to explore what it means to Dream responsibly and profitably, let's hear from a Dreamer who's faced her share of financial challenges. In a reaction to her own company's cash flow problems, this woman cofounded NOW Corp., a B2B payment company that enables small businesses to be paid immediately, using a system that functions like accepting a credit card. Previously, this CEO founded and served as chief executive officer for Nourish, a children's healthy food company. She earned a BS in aerospace engineering with highest honors from Georgia Tech and an MBA from Harvard.

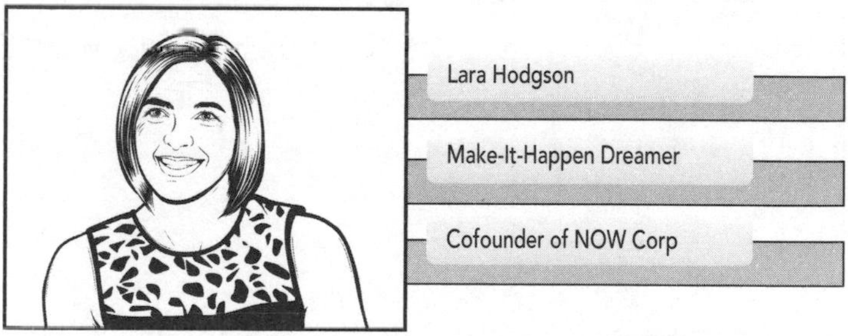

"Look at the glass ceiling this way. If I'm looking at a glass window, and I'm totally focused on the tree on the other side of the glass, I don't even see the glass. If I refocus my eyes on the window, the tree becomes blurry. I'm focused on what's in my way. Forget about the glass that might be there, because if it's there, you're going to walk through it anyway. If I think, *Oh no, there's glass in*

front of me, I've totally lost sight of my Dream. Now I'm worried about the glass, and it's going to whack me in the head."

—CEO DREAMER **LARA HODGSON**

And this week I'm pleased to offer *bonus* bonus content! Cammillia Campbell is a Careerpreneur Dreamer and serves as EGAMI's chief financial officer and chief operations officer. She's an extraordinary executive, transformational leader, and financial problem solver. Cammillia was named one of *The Network Journal*'s "40 Under Forty" for its 2016 class of achievers and was selected as a member of the *Forbes Magazine* Executive Financial Council. For financial tips from Cam, please visit TheBigStretchBook.com and download "What Would Cam Do? Business Finance Tips from a Seasoned Expert," Cam's invaluable financial "cheat sheet" to guide your Dream's finances.

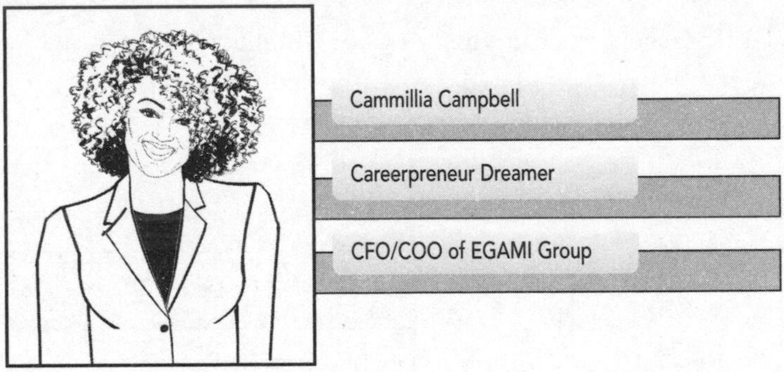

You may download this week's Dream All-Star training sessions at www.thebigstretchbook.com.

CHAPTER ELEVEN

DREAM WARRIORS FIGHT THE GIANTS

Week 11

Have you ever watched an intense boxing match? Often there's a point in the fight when both boxers are completely spent. They sway and stumble; their knees buckle; their punches look slow and weak. The fighters are evenly matched, fit, and prepared, so in the exhausted final moments, you can almost feel that the one left standing will be the one with the most heart. What does this kind of heart look like? Is it courage? Tenacity? Unbreakable determination? I would say that real heart is all of these, and you know it when you see it.

The human spirit is remarkable. There is something deep in all of us that makes us able to withstand extraordinary challenges and hardships. It is the quality that makes us Dream Warriors. You'll need this fighter's spirit as you embrace The Stretch as a lifestyle. There are many dragons you'll need to slay to protect your Dream: self-doubt, criticism, lack of resources, rejection, and fear, just to name a few. Take comfort knowing that centuries of Dream Warriors have faced such challenges and have emerged victorious. Let me introduce you to a few such Warriors who fought the obstacles that stood between them and their Dreams:

- There was once a high school student who was cut from his basketball team. He cried alone in his room, but inside this young boy lived a fighter. He fought and pushed past obstacles and went on to win six NBA championships, five NBA MVP titles, and four NBA All-Star titles. **Meet Dream Warrior Michael Jordan.**

- As a teenager, this Pakistani girl was shot by a Taliban gunman in retaliation for her activism. She recovered and went on to become a world-renowned activist in the fight for the right to education. She is also an author, Nobel Peace Prize winner, and an inspiration to people around the world. **Meet Dream Warrior Malala Yousafzai.**
- This young woman was demoted from her job as a news anchor and told she wasn't fit for television. She went on to define success her way, building an entertainment enterprise and becoming North America's first black multibillionaire. She's been called the greatest black philanthropist in American history, and her net worth is estimated at $2.9 billion. **Meet Dream Warrior Oprah Winfrey.**
- This man was fired from a newspaper for lacking imagination and the ability to generate original ideas. He redirected his energy into creating experiences that would spark the world's imagination. He was the creator of Mickey Mouse and the winner of 22 Academy Awards. **Meet Dream Warrior Walt Disney.**
- While this 13-year-old was surfing, a 14-foot tiger shark bit off most of her left arm. By the time she made it to a hospital, she'd lost 60 percent of her blood. One month later she was back on her surfboard, and two years after that she began to place in and even win major surf competitions. **Meet Dreamer Warrior Bethany Hamilton.**
- This author's book proposal was rejected by 27 publishing houses. Lucky for the children of the world, he kept writing; if he hadn't, the world might never have met the Cat in the Hat. **Meet Dream Warrior Theodor Seuss Geisel—Dr. Seuss.**
- This rapper was turned down by every major record label in the industry. He was relentless and eventually offered to pay Def Jam Records to take a chance on him. He has now recorded 13 albums, 10 of which debuted at number one on the Billboard charts. And he's the winner of 21 Grammy Awards. **Meet Dream Warrior Jay-Z.**

- When this girl was 15, she witnessed her father being shot and killed by her mother in an act of self-defense. When she was a young adult, a knee injury ended her would-be ballet career. She went on to become the first South African actress to win an Academy Award. **Meet Dream Warrior Charlize Theron.**
- She wanted to be an attorney, but her low LSAT score dashed this hope. By the age of 25 she began to develop a hosiery idea that became Spanx and made her a billionaire. In 2013 she became the first female billionaire to join Bill Gates and Warren Buffet's "Giving Pledge," a commitment through which the world's wealthiest people donate at least half of their wealth to charity. **Meet Dream Warrior Sara Blakely.**
- This man was devastated and depressed after being ousted from the company that he founded. He bounced back to lead the world's most progressive technology company, Apple. This visionary pioneered many of our modern-day communication technologies. **Meet Dream Warrior Steve Jobs.**

UNLEASH THE DREAM WARRIOR IN YOU

Those are some very well-known Dream Warriors. But there are Dream Warriors who surround you every day, too. The next time you grab a bagel from the local bakery, know that you could be standing in the realized goal of a Hobby Dreamer who pushed past the barriers of low self-esteem to open her Dream side business. When you drop off your clothes at the local cleaners, you may be experiencing the realized Dream of a CEO Dreamer who tapped into his inner warrior and courageously left the safety of his 9-to-5 job to keep a family business alive. The next time you're working out with your trainer, you might be in the presence of a Make-It-Happen Dreamer who weathered financial storms until he could establish a base of loyal clients. Keep your eyes open for the accomplishments of Dream Warriors all around you to see what you can learn from them. This chapter features stories and lessons of Dream Warriors. I hope you'll be inspired by their battles and will add some of their weapons to your own arsenal. And the exercises featured in this chapter will help prepare you to overcome obstacles, as all Dream Warriors must.

Week 11: Dream Warriors Fight the Giants

EXERCISE 11.1: The Surrender Jar
EXERCISE 11.2: Dream Warriors Expect the Best and Prepare for the Worst
EXERCISE 11.3: Life Balance Tracker

FINISHING STRONG

In the previous chapter, I mentioned that I chose the 10-10-6.2 mental strategy to help me to the finish line of the New York City Marathon. People had warned me that making it through the final 6.2 miles wasn't about training; it was about digging deep. By the time I hit mile 20, there were moments when I was so tired that I thought I couldn't possibly execute even five more strides, but I kept saying, out loud, "You will *finish*!" I even hit myself in the chest and screamed, "You will *not* quit!" And I didn't. During your Stretch, you'll have to give yourself the same reminder: do *not* quit. When running toward your Dream, when it all starts to feel like too much, remind yourself why you're running. Who is counting on you to finish the race? Which version of yourself is waiting to be born? In what miraculous ways will lives change once this Dream is alive and thriving? Remember, you're not just running for you. Other people need you to complete this race. When you're burned out, nothing feels easier than the idea of stopping, so do whatever it takes to finish strong. You *must* now finish strong, even though you're weary; if you don't summon your strength to finish strong, you'll diminish and maybe even extinguish all the miraculous work you did when you were feeling fresh.

The more you work, learn, and reach out to others on the road to achieving your goal, the more battle stories you'll hear. Let them inspire you. Let them fire you up to win the confrontations you'll eventually face. Through countless emotional, social, financial, and physical battles, true Dream Warriors fight, rebound, learn, and add Warrior Weapons to their arsenals. Let's hear from some of those Dream Warriors and see if you can add some of their weapons to your own cache.

Warrior Weapon 1: Be Patient

Make-It-Happen Dreamer Issa Rae knows that a big Dream calls for patience. The battle she endured on her way to landing on her hit show *Insecure* called for a lot of staying power. She told the Dream Project, "Honestly, I have been at this since 2006, and my business didn't start growing until 2011—that was five years of perseverance and patience. When something doesn't go according to plan, you may feel inclined to go to Plan B or to take shortcuts. And that just won't work. **The top qualities that an entrepreneur needs to have are patience, perseverance, and flexibility.**"

Hang in there. Don't let overnight success fantasies fool you about how much work really goes into a great success story. CEO Dreamer Doreen Rainey, SVP of Steve Harvey Global, reminds us of how inaccurate the term *overnight success* really is. She says, "Overnight successes take about 10 years." She advises Dreamers, "Make sure that you have a place you can go when you're feeling a little low, so that you can be encouraged and brought back up." Slow and steady wins the race.

Warrior Weapon 2: Be Prepared to Fight

Over the course of reaching your goals, you'll have to fight several obstacles you won't anticipate, but there are many relatively common battles that are somewhat easy to see coming, like battles against the old ways of doing things, battles against naysayers, and even battles against yourself. No matter what, be prepared to fight back. CEO Dreamer and founder of Harlem's Fashion Row Brandice Daniel remembers fighting back against her own self-doubt. "For me, so many times it's been about fighting the fear that comes up within myself. And the doubt. And making sure that

I never get to a place where I start questioning if this is going to happen. I try to always have my self-talk language directed toward what I want to happen. In other words, I try to make sure that my language is following my Dream, not questioning it."

Former CEO of Johnson Publishing and CEO Dreamer Desirée Rogers had to fight back against disease. After being diagnosed with breast cancer, she says that she made herself battle ready. "You say, 'This is going to be a battle in my life and I'm going to win it.' I never even considered not winning. I call it my 'Warrior Mode.' If I've got to get something done, I am a warrior. I have my spear, my gun, my axe—whatever I need to get through."

CEO Dreamer and cofounder of NOW Corp Lara Hodgson says that the first battle is with yourself. "It's your negative self-speak. It's the worry. It's going to bed at night thinking, *What if this goes wrong*? I think we probably kill our own dreams more than anybody else does. We like to talk about these glass ceilings, when in reality I think a lot of us have sticky floors. The next time you have to fight for your dream, don't be surprised if you have to fight yourself first." The second battle, she says, is with people who care about you. "There are all these people around you who aren't necessarily negative, but they're worrisome. They want you to do what you are good at *that*. You say, 'But no, my dream is over *here*.' They mean well because they're looking out for you, but at the same time, I think what a lot of people don't realize is what you're good at and what you're passionate about may not be the same thing. I think you have to fight yourself, then fight your closest friends and family who, without meaning to, can be the naysayers." And "the biggest giant you have to fight," says Lara, "is the way it's always been done. Be okay with being told 'no.' Be okay with people telling you it's a dumb idea."

Dreamers, whether it's against old ideas, other people, or even yourself, know that you're going to have to be ready to suit up.

Warrior Weapon 3: Let Your Competitor Do the Talking

A lot of successful people are used to having people listen to them, and so quite often they forget the importance of listening, if they ever knew it.

Lara Hodgson listens more than she talks, and in doing so she establishes credibility while quietly amassing invaluable information about her competitors. She says, "I think the greatest fighting technique is to know your competitors more than they know you. The first thing you do is listen, and then you ask a really good question." She's used to being underestimated, and she finds that's an advantage. Lara recalls going into a meeting to introduce NOWAccount to a banker who immediately began to explain—to Lara Hodgson, businesswoman and *professor of finance*—what lending is all about. "Before I got the first sentence out of my mouth, he said, 'Let me teach you Lending, 101.' I knew he was about to dig himself a hole, so I listened and I smiled, and at the end, I knew everything about him, and he knew nothing about me. Two meetings later, I told him I couldn't make a later meeting because I had to teach my class at Harvard Business School. His face was white as a ghost as he realized that he had been a complete idiot because he wasn't willing to listen and learn." Lara advises not to enter a fight as most men do, by coming in swinging. She says, "If you let the other person throw all the punches first, they lose all their energy. They've shared everything they have, and now you know what you have to do."

Warrior Weapon 4: Sign on for Sacrifice

Quite often, people see only the glitzy results of successful people's determination. They see influential, wealthy people being interviewed and adored, and it all looks so easy. It's not easy. One thing that I've learned from great Dreamers is that success comes at a cost called "sacrifice." In the pursuit of a Dream, you might have to say no to other opportunities including financial comfort, travel, time with loved ones—the list of things you might have to give up, temporarily or even permanently, can seem endless.

Desirée Rogers says that the road to success is a lonely one and that often a social life suffers. "Sometimes it's a lonely journey. You have to be really passionate, not emotional, about whatever it is you're doing and say, 'I am going to dedicate my full attention to this. Yes, my friends are over at the bar, but I have to stay late because I have a proposal due in the morning.' Those trade-offs are what I really think create the leaders. Some people aren't going to be as successful because they're not going to make the hard sacrifices."

Try to view your sacrifices as investments. I knew a guitar player who often spent several hours on a Friday or Saturday night practicing guitar while his buddies were at parties and bars having a blast. He knew he was missing out, but, thinking long term, he didn't mind because he viewed his sacrifice as an investment. He told me, "Tomorrow I'll have eight more hours of expertise under my belt. They'll have hangovers."

Warrior Weapon 5: Make Failure Your Friend

Anyone who has followed the careers of leaders, celebrities, successful businesspeople, etc., has heard about the value of failure. Unfortunately for most of us, the value of the failing—the lessons it can teach, the tenacity it can cultivate—isn't part of most early education curricula. Imagine how different failure might seem to us if early on we'd been taught to view failures as poorly dressed successes. I've found that the winners in the world are those who reposition failure in their minds. For them it's a perspective shift, a language choice.

Make-It-Happen Dreamer Daymond John is proud of the fact that he fails every day. He says, "I don't have a fear of failing. I have a fear of not starting. I have a fear of not continuing. I have a fear of not exploiting every single aspect of whatever I'm venturing into."

Make-It-Happen Dreamer Robbie Montgomery of Sweetie Pie's knows about choosing to view her failures in new ways. When Miss Robbie was a girl, her aunt used to say, "Joy cometh in the morning." Miss Robbie says, "I didn't understand that, but as I've gotten older, I do. Today I could be happy; tomorrow it could be raining; the next day the sun is out again. So I take my difficult moments and think positively and tell myself that a better day is coming." She's also a fan of simply redefining the experiences that go poorly. To her, a failure is another step toward getting it right. She says, "I don't call it 'failure.' I call it 'moving to the next thing.'" Be like Miss Robbie. Look your failures straight in the eye and give them new names.

Warrior Weapon 6: Expect the Unexpected

How are you supposed to expect something that's unexpected? To me the expression "expect the unexpected" is really about a willingness to pivot, to adapt to issues that you weren't planning on. I mean, what are the chances that the road to realizing your Dream will look precisely as you've envisioned it? That Yellow Brick Road might look smooth and easy to navigate, but at any turn you might face an angry flock of flying monkeys. (The good news is that along the way, you're also likely to meet helpful travelers who will teach you about things like courage and heart.)

Sometimes the unexpected comes in the form of a frustration that you can resolve with a conversation. Sometimes it's a setback that you can overcome with a little time and an adjustment or two. But what if the unexpected is life-changing, as with a medical hardship or a recession? Patrice Washington is a CEO Dreamer and the CEO of Seek Wisdom, Find Wealth, a personal finance consulting firm, who experienced both of those massive setbacks at the same time. To prevent giving birth prematurely, she ended up in Cedars-Sinai hospital on 10 weeks of bed rest. Patrice had become extremely successful in real estate, earning seven figures annually. Then, as her hospital stay led to over $400,000 in medical bills, the housing market crashed, and her stress began to put her health and her unborn baby's health in jeopardy.

She recalls, "My doctor came in one day telling me, 'If you don't stop stressing out, you're going to leave this hospital with no baby.' I realized that I'd spent my entire life chasing money, and I went from a seven-figure business to scraping up change to feed my daughter." She left California for Atlanta to rebuild her life with the help of relatives. She says, "I'm a poster child for financial loss." A major lesson Patrice learned about expecting the unexpected has to do with insurance. As soon as she could afford to, she bought a $50,000 policy, because, she says, "That's what I could afford at the time. I've rebuilt to now have multiple six-figure businesses, and my husband has a seven-figure business. What was a $50,000 policy is now $4 million or $5 million worth of different types of insurance." Patrice now expects the unexpected by being fully insured and by regularly consulting with her financial planner. "Don't wait until you think you have it together to have the conversation to start planning for the future," she advises. "Seek a financial planner and advisor now."

Warrior Weapon 7: Find Ways to Turn Your Pain into Purpose

It's inevitable—life is destined to hand you lemons. When this happens, be ready to make lemonade, and remember that even the sourest lemons can offer a redeeming opportunity, if you just look for it. Tarana Burke, founder of the #MeToo movement, offers a dramatic example of how to turn something terrible into something valuable. Throughout her childhood and teen years, Tarana was a victim of sexual abuse and rape. As part of her recovery, she reached out to other such victims in an effort to help them thrive and to increase awareness of the prevalence of rape and sexual assault in our society. And then she created #MeToo, the effects of which have been heard around the world—in countless businesses and other organizations, on sports teams, in schools, and in homes. Thanks to Tarana's courage to shift her pain to purpose, women and men around the world feel more heard than ever, and positive change is happening. When you experience pain, do your best to turn it into purpose.

Warrior Weapon 8: Know When to Surrender

At some point, all Dream Warriors realize that they can't do it all. You have to find people you can trust, and you have to be willing to, at least somewhat, loosen your grip on the reins. I'll never forget the day that I came very close to calling it quits on my Dream to build EGAMI. It was in the midst of a long season of difficulty. In Chapters Nine and Ten, I shared the rookie mistake I made because I didn't understand the importance of cash flow. That mistake had ripple effects with waves so big that I thought they would wash away my Dream. I have a theory that when a small business is close to failure, a cyber alert is sent to all banking institutions and creditors that the business is stretched to the limit. Instead of my banks stepping up to save the day, my business lines of credit were suddenly decreased.

I found myself on the phone with my banking institutions and creditors demanding, "*Why* did you decrease our credit line? We pay it to zero each month. We've *never* been late. We established our credit for moments like this!" I heard answers like, "Mrs. Warner, we are sorry, but we are concerned that your company is too strained. We've decided to minimize our risk." Looking back with a clear head, I understand why our lending partners took steps to protect themselves. But in the midst of the battle, it just felt like another blow.

My worry during this season of difficulty was made even worse when my accountant called to say that unless one of our clients paid us in the next day or two, we wouldn't be able to meet our payroll. This was rock bottom. What would I tell my employees? They trusted our company, and they trusted me. I went outside and cried aloud to God, "*How* could you give me this Dream and have it all come to *this*? I *trusted* you." In the midst of the cry, I began to feel strongly that it was time for me to let go of my control of EGAMI Group. I had done all that I could, and it was time for me to surrender. In that moment, I said a prayer that I've heard often, "Thy will be done." And on that same day I experienced the miracle of Cammillia Campbell calling to ask if I needed help with anything. I felt as if God had sent an angel my way. Cam ended up helping us move through that difficult time, and, as you know, later became the CFO who would push EGAMI into the black. That year, EGAMI tripled its revenue.

CEO Dreamer and author of *God Is My CEO* Larry Julian says that some of the best advice he's ever gotten was about surrendering control. Trying to get his book written and sold was, he says, "a seven-year journey of failure and rejection." He was just about to give up and told his mentor that he was done. His mentor read from the Bible and asked Larry to consider whether his Dream journey was about only himself. "He said, 'If this journey is just about you, you may want to quit. But if this is really your calling and purpose, if this is what you were called to do, then you may want to continue.' I remember it was a defining moment in my life, and I made the decision to go on, no matter what. For one year, I lived this—if you would—surrender, meaning I'm not going to give up the book. I'm going to keep doing what I'm called to do and not worry about finding a publisher. That's beyond my control. One year later, I found a publisher, and then, by the grace of God, it became a bestseller."

Sometimes when you're about to throw in the towel, you're actually on the edge of achieving your wildest Dreams (I called these Mega Dreams; more on that in our final chapter). I'm grateful to say that in the decade-long history of our firm, we have never missed payroll. Thanks to God, the miracles keep flowing. God saved my Dream and helped me discover the Dream Warrior's power of surrender.

Remember, it is not "if" a battle is coming, it's "when." I've yet to meet a Dreamer who's been exempt from having to fight giants. So steel yourself. Keep working your warrior muscles. Dreamers, are you ready for some exercises? Let's do it.

EXERCISE 11.1

THE SURRENDER JAR

As a Dreamer, you'll be faced with roadblocks that are beyond your control. One symbolic way to let go of the worries that accompany such roadblocks is to keep a jar on your desk or beside your bed at night labeled "surrender." Before you leave your office each day or before you close your eyes at night, if there's anything still troubling you, write it on a small piece of paper and drop it into your Surrender Jar. I know this sounds a little "out there," but try it. Giving yourself permission to surrender your fears at the end of the day can help you release your worries and replace your anxiety with peace.

Specifically, during these last two weeks of The Stretch, think about three things within your Dream that you can let go of. At the end of The Stretch, revisit your Surrender Jar and give yourself the joy of looking back through some of those small sheets of paper and recognize that indeed things fell into place.

Take a few minutes for yourself and write down all of your troubles on individual pieces of paper and place them in the jar. You can revisit and add to this jar whenever you need.

EXERCISE 11.2

DREAM WARRIORS EXPECT THE BEST AND PREPARE FOR THE WORST

The best time to prepare for a crisis is before it happens, so in this exercise you'll explore some worst-case scenarios that you can imagine crashing down around your Dream. There will be many occasions that make you want to give up and go back to your "easy" life. Don't let these take you by surprise. Let's look at some common Dream enemies and ways you can arm yourself to battle them.

Embracing Your Big Fears

You've heard this over and over, and it is indeed true: failure throughout the Dreaming process is inevitable. From a new business pitch that goes wrong to losing it all and having to rebuild, there will be failures. So relative to the Dream you're currently working on, what are your biggest fears? Let's make a short list of your biggest fears below, and for every fear let's offer a possible mitigating action. Here's the good news: nothing you list will warrant your quitting.

Big Fear: Losing your job

Mitigating Action: Keep a list of jobs of interest and review it once a quarter. Update the list regularly.

Big Fear: Company going bankrupt

Mitigating Action: Go back to a "regular" job and rebuild your savings. Use the time to assess what went wrong.

Big Fear: Not being qualified for the Dream you really want

Mitigating Action: Go back to school to earn additional degree and certification.

Now that you've seen some examples in action, go ahead and list four of your fears followed by action you might take to mitigate the effects of that fear.

1. **Big Fear:** ______________________________

   Mitigating Action: ______________________________

   ____

2. **Big Fear:** ______________________________

   Mitigating Action: ______________________________

   ____

3. **Big Fear:** ______________________________

   Mitigating Action: ______________________________

   ____

4. **Big Fear:** ______________________________

   Mitigating Action: ______________________________

   ____

Entering "Never Been Done Before" Territory

It can be very challenging to build something for which you have no reference point. It can feel like a game of trial and error, which can tire your soul and make you want to give up. Planning for these moments of frustration can help. Create a list of three to five people who have already walked a similar road. Some of these people may already be on your networking list. Identify these Dream Pioneers, and then reach out to them—before you need them—to let them know that you're about to walk a path they've already been on. Ask them if it is okay for you to reach out when you step into potholes. And then keep them on "speed dial," so that you can reach out to them quickly when frustration hits.

Dream Pioneers

Name: ______________________________

Title: ______________________________

Phone: ______________________________

E-mail: ______________________________

What experience does this Dream Pioneer have that you can tap into?

____

Name: ______________________________

Title: ______________________________

Phone: ______________________________

E-mail: ______________________________

What experience does this Dream Pioneer have that you can tap into?

____

Name: ______________________________

Title: ______________________________

Phone: ______________________________

E-mail: ______________________________

What experience does this Dream Pioneer have that you can tap into?

____

Name: ______________________________

Title: ______________________________

Phone: ______________________________

E-mail: ______________________________

What experience does this Dream Pioneer have that you can tap into?

____

Creating the Motivation to Continue

The Dream journey is a long one. Don't try it without a hype man. Where would Rocky have been without Mickey to keep pushing him? And, of course, your biggest cheerleader should be you. Here are two things I recommend that you do to keep your motivation humming.

Find a Hype Man

Create a list of three to five people who are well suited to fire you up when your motivation starts to fade. Reach out to at least one of those people this week and ask if the person is willing to sign up to be your motivation coach. Let people know that in the future, you may be calling them at your lowest point and that their number one responsibility will be to make sure that you do not quit, *no matter what*.

1. Name and contact info:
2. Name and contact info:
3. Name and contact info:

Encourage Yourself with a Rainy Day Note

On a day when you're feeling on top of the world, I want you to write a letter to yourself that includes:

- Why you're qualified for this Dream
- A detailed list of your greatest attributes
- Why this Dream is so important to you
- A minimum of 25 reasons why you should not give up

After you write the letter, seal it. Then, on a day when you think that your idea isn't going to work and it's just not worth it, open the letter and read it.

Developing a Growth Strategy

Remember when CEO Dreamer Lara Hodgson said that when a business fails, people often incorrectly assume it's because the idea wasn't good, the market wasn't there, or the person who was running the business wasn't capable? A lot of businesses fail because they grow too fast, which means that they do have a good product and the market is there, but demand can strain their infrastructure and their cash flow. Let's look down the road at your company's growth and create a growth plan strategy to lay a growth foundation in advance.

Take a look at your current business model. Let's make an assumption that you may receive an influx of clients or growth, and let's plan for you to do three to four times the volume of what your business is currently doing. If this growth forecast were to hold true, how would it impact the following areas?

Employees

How many employees, contractors, or volunteers would you have to hire to handle the increase in volume? What type of roles would these employees, contractors, or volunteers fill? What would the salary ranges of these employees be?

Make a list of each employee's type (title), role, and salary range.

Title:	
Role Description:	
Salary Range:	

Title:	
Role Description:	
Salary Range:	

Title:	
Role Description:	
Salary Range:	

Title:	
Role Description:	
Salary Range:	

Finding the Right Talent

How would you find these employees, contractors, or volunteers? Should you hire a recruiter, start an intern program, or create a job posting? Thinking future forward, identify sources you can tap to assist you with finding this talent.

Talent Sourcing Option 1: ________________________________
____

Talent Sourcing Option 2: ________________________________
____

Talent Sourcing Option 3:________________________________
____

Running List of Great Talent

Great leaders are always keeping their eyes open for talent. Although you may not be ready to make a hire, keep a running list of qualified talent that you could maybe one day bring on board as employee, intern, partner, or volunteer.

Name:	
Title:	
Description of Talent's Winning Skill:	

Name:	
Title:	
Description of Talent's Winning Skill:	

Name:	
Title:	
Description of Talent's Winning Skill:	

Name:	
Title:	
Description of Talent's Winning Skill:	

Facilities

Will your current working space and location be sufficient? What type of additional facilities would you need? Identify two to three facility options that you can leverage to support the growth (such as office spaces, manufacturing facilities, etc.). Perhaps you can explore some of the coworking spaces to accommodate the additional team (such as Knotel, WeWork, etc.). Your options can include identifying overflow space or upgrading into new space.

Office Space or Manufacturing Location: ___________________________

Office Space or Manufacturing Location: ___________________________

Office Space or Manufacturing Location: ___________________________

Working Capital

How much working capital would you need to fund your growth needs? Prior to needing the capital, create a list of funding sources that you can tap. This can be a range of banking institutions, friends and family investors, government agencies, angel investors, angel groups, accelerators, and incubators. Take time to do the research, determine the criteria, and identify matches that may work for you.

Funding Source Option 1: ______________________________

____

Funding Source Option 2: ______________________________

____

Funding Source Option 3: ______________________________

____

Avoiding Slow Business Growth

Perhaps your business isn't generating enough revenue to cover day-to-day operation costs. When you hit slow times like this, you have a few options available:

Generate New Revenue Ideas

Explore ways to increase sales and add new business to what you already offer. Is there an opportunity to innovate and deliver your service in new ways? List three to five ways you might expedite sales.

1. ______________________________________
2. ______________________________________
3. ______________________________________
4. ______________________________________
5. ______________________________________

Identify New Channels to Reach Your Target

Brainstorm with your team new channels that you can leverage to reach your clients. List three to five new channels to reach your clients in new ways (e.g., targeted digital promotion, conferences, referral program, etc.).

1. ______________________________
2. ______________________________
3. ______________________________
4. ______________________________
5. ______________________________

Seek Partnerships

Collaboration can be very effective. Are there any potential strategic partners you can work with that might lead to more clients for you? Make a target list of three to five potential partnerships.

1. ______________________________
2. ______________________________
3. ______________________________
4. ______________________________
5. ______________________________

Remember, necessity is the mother of innovation! Embrace the slow periods. Use them to work on creative ways to grow your business.

Managing Lack of Funding and Cash Flow Issues

As Daymond John shared, there is nothing like the "power of broke" to create innovative entrepreneurs. When you're broke, you have no choice but to be resourceful. Here are three strategies to combat lack of funding or cash flow issues.

Ask for a Line of Credit

Talk to your business banker. Make a list of programs that are available to business owners that match your criteria.

Program 1:____

Program 2:____

Program 3:____

Negotiate Better Payment Terms

List one to three of your clients that you will negotiate more favorable payment terms with.

Client 1: ____

Client 2: ____

Client 3:____

Look for Creative Ways to Cut Expenses

There are many ways to reduce operating expenses. For example, you could sublet an office, share an office, or merge with a company and share costs. Review your operating budget. How many expenses can you cut or reduce?

Expense Reduction 1: ________________________________

Expense Reduction 2: ________________________________

Expense Reduction 3: ________________________________

Navigating an Unexpected Layoff

Careerpreneur Dreamers who unexpectedly lose their executive jobs can end up not only shocked but suffering an identity crisis based in "Who am I without the title?" They can also find themselves very financially stressed. It's important to always have some exploratory options available so you're never blindsided and needing to start from scratch. Below are a few tips to help you prepare for a layoff.

Work with a Headhunter

Choose a good headhunter and stay in contact. Have the person periodically send you career options that align with your skills and purpose. List three to five possible headhunters you can work with if needed.

1. ____
2. ____
3. ____
4. ____
5. ____

Create a "Great Places to Work" List

List two or three companies you'd love to work for, and explain why those places appeal to you. Stay aware of their innovations, staff changes, developments, etc.

1. ____
2. ____
3. ____

Keep a Rock Star List

Keep a fresh list of your skills, accomplishments, and career highlights so that you can quickly update a résumé at any time. List five of these assets below. Keep this list current and use it both to stay prepared and to remind yourself of your greatness.

1. ____
2. ____
3. ____
4. ____
5. ____

Make a habit of "keeping your door open" and have exploratory conversations with potential employers, headhunters, or partners. There is no better time to search for the next big opportunity than before you need it.

EXERCISE 11.3

LIFE BALANCE TRACKER

This chapter has been about making sure that you're able to kick into Warrior Mode whenever you need to. A key component of this readiness is making sure that you're also taking care of yourself. The following life tracker is a tool for you to outline your key activities over the next two weeks to see how well you're keeping your life in balance.

Fill in the two-week chart below with your daily activities. I've included six specific categories:

- Health/Wellness (Physical)
- Health/Wellness (Mental/Spiritual)
- Business/Work
- Entertainment
- Family Time
- Household/Work

As you will see, there are also spaces for you to customize your own categories. Over two weeks, chart your activities using the applicable categories. Describe what you do and the amount of time you spend doing it. Be specific, just as if you were listing them in a planner or calendar. If you use colored pens or pencils and use a different color for each category of activity, you'll create a simple visual representation of how well balanced your days are. For example, you might list fitness/health/nutrition activities in blue, mental health activities in green, business activities in black, and so on. After filling in the chart, take some time to think about how you're dividing your time. If one category dominates the chart, make the necessary shifts, and remember that your Dream mentor is available for support and advice.

Sample Life Tracker

Week 1	Sunday	Monday	Tuesday	Wednesday	Thursday	Friday	Saturday
Health/Wellness (Physical)	Went for an evening run: 1.5 hours	Spin class at local gym: 2 hours		Spin class at local gym: 2 hours		Spin class at local gym: 2 hours	
Health/Wellness (Mental/ Spriitual)	Attended church: 3 hours		Attended early-morning yoga and meditation class: 2 hours				
Business/Work		Spent entire day at work and worked overtime on project: 12 hours	Spent etnrie day at work: 8 hours	Spent day at work: 8 hours Lunch with headhunter: 1.5 hours	Spent entire day at work and worked overtime on project: 12 hours	Spent entire day at work and worked overtime on project: 12 hours	
Entertainment							Date night with husband: 4 hours
Family Time	Spent entire day and evening with family: 8 hours			Dinner with family: 2 hours			Attended son's soccer game: 3 hours
Household/ Work	Cleaned house and prepared for week: 3 hours		Worked in the garden in the evening: 2 hours				Entire day cleaning, picked up dry cleaning, dropped dry cleaning: 8 hours
Customize							
Customize							

Now it is your turn to complete your Life Tracker chart. You can download a larger version of the chart at www.TheBigStretchBook.com.

Life Tracker

Week 1	Sunday	Monday	Tuesday	Wednesday	Thursday	Friday	Saturday
Health/Wellness (Physical)							
Health/Wellness (Mental/ Spriitual)							
Business/Work							
Entertainment							
Family Time							
Household/ Work							
Customize							
Customize							

Week 2	Sunday	Monday	Tuesday	Wednesday	Thursday	Friday	Saturday
Health/Wellness (Physical)							
Health/Wellness (Mental/ Spriitual)							
Business/Work							
Entertainment							
Family Time							
Household/ Work							
Customize							
Customize							

YOUR 90-DAY STRETCH PLAN GOAL CRUSH REMINDER

Here I am, asking you once again to review your 90-Day Stretch Plan. You're near the 90-day mark now. Never forget the importance of finishing strong! Review those goals you set for yourself to make sure you're hitting them.

All right, Dreamers, we're headed into the last leg of your Stretch, but before we do so, get ready to spend time a with a world-renowned Activist Dreamer! The #MeToo movement is one of the most significant social phenomena in decades. We have witnessed the empowering of thousands of women and men who are now speaking out and taking action against sexual violence. The woman behind this movement is the epitome of an Activist Dreamer, a warrior who will do whatever it takes to stand against injustice. She saw a problem, and like a true activist, she chose to be part of the solution.

Tarana Burke

Activist Dreamer

Founder of the #MeToo Movement

"Unless you're looking for fame or looking to be a huge platform out of the gate, there's absolutely nothing hindering anybody who's passionate about doing social justice work from doing it. Whether you're doing it in a small community, on your college campus, in

> your church, wherever it is that you decide to do the work, people who do this work do it because they are completely compelled.
>
> —Activist Dreamer **Tarana Burke**

You may download this week's Dream All-Star training session at www.thebigstretchbook.com.

CHAPTER TWELVE

LEAVE ROOM FOR THE MEGA DREAM

Week 12

You've made your way to the final week of The Stretch. For the past 11 weeks, you have been diligent and imaginative, bold and consistent. I can't tell you how proud I am of you for beginning this journey and seeing it all the way through. Because of the work you've done, your life and the lives of others will change in magnificent ways. But before I wear myself out applauding you, I want to challenge you to Dream even bigger. What if the biggest Dream you've ever imagined is small in God's eyes? Have you ever considered that your most ambitious plan may not be nearly as grand as the one that God wants to bless you with? As pleased as you are with your progress and with the brightness of the light ahead, I urge you not to become so attached to your current vision that it blinds you to your Dream's massive potential. I want to use this final chapter to offer my personal experiences of witnessing a Dream's ability to expand well beyond initial desires and goals. It is my hope that these examples will inspire you to allow space for your Dream to grow into a Mega Dream.

Near the end of this chapter, I'll share two final exercises to help you Stretch your Dreams beyond where you've allowed your imagination to go so far:

Week 12: Leave Room for the Mega Dream

EXERCISE 12.1: Keeping Your Dream in Flight

EXERCISE 12.2: Your Mega Dream Wild Card

Let's get ready to explore the Dream for your Dream!

WHAT IS THE DREAM FOR YOUR DREAM?

Throughout The Stretch, you've read references to my yearly symposium, the Dream Project. The Dream Project came to me during my solitude in a cabin back in 2012. When it became a reality, the symposium attracted more than 400 attendees each year. Much of the wisdom I've shared with you throughout The Stretch came from the speakers who joined forces with us in this vision.

In 2015, we had an All-Star lineup scheduled, including Soledad O'Brien, India.Arie, and the author of my favorite book, *The Dream Giver*, Dr. Bruce Wilkinson. Dr. Bruce has been a great influence during my journey. In his book, I truly believe that he offers the ultimate Dreamer's blueprint. When he accepted my invitation to deliver a keynote at the Dream Project, I knew the crowd was in for an unforgettable experience.

As part of our production process, my team and I conducted preparatory meetings with all the keynote speakers. During Dr. Bruce's prep call, I worked my way down the logistical checklist and also made sure that he understood the purpose and audience of the conference. As I was winding down our call, Dr. Bruce asked one of the most memorable questions I've ever been asked, "What is the Dream for *your* Dream?"

I replied, "Dr. Bruce, I don't think I understand the question."

He said, "I mean exactly what I asked. What is your Dream for *this* Dream?" Planning and executing the Dream Project requires a lot of hustle, but I don't know that I ever found myself in a conversation about my original vision or the potential of my Dream. And certainly, no one had asked a question like this one.

I closed my eyes and brought an image to mind. After a long pause, I said, "Dr. Bruce, my Dream for the Dream Project is that we'll build a terrific experience and one day attract 1,000 people to attend." I was beaming, just imagining the crowd growing to that size. He was silent. I said, "Dr. Bruce, did you hear me?"

His next words nearly pierced my heart. "My, my," he said, "how small you hold our God." I sat silently and thought about what he was telling me. Indeed, how small. Did I really think that the Dream Project had such little potential? My time with Dr. Bruce expanded my mind and my imagination. He showed me not only what I could achieve but what God could help me achieve. Dr. Bruce taught me how to Mega Dream.

HOW SMALL ARE YOU HOLDING GOD?

Throughout this book, I've asked you to reflect on your Dream. I've asked you to spend time with this goal in your mind. By now, you and your Dream should be intertwined. So let me ask you now, what is your Dream for your Dream? What is your greatest hope for what this Dream will someday become? While reading this chapter, I want to open your soul to the divine possibilities for your Dream. Close your eyes and bring the image of the idea into your vision. What long-term effects do you hope for? Whose lives will be affected? And how? How many people will be touched by it? How much money will it make that you'll be able to save? How many people will it employ? How much money will it produce that you can contribute to causes you care about? How many years will it last?

I thought I'd been reaching high to hope for a venue that would one day inspire up to 1,000 Dreamers. Then, leading into the 2016 Dream Project, we had problems. Although we had 300 to 400 attendees each year and iconic All-Stars eager to share their stories with participants, we kept ending up in the red. I hadn't figured out how to execute this annual production in a way that yielded my company profit. The time and resources that I deployed from EGAMI to execute this event each year kept my team from focusing on our clients and growing our business. As a result, during all five Dream Project years, EGAMI experienced slowed growth, and we missed our goals. I was frustrated, and I knew that something needed to change, because one Dream shouldn't rob another. My business partners and advisors were adamant that it was time for me to end the Dream Project, but I wasn't about to let that happen, so I gave myself a year to turn the conference around and prayed and believed that it would happen.

A few days before flying to Atlanta to produce the 2016 Dream Project, I knew that I had failed. The sponsorships weren't enough to cover the total production experience. Once again, I would end up in the red, and that year we barely reached 400 attendees. This wasn't even close to my *big* goal of hosting 1,000 people. I was beyond frustrated; I was heartbroken. Prior to leaving Atlanta, I went into my prayer closet to meditate and still my mind. On that day, I had taken my laptop into my sacred space with me, and after meditating, I turned on the computer and wrote Dr. Bruce Wilkinson a note from my weary heart. I asked, "What do you do when a Dream doesn't work out?"

Dr. Bruce travels throughout the world, and I didn't expect him to answer for days or even weeks. I sent the e-mail and then quietly cried a while in the closet. Then I picked myself up and wiped my tears. Regardless of my heartache, people had paid to attend the Dream Project, and I was going to give them an outstanding experience.

After getting out of the shower, I checked my e-mail, and to my surprise there was a note from Dr. Bruce waiting in my inbox. He wrote that he was sorry my Dream hadn't worked as expected. He told me that he truly believed I had a solid foundation but that perhaps I was a bit too tied to my vision of it. He asked me if I had thought of other possibilities, such as engaging in a collaboration or partnership. Then there was an odd question at the end. He asked, "Have you ever thought of partnership with Bishop T.D. Jakes?" Was Dr. Bruce crazy? *Bishop T.D. Jakes*? Bishop Jakes is a world-renowned preacher, speaker, *New York Times* bestselling author, and founder of The Potter's House Ministries. How in the world did Dr. Bruce think I'd score *that* kind of partnership? It was light-years beyond my hopes.

My team and I went on to deliver the 2016 Dream Project in excellence, but when attendees asked about the next year's symposium, I didn't have an answer. I knew that what I'd been doing wasn't working, but I promised myself to give it one more shot. If it didn't work, I would step back and put the project on hold until I could figure out how to run the Dream Project successfully. To continue running the Dream Project using an unprofitable business model would have been potentially harmful to EGAMI's growth and simply unfair to my team.

THE HOLDING PATTERN

Have you ever been in the midst of a project, knowing that you can't continue as you are but having no idea how to do things differently? I call these periods "holding patterns." During a holding pattern, sometimes it's best to do nothing. Yes, nothing. There's power in knowing when to be still. I've learned that during holding patterns, when I'm too scared to do anything, it's best to wait for clarity. When attendees and sponsors asked for the next location and dates for the Dream Project, I simply replied, "We're re-envisioning the platform and will let all of you know once we're ready for the announcement." Then for months I did nothing.

The following summer, I was again working at the Essence Music Festival. Before one of the nightly concerts, I entered the VIP room, and there was Bishop T.D. Jakes, surrounded by other community leaders and celebrities. I couldn't believe the serendipity! Dr. Bruce's words came rushing back to me. You know enough about The Stretch by now that you can probably guess my next move.

I walked over to Bishop T.D. Jakes, introduced myself, and made a Big Ask. I asked him if he was looking for partners. He replied that he'd *just* been talking about the importance of partnerships, and he introduced me to a member of his team. A few months later, we had a series of exploratory meetings and then closed on a partnership between the Dream Project and Bishop Jakes's biannual, faith-based platform MegaFest. It was my Mega Dream, and I was standing right in the middle of it!

We created a partnership that provided the Dream Project an opportunity to deliver a three-day experience called Mega Dream at Bishop T.D. Jakes's biannual event, MegaFest. The Mega Dream experience included a variety of panel subjects, like "The Dreamer's Blueprint Panel," "Good Idea or God-Given Idea?," "Dream Catchers," and "In the Mind and Body of a Dreamer." Does that content seem familiar? It should. It's some of the basis of this book. Our breakout session hosted nearly 4,000 participants at each panel! And more than once I stood on the main stage of MegaFest, sharing my words of inspiration with 100,000 Dreamers! To think that I'd allowed myself to fantasize about a maximum of *1,000* people attending my event. No wonder Dr. Bruce had shaken his head at my description of my "wildest dream." God had something much bigger in mind, a Mega Dream, and I just had to go after it. Little old me—back then I thought I already knew how to Dream big. I assure you, I'll never limit myself that way again. I won't even limit myself to one Mega Dream at a time. As I was dazzled by the miraculous Stretching power of the Dream Project, my second Dream Baby, EGAMI Group, began to bloom.

CREATING A DREAM BIGGER THAN YOU CAN IMAGINE

It was the night of the Cannes Lions International Festival of Creativity, a global event for people in creative communications, advertising, and related fields. It is considered to be the largest gathering of the advertising and creative communications industry. It's essentially the Oscars for advertising. The spotlight was shining on my friend and client, Damon Jones, vice president, global communications and advocacy at Procter & Gamble, and me, and the crowd erupted in applause. My husband and I exchanged looks of shock. Through a sea of applause, tears, handshakes, and pats on the back, Damon and I made our way to the stage along with other team members from our partner agency, BBDO. I crossed to center stage and was handed the trophy for The Cannes Grand Prix in Film for "The Talk" campaign, which EGAMI and BBDO created and executed for Procter & Gamble. I accepted the award, along with our partner agency and client. Then the rest of the night was a blur of photos and congratulations. Somewhere in the swirl of flashing cameras and popping champagne corks, an executive from Google named Xanthe Wells approached me and said, "When you walked on to the stage, it signaled to other women, and especially women of color, that we belong there."

I smiled and said, "Thank you."

She paused as if waiting for me to say more. Then she said, "You really don't get what happened tonight, do you? I've been in this industry for more than 20 years, and I've never seen a black woman accept a Grand Prix award." That's when it hit me. Tears filled my eyes, and I knew that I was experiencing something much bigger than I'd thought. *Fast Company* magazine would later write an article documenting the historic moment. The campaign would also go on to win an Emmy.

For many parents, "the talk" refers to the conversation they'll have with their kids about reproduction, sex, the body—the birds and the bees. But in an African American family, "the talk" refers to the first conversation parents have with their children about racial bias. We created a film that spans several decades, showing that while many elements surrounding the issue of race have changed for the better, "the talk" has remained a grim rite of passage for black Americans for too many generations. The film features intimate moments in which African American mothers from various eras and social classes prepare their sons and daughters for race-related issues, from insults in the form of racial slurs to potentially dangerous interactions with police. The film ends with a call for people to be part of a larger conversation about racial bias, so that one day black families will no longer need to have "the talk."

Our team and our client felt that it was time for America to have a talk about "the talk." My colleagues and I took our collective frustration about injustice and our country's escalating racial division, and we crafted that energy into a purpose-inspired work. "The Talk" went on to be one of the most awarded campaigns in Procter & Gamble's history.

It's taken some time for me to fully process what that campaign has meant to other people and to me, but I'm getting there. I went from being a girl who Googled "What is an agency?" to becoming the head of the first African American–owned firm to win a Grand Prix Award. I offer this story to you because, friends, that's not a Dream—that's a Mega Dream!

If you'd like to watch Procter & Gamble: "The Talk," visit https://www.youtube.com/watch?v=ovY6yjTe1LE.

DIVINE TIMING OF MEGA DREAMS

I've also come to learn that Dreams can have divine timing. Keep a journal of your ideas and Dreams, and don't be frustrated if you can't see where they're headed yet. It may simply not be their time. When the time is right, your Dreams will take off and maybe even become Mega Dreams.

Do you remember back in Chapter One when I talked about the importance of Dreaming in color? It's about letting your imagination soar, without boundaries or the limits of internal or external criticism. During one of my trips to escape to nature, I was Dreaming in color and developed a vision of a sacred place that would be designed for Dreamers. I had the idea to create a wonderful, freeing, peaceful space where people could get away, unplug, and Dream. I imagined calling this magical place "the Dream Maker," and the idea marinated for about five years.

I believe that sometimes there's a divine season for each idea, and I instinctively knew that it was not time for that Dream. During that trip, I went on a long walk and stumbled upon the most beautiful log cabin I'd ever seen. It was situated at the top of a hill. It was chocolate brown with a red door, and lime green rocking chairs sat on the front porch. There was something mystical about the place. Brenda, the owner, wandered outside, and we began talking about our daydreams and the magical effects of being surrounded by nature. She took me inside and showed me all the wonderful accent pieces she'd collected just for the cabin: lovely ceramics from antique stores, handmade pillows, a toilet paper holder made from a horseshoe. On a counter were stones she'd found and welded together. I shared with her my fantasy of "the Dream Maker," and then we exchanged phone numbers, but for years I didn't call her.

Five years later, I walked that road again. I was exhausted from work and was taking a clarity break in my beloved Georgia woods. I stood in front of her beautiful cabin, and this time a big "for sale" sign dominated the cabin's lawn. My heart began to race. I dialed Brenda's number and was delighted that she answered and remembered me. *Could this be the right time for this Dream?* The Dream had been tucked away for the five years, but now all the images and ideas I'd had about this sacred space came flooding back. I prayed, called my husband, and we talked about it. Then I told Brenda that she should expect a bid from me within the week.

All week long the cabin stayed on my mind. I ran numbers and made calls to my financial institution. By the end of the week, I was convinced that it was "time," and I e-mailed a bid to Brenda's Realtor. I just knew this was my cabin. Then I received an e-mail that read, "I apologize, but Brenda accepted another offer just hours before yours." I was devastated. I called Brenda, and she said that our timing was off. She waited all week for my bid, and when she didn't hear back, she assumed I'd changed my mind, so she accepted another offer. I cried all night. My husband said, "That just means God has something better." I cried, "You don't understand! This was *my Dream cabin*!" And I cried myself to sleep.

A few months later, I was moved to start looking for another cabin. I was sure that there could never be another cabin as exquisite as Brenda's, certainly not one that I could afford, but I began a search for a close second. After looking at more than 20 cabins, I was ready to give up, but there was one more on my list. As my real estate agent (my mom) and I drove up a winding road, we saw a beautiful three-story cabin, secluded and perched on the top of a mountain. Could this be the place that God wanted for me? After losing Brenda's cabin, I couldn't imagine finding another that could make my heart jump, and yet there I was, standing in front of my Dream cabin, a lovely home with a fireplace, three wrap-around porches, and a private writer's room. And it's perched atop a mountain! We moved quickly, and that beautiful place became our Dream Maker. I'm writing these words to you right now from a desk inside my Mega Dream. Is it possible that God wants to move your "regular" Dream to the side to make room for a Mega Dream? Yes!

STRETCHING DREAMS TO MEGA DREAMS

Throughout this book, you've read countless stories about Dreamers who reached higher than they thought they could—despite discouraging roadblocks. Let's do a quick review of how some of them Stretched beyond their Dreams to Mega Dreams.

- A young kid from Baltimore with a love of music went from quirky intern to become president of Def Jam Records. **Meet Make-It-Happen Dreamer Kevin Liles.**
- A Memphis country girl with a vision to elevate designers of color shook up the city of New York and changed the fashion industry forever. **Meet CEO Dreamer Brandice Daniel.**
- The little "unwanted" girl who was given up for adoption created the largest anti–human trafficking organization in the world. **Meet Activist Dreamer Christine Caine.**
- A hobbyist with a love for fragrances went from selling products out of her kitchen to selling her company to L'Oréal. **Meet CEO Dreamer Lisa Price.**
- A little boy from Michigan who didn't think that people who looked "like him" could be successful in business not only became a world-class athlete but runs businesses worth nearly a billion dollars. **Meet CEO Dreamer Earvin "Magic" Johnson.**
- A risk-averse single mother created the largest online network of female bloggers. **Meet CEO Dreamer Lisa Stone.**
- His family told him that everyone in Hollywood is going to hell, but he moved there anyway and proceeded to produce multimillion-dollar box office hits. **Meet CEO Dreamer DeVon Franklin.**
- As a girl, she listened to the records of her idol, Stevie Wonder. Then, after years of singing and practicing her guitar, she eventu-

ally went on to tour with Stevie Wonder himself. **Meet Make-It-Happen Dreamer India.Arie.**

- A college student had a hunch that women would pay to rent luxury clothing. She filled her dorm room with samples and tested her idea on fellow coeds. Her idea, Rent the Runway, changed the fashion industry forever. **Meet Make-It-Happen Dreamer Jennifer Fleiss.**
- A courageous warrior who was willing to talk openly about her sexual abuse with the goal of empowering other abuse survivors started a movement that changed the world. **Meet Activist Dreamer and #MeToo founder Tarana Burke.**
- When this Alabama country girl used to watch movies, she found herself focused on the on-screen food. "What's in those recipes?" she wanted to know. She went on to be crowned a winner of Bravo's *Top Chef*. **Meet Kelsey Barnard.**

Those are only a few people whose Dreams surprised them by evolving into much greater Mega Dreams. And they are no different from you or me. They're hard workers who stayed with it. This kind of Dream expansion (sometimes it can feel like an explosion!) might seem miraculous, as if there are powers involved that you can't see. Well, there just might be. It's as if a willingness to Stretch is consecrated by a higher power. I believe that when you work hard, try to be your best, and Dare to Stretch toward greatness, that higher power shines a light on the effort to pave the way.

WHAT'S YOUR MEGA DREAM?

Dreamer, you've done a great job in this pursuit. You've gone for it. And now I want you to ponder the following two questions: "What is your Dream?" and "What is your Dream *for* your Dream?" The answer to the second question becomes your Mega Dream. Keep your Dream watered with prayer, consistent action, and determination. And keep your mind open for the magic.

Thank you for joining me on this journey. You're ready. It's time for your Mega Dream.

EXERCISE 12.1

KEEPING YOUR DREAM IN FLIGHT

Now that your Dream is in flight, you need to develop a plan to keep it soaring. Use the form below to create Your Dream Flight Plan.

Your Dream Flight Plan

Copilot: The person you will need by your side throughout this journey.

Flight Crew: Team members, mentors, and strategic advisors who will help keep your Dream in flight.

Fuel Source: Sources of important inspiration and information, like books, podcasts, workshops, etc.

First-Class Upgrade: Tools or strategies you can use to boost your Dream, like extra funding, new technologies, or new methods.

Emergency Preparedness Training: Try to anticipate emergencies that your new company might encounter, and list some "emergency equipment" you'll have on hand to avert those crises, like insurance, savings, backup team members, network resources, etc. For example:

- **Emergency:** Your trusted office manager says she's quitting in one week
- **Emergency Equipment:** Temp agency phone numbers, network members for referrals

Dream Destinations: List a goal for your Dream—a one-year goal, five-year goal, or longer-term goal.

A Sample Dream Flight Plan for a Nonprofit for Survivors of Gun Violence

Copilot: Marcus, husband

Flight Crew:

- Sarah Jane, cofounder
- Michelle, CFO
- Randall, mentor and coach
- Virgil, administrative assistant

Fuel Source: God, stories of families that have lost someone to gun violence, books about the psychological impact of traumatic experiences, gun-ownership websites.

First-Class Upgrade: Hosting fundraiser, expanding your reach from one state to multiple states, partnering with other organizations that are fighting gun violence, creating a 1-800 support hotline.

Emergency Preparedness Training:

- **Emergency:** Start-up costs proving to be more than expected
- **Emergency Equipment:** 401(k), small investor loans, Kickstarter or GoFundMe campaign

Dream Destinations: Developing 10 locations for the program within the next five years.

Your Dream Flight Plan

Copilot: ______________________________

Flight Crew:

____

____

____

____

Fuel Source: ______________________________

First-Class Upgrade: ______________________________

Emergency Preparedness Training:

____

____

____

- **Emergency:** ______________________________
- **Emergency Equipment:** ______________________________

Dream Destinations: ______________________________

EXERCISE 12.2

YOUR MEGA DREAM WILD CARD

A wild card is an unpredictable person or thing. When there's a wild card involved, you really don't know what might happen. Let's talk about the wild card aspect of your Stretch, the limitless possibilities if only you'll let yourself imagine. What if this Dream could expand into anything you wanted?

Right now I want you to think about your goal and imagine it expanded 1,000 times greater than you've ever thought possible. No limits. Write that down. It's okay if that Dream feels so big that you might feel a little embarrassed if someone found this and read it. Now answer one last question: if there were a divine Dream for your Dream, what might that be?

Take your time and play out this success scenario in your mind and then commit it all to paper.

Remember that The Stretch is a lifestyle. Meet me in the Epilogue to find out how you can continue to Stretch and also invite others along on your journey.

EPILOGUE

THE STRETCH EFFECT

Running the Race of Your Dreams

I'm *so* proud of you. For the past 12 weeks, you've proved that you're willing to Stretch toward your Dreams. These 12 weeks are much bigger than what you can see now. Many people will be affected by the Dream that you are bringing forth. The effects of your efforts will be felt throughout your community, your workplace, and beyond. This is The Stretch Effect. As you move forward, it's important that you realize that finishing this book in no way signals an ending. The Stretch is a lifetime commitment. Let's review the phases you've just worked through.

- **Phase 1: Dream.** You now understand what it means to Dream and believe. You gave yourself time to imagine freely, you're more aware of your ideal Dream environments, and you identified your Dream Champions and Dream Bullies. You understand your Dream Ancestry and how that influences you today. Use the power of your Dreams to fuel you every day.
- **Phase 2: Design.** You now know that great Dreamers are planners. They design the framework and infrastructure for their goals. You can now use your Design techniques to design a blueprint for your ideas to thrive.
- **Phase 3: Dare.** Nothing great was ever achieved from inside the zip code of a comfort zone. You understand this, and you will courageously be bold and take risks.

- **Phase 4: Do.** You now understand that Dreams come to life because of action. And great Dreamers know what it means to *do* the Dream for the long term. This is not a 5K; it's a marathon.

Always remember that The Stretch is a lifestyle. From this point forward, you will be required to Stretch over and over again, so I think it's fitting that I end this book with a commitment from you to continue in your Stretch.

THE STRETCH AGREEMENT: COMMITTING TO THE STRETCH AS A LIFESTYLE

When you started this book, I asked you to sign a contract to demonstrate your willingness to remain committed over the 12-week period. Now I want you to commit to a long-term continuation of your Stretch.

> I ______________________ commit to The Stretch as a lifestyle.
> I commit to challenging myself *at least* once a year by
> Stretching toward a new goal, Dream, or expanded Dream.
>
> ____
>
> Signature, Date

Remember, you can use this book and the tools from The Stretch toward as many kinds of Dreams as you can imagine. This program is designed to be used again and again.

EXERCISE E.1

DREAMERS DON'T DREAM ALONE

Do you remember my sharing with you that when you Dream, you inspire others to Dream? Within your network, think about how many friends, relatives, and champions were thrilled to see you Stretch toward your goal. Do you know why? They want to see you become the very best you. So whose Dreams would *you* like to support?

Think of three people who might have Dreams that you can help become realities. List their names below along with tangible ways you can help them Stretch—buying them a copy of this book could be an ideal way for them to get started! Make a commitment to take action to support them.

1. ____

2. ____

3. ____

EXERCISE E.2

SHARE YOUR STRETCH EFFECT

Last but not least, I want to hear from *you*! I am very interested in hearing about the effects of your Stretch. You're going to discover new things about yourself, expand in new ways, accomplish exciting results, and change people's lives, and I want to hear all about it. I believe in you so much that I'm already moving onto part two of this journey. I'm going to curate stories of people who have worked through the book and share those stories on www.TheBigStretch.com to inspire other Dreamers. Please join us by visiting TheBigStretchBook.com and telling us about The Stretch Effect on your life.

Beloved Dreamer, you've completed all 90 days! It's been a wonderful 12 weeks, and my prayer for you now is that you know you're destined for the life of your Dreams. I want you to realize that you're capable and ready and that you will have support along the way. There will be surprises, setbacks, and challenges. But know that your willingness to Stretch will always be greater than any impediments.

You're stronger, tougher, and now equipped to realize your God-given, extraordinary Mega Dream.

It's been a blessing and an honor to be with you.

Forever Your Dream Coach,
T

INDEX

ABOUT THE AUTHOR

TENESHIA JACKSON WARNER is the founder and CEO of the Manhattan-based EGAMI Group. As the founder, Teneshia took a Dream idea and grew it into a multimillion-dollar multicultural marketing and communications agency serving major clients including P&G, My Black Is Beautiful, Verizon Wireless, Pfizer, Target, Hennessy, Major League Baseball, and more. Under her leadership, EGAMI Group made history working on the eye-opening P&G campaign, "The Talk," for which the firm became the first black-woman-led company to win the Cannes Lion Grand Prix Award. The campaign also earned EGAMI a 2018 Emmy Award for Outstanding Commercial. EGAMI Group was also named to *Adweek*'s 100: Fastest Growing Agency List.

Teneshia is also the founder and creator of The Dream Project, an empowerment platform designed to support professionals, entrepreneurs, and creatives as they reach toward their business goals and Dreams. Through this platform, Teneshia has empowered more than 150,000 professionals to achieve their goals and has featured over 200 speakers, including global business leaders, professional athletes, world-changing activists, and Teneshia herself.

A graduate of Alabama A&M University, Teneshia has been acknowledged as one of *Black Enterprise*'s "Rising Stars" and "40 Under 40" and *The Network Journal*'s "Forty Under 40." She's also the recipient of AdColor's

MVP Award and has been featured in *Forbes, Fast Company, Entrepreneur Magazine, Essence Magazine, Black Enterprise*, and *PR Week.* She has also appeared on *ABC News* and *The Steve Harvey Show.*

Teneshia is a frequent public speaker who joyfully inspires audiences to go after their Dreams at major conferences like BlogHer, Cannes Lion International Festival of Creativity, Leading Women Defined, and T.D. Jakes's MegaFest. She lives in New Jersey with her husband/business partner, Michael Warner, and their poodle, Tully.

For more information on Teneshia J. Warner:
www.teneshiajwarner.com
www.thebigstretchbook.com

For more information on The Dream Project:
www.dreamprojectonline.com

For more information on EGAMI Group:
www.egamigroup.com